T0214997

Communications in Computer and Information Science   **757**

Commenced Publication in 2007
Founding and Former Series Editors:
Alfredo Cuzzocrea, Xiaoyong Du, Orhun Kara, Ting Liu, Dominik Ślęzak,
and Xiaokang Yang

More information about this series at http://www.springer.com/series/7899

Yongtian Wang · Shengjin Wang
Yue Liu · Jian Yang
Xiaoru Yuan · Ran He
Henry Been-Lirn Duh (Eds.)

Advances in Image and Graphics Technologics

12th Chinese conference, IGTA 2017
Beijing, China, June 30 – July 1, 2017
Revised Selected Papers

Springer

Editors
Yongtian Wang
Beijing Institute of Technology
Beijing
China

Shengjin Wang
Tsinghua University
Beijing
China

Yue Liu
Beijing Institute of Technology
Beijing
China

Jian Yang
Beijing Institute of Technology
Beijing
China

Xiaoru Yuan
School of EECS, Center for Information
 Science
Peking University
Beijing
China

Ran He
Institute of Automation
Chinese Academy of Sciences
Beijing
China

Henry Been-Lirn Duh
La Trobe University
Melbourne, VIC
Australia

ISSN 1865-0929   ISSN 1865-0937 (electronic)
Communications in Computer and Information Science
ISBN 978-981-10-7388-5   ISBN 978-981-10-7389-2 (eBook)
https://doi.org/10.1007/978-981-10-7389-2

Library of Congress Control Number: 2017960861

Printed on acid-free paper

This Springer imprint is published by Springer Nature
The registered company is Springer Nature Singapore Pte Ltd.
The registered company address is: 152 Beach Road, #21-01/04 Gateway East, Singapore 189721, Singapore

Preface

It was a pleasure and an honor to have organized the 12th Conference on Image and Graphics Technologies and Applications. The conference was held from June 30 to July 1, 2017 in Beijing, China. The conference series is the premier forum for presenting research in image processing and graphics and their related topics. The conference provides a rich forum for sharing the progress in the areas of image processing technology, image analysis and understanding, computer vision and pattern recognition, big data mining, computer graphics and VR, image technology application, with the generation of new ideas, new approaches, new techniques, new applications, and new evaluations. The conference was organized under the auspices of Beijing Society of Image and Graphics, at Beijing Institute of Technology, Beijing, China.

The conference program included keynotes, oral papers, posters, demos, and exhibitions. For the conference, we received 78 papers for review. Each of these was assessed by at least two reviewers, with some of papers being assessed by three reviewers, in all, 26 submissions were selected for oral and poster presentation.

We are grateful for the efforts of everyone who helped to make this conference a reality. We are grateful to the reviewers who completed the reviewing process on time. The local host, Beijing Institute of Technology, took care of the local arrangements for the conference, and welcomed all of the delegates.

The conference continues to provide a leading forum for cutting-edge research and case studies in image and graphics. We hope you enjoy the proceedings of this conference.

June 2017

Yongtian Wang

Organization

General Conference Chair

Yongtian Wang   Beijing Institute of Technology, China

Executive and Coordination Committee

Guoping Wang	Peking University, China
Chaowu Chen	The First Research Institute of the Ministry of Public Security of P.R.C.
Mingquan Zhou	Beijing Normal University, China
Zhiguo Jiang	Beihang University, China
Shengjin Wang	Tsinghua University, China
Chenglin Liu	Institute of Automation, Chinese Academy of Sciences, China
Yao Zhao	Beijing Jiaotong University, China
Qingming Huang	University of Chinese Academy of Sciences, China

Program Committee Chairs

Xiaoru Yuan	Peking University, China
Ran He	Institute of Automation, Chinese Academy of Sciences, China
Jian Yang	Beijing Institute of Technology, China

Organizing Chairs

Xiangyang Ji	Tsinghua University, China
Yue Liu	Beijing Institute of Technology, China

Organizing Committee

Lei Yang	Communication University of China, China
Fengjun Zhang	Institute of Software, Chinese Academy of Sciences, China
Xiaohui Liang	Beijing University of Aeronautics and Astronautics, China

Program Committee

Xiaochun Cao	Institute of Information Engineering, Chinese Academy of Sciences, China
Weiqun Cao	Beijing Forestry University, China
Mingzhi Cheng	Beijing Institute of Graphic Communication, China
Jing Dong	Institute of Automation, Chinese Academy of Sciences, China

Kaihang Di	Institute of Remote Sensing and Digital Earth, Chinese Academy of Sciences, China
Fuping Gan	Ministry of Land and Resources of the People's Republic of China, China
Henry Been-Lirn Duh	La Trobe University, Australia
Yan Jiang	Beijing Institute of Fashion Technology, China
Hua Li	Institute of Computing Technology, Chinese Academy of Sciences, China
Qingyuan Li	Chinese Academy of Surveying & Mapping, China
Jianbo Liu	Communication University of China, China
Hua Lin	Tsinghua University, China
Li Zhuo	Beijing University of Technology, China
Liang Liu	Beijing University of Posts and Telecommunications Sciences, China
Xiaozhu Lin	Beijing Institute of Petrochemical Technology, China
Xueqiang Lu	Beijing Information Science & Technology University, China
Huimin Ma	Tsinghua University, China
Siwei Ma	Peking University, China
Nobuchika Sakata	Osaka University, Japan
Seokhee Jeon	Kyunghee University, Korea
Yankui Sun	Tsinghua University, China
Takafumi Taketomi	NAIST, Japan
Yahui Wang	Beijing University of Civil Engineering and Architecture, China
Yiding Wang	North China University of Technology, China
Zhongke Wu	Beijing Normal University, China
Shihong Xia	Institute of Computing Technology, Chinese Academy of Sciences, China
Guoqiang Yao	Beijing Film Academy, China
Jun Yan	Journal of Image and Graphics, China
Cheng Yang	Communication University of China, China
Youngho Lee	Mokpo National University, Korea
Yiping Huang	Taiwan University, China
Xucheng Yin	University of Science and Technology Beijing, China
Jiazheng Yuan	Beijing Union University, China
Aiwu Zhang	Capital Normal University, China
Danpei Zhao	Beijing University of Aeronautics and Astronautics, China
Huijie Zhao	Beijing University of Aeronautics and Astronautics, China

Contents

SAR Image Registration Using Cluster Analysis and Anisotropic Diffusion-Based SIFT

Yanzhao Wang[1,2(✉)], Zhiqiang Ge[2], Juan Su[1], and Wei Wu[1]

[1] Xi'an High-Tech Institution, No. 2, Tongxin Road, Baqiao District, Xi'an 710025, China
wyzhao1874@foxmail.com
[2] Beijing Institute of Remote Sensing Equipment, Yongding Road, Beijing 100854, China

Abstract. The scale-invariant feature transform (SIFT) algorithm has been widely used in remote sensing image registration. However, it may be difficult to obtain satisfactory registration precision for SAR image pairs that contain much speckle noise. In this letter, an anisotropic scale space constructed with speckle reducing anisotropic diffusion (SRAD) is introduced to reduce the influence of noise on feature extraction. Then, dual-matching strategy is utilized to obtain initial feature matches, and feature cluster analysis is introduced to refine the matches in relative distance domain, which increases the probability of correct matching. Finally, the affine transformation parameters for image registration are obtained by RANSAC algorithm. The experimental results demonstrate that the proposed method can enhance the stability of feature extraction, and provide better registration performance compared with the standard SIFT algorithm in terms of number of correct matches and aligning accuracy.

Keywords: SAR image registration · Scale-invariant feature transform (SIFT)
Speckle reducing anisotropic diffusion (SRAD) · Cluster analysis

1 Introduction

Synthetic aperture radar (SAR) image registration is one of many key procedures in applications such as matching guidance, information fusion, change detection, and three-dimensional reconstruction [1]. Due to complex geometric deformations and grayscale differences between SAR image pairs, it's difficult for traditional approaches that may suffer from poor robustness to obtain a satisfactory registration precision [2].

The feature-based methods are the mainstream methods for SAR image registration. These methods extract and match significant features from two images and the correlation between those features is used to determine the alignment. Generally, features extracted include point, edge, and the centroid of a specific area [3]. Among feature-based methods, scale-invariant feature transform (SIFT) [4] is a representative algorithm. It has been widely used in image registration for its invariance to image rotation and scaling and partial invariance to changes in camera viewpoint and illumination [5]. Chen *et al.* [6] proposed a new definition of gradient computation with ROEWA operator and reduced the dimension of feature descriptors, which improved the computational efficiency. Schwind *et al.* [7] proposed SIFT-OCT, in which the performance of feature

© Springer Nature Singapore Pte Ltd. 2018
Y. Wang et al. (Eds.): IGTA 2017, CCIS 757, pp. 1–11, 2018.
https://doi.org/10.1007/978-981-10-7389-2_1

detectors is analyzed to improve the robustness of the algorithm. Many false keypoints may be detected when traditional SIFT is directly adopted in SAR image registration as a result of complex imaging conditions of SAR, especially the existence of speckle noise in the image. These points are randomly distributed with a poor repeatability rate, which will lead to fewer feature matches and more mismatches.

In order to reduce the negative effect of speckle noise, some improved SIFT algorithms based on anisotropic scale space (ASS-SIFT) were proposed. Wang *et al.* [5] proposed BFSIFT by analyzing the similarity between the bilateral filter and the thermal diffusion equation, which increased the number of correct matches. According to local structural characteristics of the image, an anisotropic Gaussian scale space was established [8], improving the robustness of features. Fan *et al.* [9] adopted Perona-Malik (PM) equation to establish a nonlinear diffusion scale space and proposed a new definition of gradient computation with ROEWA operator, which increased the probability of correct matching. Compared with traditional SIFT, ASS-SIFT algorithms effectively preserve fine details and suppress the speckle noise in SAR images, and the local information of the images is described more comprehensively. As a result, the number of keypoints is increased and the positioning accuracy of control points is improved. However, they cannot effectively reduce the unstable keypoints caused by the speckle noise from SAR images. The reason for this is that in the existing ASS-SIFT approaches, the anisotropic diffusion filters adaptively smooth the noises and preserve the edges due to their different image gradient magnitudes [10]. If the images contain strong multiplicative noises such as speckles, then the image edges are difficult to distinguish from the speckled homogeneous region, since both the image boundaries and the multiplicative noises lead to high image gradient magnitudes. As a result, the speckle noises from the SAR images will be preserved instead of being smoothed by the anisotropic diffusion filters and then identified as unstable keypoints in the ASS.

In this paper, we proposed a speckle reducing SIFT match method to obtain stable keypoints and precise matches for the SAR image registration. The contributions of this paper are as follows. First, a speckle reducing anisotropic scale space is constructed based on the speckle reducing anisotropic diffusion (SRAD). Due to the gradient magnitude operator and the Laplacian operator of SRAD, speckle noises are greatly reduced and the edges of the images are preserved, then the stable keypoints can be obtained. Second, we utilize dual-matching strategy to obtain initial matches and cluster analysis in relative distance domain is introduced to eliminate false matches caused by speckle noise and geometric deformations. With cluster analysis, the keypoint correct match rate is significantly enhanced. Finally, the affine transformation parameters for image registration are obtained by random sample consensus (RANSAC) algorithm with removing the false matches simultaneously. We validate our method on simulated images and real SAR images and the experimental results demonstrate the effectiveness of our method.

2 Traditional SIFT Algorithm

SIFT is a famous matching algorithm which was proposed by David Lowe in 1999 and consummated in 2004. It was created based on local invariant feature of the image, with good rotation, scale, local affine and gray invariance [6]. Traditional SIFT algorithm consists of three major stages: multiscale space construction, feature detection and description, and feature matching.

Firstly, Gaussian scale space is constructed by convolving the original image with Gaussian kernel at different scales

$$\left. \begin{array}{l} L(x, y; \sigma) = I(x, y) * G(x, y; \sigma) \\ L(x, y; k\sigma) = I(x, y) * G(x, y; k\sigma) \end{array} \right\} \tag{1}$$

Where $I(x, y)$ is the original image and $L(x, y; \sigma)$ is the Gaussian scale space. $G(x, y; \sigma)$ is the Gaussian function with standard deviation σ and k is the scale parameter. A series of difference of Gaussian (DoG) images are achieved by subtracting adjacent Gaussian images, and extrema of the DoG images are detected as the candidate features.

$$\begin{aligned} D(x, y; \sigma) &= L(x, y, k\sigma) - L(x, y, \sigma) \\ &= (k - 1)\sigma^2 \nabla^2 G * I(x, y) \end{aligned} \tag{2}$$

Where $D(x, y; \sigma)$ is the Gaussian differential scale space.

Secondly, dominant orientation of each keypoint is calculated for each keypoint, and a 128-element feature descriptor is constructed based on the gradients in the local image patches aligned by its dominant orientation.

Finally, feature points are matched using the nearest neighbor distance ratio (NNDR), and the matching result is optimized by RANSAC algorithm. More details about SIFT can be found in [4].

3 Description of the Proposed Method

Traditional SIFT has been successfully employed to the registration of optical remote sensing images. However, it usually fails to provide favorable results when directly used to SAR images. As is known, SAR images are obtained by coherent processing of the target scattered signal. The coherent superposition of the scattered electromagnetic waves usually forms a large number of multiplicative speckle noises, which causes many false keypoints while real features are buried in the noise. Speckle noises may also blur the adjacent area of features, which reduces the robustness and distinctiveness of feature descriptors that are expected to be correctly matched. Therefore, it's necessary to effectively reduce the negative effect of speckle noises when using SIFT for SAR image registration.

3.1 Speckle Reducing Anisotropic Scale Space

Gaussian blurring is one instance of isotropic diffusion filtering which is sensitive to speckle noise and does not respect the natural boundaries of the object. As a consequence, many unstable keypoints are brought from the Gaussian scale space of SIFT and then the matching performance is degraded. The existing ASS-SIFT methods overcome the shortcomings of the conventional SIFT algorithm based on anisotropic diffusion filtering. However, they suffer from unstable keypoints caused by speckle noises in SAR images, since the anisotropic diffusion filters detect edges depending upon image gradient magnitude and would not smooth the speckled homogeneous regions.

SRAD [11] is an edge-sensitive partial differential equation version of the conventional speckle reducing filters, which has better properties of speckle reduction and edge preserving. To enhance the stability of the keypoint detection, we construct an anisotropic scale space with SRAD. Then the keypoints are detected in the space.

3.1.1 SRAD

Anisotropic diffusion based on partial differential equation is widely used in image denoising and edge detection [12]. The main idea is heterogeneous diffusion and iterative smoothing. The partial differential equation of SRAD can be expressed as:

$$\begin{cases} \partial I(x,y;t)/\partial t = \mathrm{div}[c(q) \cdot \nabla I(x,y;t)] \\ I(x,y;0) = I_0(x,y) \end{cases} \tag{4}$$

where $I_0(x,y)$ is the origin image and $I(x,y;t)$ is the filtered image. div and ∇ are divergence and gradient operators, and the time t is the scale parameter. In Eq. (4), $c(q)$ refers to the conductivity coefficient defined as

$$c(q) = \frac{1}{1 + [q^2(x,y;t) - q_0^2(t)]/\{q_0^2(t)[1 + q_0^2(t)]\}} \tag{5}$$

Where $q(x,y;t)$ severs as an edge detector for SRAD determined by

$$q(x,y;t) = \sqrt{\frac{(1/2)(|\nabla|/I)^2 - (1/16)(\nabla^2 I/I)^2}{[1 + (1/4)(\nabla^2 I/I)]^2}} \tag{6}$$

In Eq. (5), $q_0(t)$ is the diffusion threshold which determines the total amount of diffusion. It can be approximately calculated by Eq. (7).

$$q_0(t) \approx q_0 \exp[-\rho t] \tag{7}$$

In practical applications, ρ generally takes $1/6$. $c(q)$ controls the process of diffusion according to the relationship between the edge intensity and the diffusion threshold. At the center of an edge, the Laplacian term undergoes zero crossing and the gradient term dominates, leading to a relatively large $q(x,y;t)$. Then the conductivity coefficient approaches 0 and the edge is preserved. While in the speckled homogeneous regions, the normalized image divergence is approximately equal to the normalized gradient magnitude, resulting in a relatively small $q(x,y;t)$. Thus the conductivity coefficient closes to 1 and the speckle noise is smoothed.

The edge detector $q(x,y;t)$ contains a normalized gradient magnitude operator and a normalized Laplacian operator. The second derivative properties of Laplacian operator can distinguish whether the local grayscale of the image is caused by noise or by the edge. It is a constant false alarm for speckle noises, thus edges can be detected more accurately from the speckle noise regions.

3.1.2 Anisotropic Scale Space Construction

The process of image filtering can be transformed into a continuous evolution with time scale t_i. The solution (filtered image) solved by numerical method can correspond to the image of the discrete scale in the scale space. Thus the anisotropic scale space of the image can be constructed by obtaining all successive scale images with numerical iterations.

By means of the semi-implicit schema [13], Eq. (4) can be discretized and reconstructed as an iterative form

$$I^{i+1} = \left[E - (t_{i+1} - t_i) \sum_{l=1}^{m} A_l(I^i) \right]^{-1} I^i \tag{8}$$

where I^i and I^{i+1} are the image vector representations at time t_i and t_{i+1}, E is the identity matrix, and $A_l(I^i)$ is a coefficient matrix. m represents the dimension of the image. The two-dimensional diffusion filtering can be decomposed into two independent one-dimensional diffusion processes by additive operator splitting (AOS), and the corresponding linear equations are solved in both x and y directions. Let I^i and I^{i+1} be the images of x and y directions at time t_{i+1}, then the image at time t_{i+1} can be determined by the images from two directions:

$$I^{i+1} = \left(I_x^{i+1} + I_y^{i+1} \right) \Big/ 2 \tag{9}$$

Since the anisotropic diffusion filtering is defined in time terms, the discrete scale σ_i is required to be converted into time units using the equation [9]:

$$t_i = \sigma_i^2 / 2 \tag{10}$$

Thus, the anisotropic scale space L can be formed by a stack of smoothed images generated by Eqs. (9) and (10)

$$L = \left\{ I^0(t_0), I^1(t_1), \ldots, I^{W-1}(t_{W-1}) \right\} \tag{11}$$

where $\left\{ t_0, t_1, \cdots, t_{W-1} \right\}$ is a series of discrete evolution times, and W is the total number of images in the scale space. We take the same approach as done in SIFT, discretizing the scale space into a series of O octaves and S sublevels

$$\sigma_i(o, s) = \sigma_0 2^{0 + \frac{s}{S}}, o \in [0, O-1], s \in [0, S+2], i \in [0, W-1] \tag{12}$$

where σ_0 is the basic scale, O and S are the number of octaves and sublevels in the space, while o and s are the index of octave O and interval S. It is noteworthy that, when we reach the last sublevel in each octave, we downsample the image, as described in SIFT, and use the downsample image as the initial image for next octave.

As Fig. 1 shows, we use a RadarSat image and an ALOS-PALSAR image as the reference images. The Gaussian scale space and SRAD anisotropic scale space of the two images are constructed. O and S are set to 4 and 3. Fig. 1(b)–(c) in the first row are the images at the second sublevel within the second octave, and Fig. 1(b)–(c) in the second row are the images at the third sublevel within the second octave. As it can be observed, due to the influence of linear filtering, Gaussian scale space images are blurred with increasing scale values and fine details such as contours and edges are seriously destroyed. In contrast, strong speckle noises are smoothed and prominent structures are preserved in the SRAD anisotropic scale space. Thus more stable keypoints can be extracted.

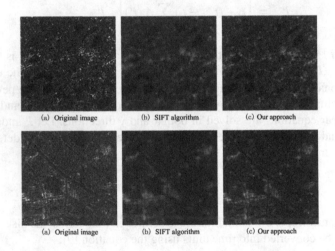

Fig. 1. Scale space comparison

After the SRAD anisotropic scale space has been constructed, the difference between adjacent smoothed images in the SRASS is performed. Then the keypoints are detected as done in the SIFT algorithm.

3.2 Feature Matching and Outlier Removal

Due to the existence of multiplicative speckle noises in SAR images, a large number of unreliable keypoints will inevitably appear within the initial keypoints, which will lead to inaccurate correspondence and further affect the correct calculation of the transformation parameters. So it is necessary to eliminate the false matches within the initial keypoints effectively.

3.2.1 Dual-Matching Strategy

When there are repeated patterns in the image, many keypoints in the sensed image are matched to the same one in the reference image using the SIFT matching strategy (distance ratio). Therefore, we use dual-matching strategy (use the distance ratio twice) [5], namely, keypoint A in the sensed image and keypoint B in the reference image are accepted as a correspondence only when A and B are matched to each other by the distance ratio, which improves the possibility of correct matches.

3.2.2 False Matches Removal Using Cluster Analysis

A lot of false matches still exist in the initial matching results directly obtained by dual-matching strategy. Due to the strong randomness in the distribution of speckle noises, most of false matches are random while correct matches often have some consistent inner connections. In addition, geometric differences between images cause a difference in the position of the feature matches, but the relative distances of correct matches should maintain a high consistency.

We first calculate the relative distances Δx and Δy between feature matches in both horizontal and vertical directions. Then the relative distance domain is established and distance relations of the feature matches are mapped into the domain. $(\Delta x, \Delta y)$ is used as the cluster feature to make K-means cluster analysis of the relative distances. False matches are randomly distributed in the domain and scatter in smaller classes for their poor consistency in distance. In contrast, the correct matches are more concentrated in distribution, so they can be selected by maintaining the largest class in the domain. In this paper, the relationship between the number of classes and the number of correct matches is observed in all experiments. It can be observed that with the increase of the number of classes, the number of correct matches increases, but does not satisfy a monotonically increase.

3.2.3 Matching Result Optimized by RANSAC

After above steps, correct matches have accounted for the vast majority in the matching result. The result can be further optimized by random sample consensus (RANSAC) algorithm [14]. The commonly used affine transformation is chosen as the transformation model, and the registration parameters are obtained with the least squares method.

4 Experimental Results and Analysis

4.1 Stability Analysis of Feature Extraction

To verify the improvement on feature extraction stability, A SAR image with a size of 450×287 is tested. A comparison of the performance in feature extraction between our approach and Ref. [9] is made under the conditions of noise changes, scale changes and rotation transformation. The Gaussian noise model with mean 1 and variance $0.1 \times i$ ($i = 1, \ldots, 10$) is utilized to add multiplicative noise to the reference image. Figure 2(a) shows the reference image. Figure 2(b) and (c) shows the simulated noise image with variances 0.2 and 0.5.

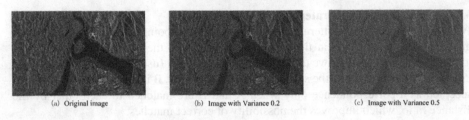

(a) Original image   (b) Image with Variance 0.2   (c) Image with Variance 0.5

Fig. 2. Partial simulated images

The repeatability rate refers to the proportion of the number of keypoints that are repeatedly extracted from two images to the total number of the keypoints within the range of a positioning error (1.2 is taken in our paper). The higher the repeatability rate is, the stronger the stability of feature extraction will be.

Figure 3(a) shows the changes of the repeatability rates between the reference images and the simulated images with different noise variances. It can be seen that the repeatability rates obtained by our method are always higher than those of Ref. [9]. Meanwhile, with the increase of the variance, the repeatability rates decrease sharply in Ref. [9], while those obtained by our method keep a stable decrease. The reason is that speckle noises are effectively smoothed by SRAD, thus the probability that noises are erroneously extracted as keypoints is reduced and the positioning accuracy of the keypoints is improved.

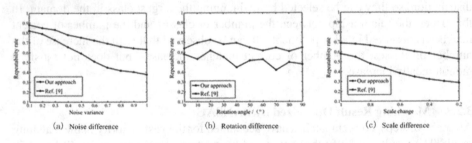

(a) Noise difference   (b) Rotation difference   (c) Scale difference

Fig. 3. Repeatability rates comparison

In addition, let Fig. 2(b) be the reference image, and Fig. 2(c) is rotated and scaled as the transformed images. Figure 3(b) and (c) show the changes of the repeatability rates between the reference images and the images transformed. Compared with Ref. [9], the repeatability rates obtained by our method are higher and keep a more stable change. The results show that the keypoints extracted by our method still keep a greater stability for images with different rotation and scale differences.

4.2 Comparisons with Other Registration Algorithms

To evaluate the registration performance of the proposed method, we experimentally validate it on three SAR image pairs with different time, different bands and different polarization modes. Registration comparisons between the proposed method and the traditional SIFT and Ref. [9] are implemented to demonstrate the superiority of our method in registration performance.

The first pair is two ALOS-PALSAR images from the same region. These two images were taken at different time and the resolution of them is 10 m. To increase the difficulty of the test, the sensed image is simulated with a rotation of 30°. The second pair is two multi-band images from the same region. One image with a size of 500×500 form C-band taken by Radarsat-2 is selected as the reference image, and the other one with a size of 450×450 from X-band taken by TerraSAR is selected as the sensed image. The third pair is two 512×512 multi-polarization images with the reference image obtained from the HV mode, and the sensed image of the same scene obtained from the VV mode. All of the three image pairs are contaminated by speckle noises.

The quantitative evaluation results for each method are listed in Table 1 and Fig. 4 is the registration result of our method. Compared with traditional SIFT, the number of keypoints detected and correct matches obtained by our method is larger and the registration accuracy has been greatly improved. Although the number of feature points extracted by the Ref. [9] is more than that of ours, the correct matches are relatively fewer and the registration accuracy is not satisfactory.

Table 1. Quantitative comparison of different algorithms

Data sets	Method	Number of keypoints		Match	RMSE/pixel
		Reference image	Sensed image		
1	SIFT	342	326	5	6.81
	Ref. [9]	448	412	10	2.13
	Our approach	427	395	14	1.26
2	SIFT	1397	631	8	4.06
	Ref. [9]	1693	801	21	2.07
	Our approach	1642	763	29	1.19
3	SIFT	1105	1090	8	5.67
	Ref. [9]	1549	1467	17	2.31
	Our approach	1454	1325	24	0.94

It is found that SRAD has a better filtering performance than the Gaussian function, and it can preserve edges of the image while smoothing speckle noise. Thus the number of false feature matches is reduced and the real keypoints contained in the important targets such as edges, contours and textures are preserved, which increases the number of keypoints detected and the probability of correct matching. Traditional SIFT is seriously affected by speckle noise. Many false keypoints are detected while a large amount of real points are lost as the edges are blurred, which greatly reduces the number of keypoints. Due to the use of nonlinear diffusion filtering in Ref. [9], the keypoints extracted is even more than that of our method. But it can't be ignored that many speckle noises are mixed with the real ones, which reduces the stability of feature extraction.

In the stage of feature matching, due to the existence of false keypoints as well as complex geometric changes and texture differences between the three image pairs, the registration accuracy is difficult to be ensured if only European distance is chosen as the

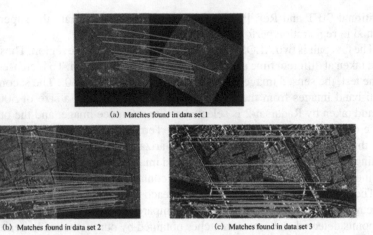

(a) Matches found in data set 1

(b) Matches found in data set 2   (c) Matches found in data set 3

Fig. 4. Matches found by the method proposed

similarity measure to make a feature matching. In Ref. [9], false points are eliminated with phase congruency of the points before matching, but the threshold of phase congruency is difficult to select. It is unreliable to remove the false keypoints from the real ones relying on the empirical threshold as a result of the randomness of speckle noises. By contrast, dual-matching strategy used in our approach overcomes the limitation of unidirectional ratio method. The relative position information between features is analyzed and the cluster analysis is utilized to effectively remove the mismatches, improving the registration accuracy. In addition, our approach can obtain better registration performance even rotation, scale and grayscale changes exist between the images, which inherits the superiority of SIFT.

5   Conclusions

In this paper, a SAR image registration approach based on improved SIFT is proposed. An anisotropic scale space of the image is constructed by SRAD with good properties of noise reduction and edge preserving, which improves the number and the stability of the keypoints and weakens the negative effect of speckle noises. Dual-matching strategy and cluster analysis in relative distance domain are introduced to refine the matches, which eliminates the false matches caused by speckle noises. The number of correct matches is increased and the registration precision is improved. Experimental results show that the method proposed has strong robustness to speckle noises and good adaptability to grayscale, rotation and scale differences of the images.

References

1. Zitova, B., Flusser, J.: Image registration methods: a survey. Image Vis. Comput. **21**(11), 977–1000 (2003)
2. Zhu, H., Ma, W.P., Hou, B., et al.: SAR image registration based on multifeature detection and arborescence network matching. J. IEEE Geosci. Remote Sens. Lett. **13**(5), 706–710 (2016)
3. Su, J., Li, B., Wang, Y.Z.: A SAR image registration algorithm based on closed uniform regions. J. Electron. Inform. Technol. **38**(12), 3282–3288 (2016)
4. Lowe, D.G.: Distinctive image features from scale-invariant keypoints. Int. J. Comput. Vis. **60**(2), 91–110 (2004)
5. Wang, S.H., You, H.J., Fu, K.: BFSIFT: a novel method to find feature matches for SAR image registration. IEEE Geosci. Remote Sens. Lett. **9**(4), 649–653 (2012)
6. Chen, Y., Zhao, H.C., Chen, S., Zhang, S.N.: Image matching algorithm based on SIFT for missile-borne SAR. Syst. Eng. Electron. **38**(6), 1276–1280 (2016)
7. Schwind, P., Suri, S., Reinartz, P., et al.: Applicability of the SIFT operator to geometric SAR image registration. Int. J. Remote Sens. **31**(8), 1959–1980 (2010)
8. Wang, F., You, H.J., Fu, K.: Adapted anisotropic Gaussian sift matching strategy for SAR registration. IEEE Geosci. Remote Sens. Lett. **12**(1), 160–164 (2015)
9. Fan, J.W., Wu, Y., Wang, F., et al.: SAR image registration using phase congruency and nonlinear diffusion-based SIFT. IEEE Geosci. Remote Sens. Lett. **12**(3), 562–566 (2015)
10. Weickert, J.: A review of nonlinear diffusion filtering. In: Haar Romeny, B., Florack, L., Koenderink, J., Viergever, M. (eds.) Scale-Space 1997. LNCS, vol. 1252, pp. 1–28. Springer, Heidelberg (1997). https://doi.org/10.1007/3-540-63167-4_37
11. Yu, Y., Acton, S.T.: Speckle reducing anisotropic diffusion. IEEE Trans. Image Process. **11**(11), 1260–1270 (2002)
12. Perona, P., Malik, J.: Scale space and edge detection using anisotropic diffusion. IEEE Trans. Pattern Anal. Mach. Intell. **12**(7), 629–639 (1990)
13. Weickert, J., Romeny, B.M.H., Viergever, M.A.: Efficient and reliable schemes for nonlinear diffusion filtering. IEEE Trans. Image Process. **7**(3), 398–410 (1998)
14. Fischler, M.A., Bolles, R.C.: Random sample consensus: a paradigm for model fitting with applications to image analysis and automated cartography. Commun. ACM **24**(6), 381–395 (1981)

Palmprint Recognition with Deep Convolutional Features

Qiule Sun, Jianxin Zhang[✉], Aoqi Yang, and Qiang Zhang

Key Laboratory of Advanced Design and Intelligent Computing, Ministry of Education,
Dalian University Dalian, Dalian, People's Republic of China
jxzhang0411@163.com

Abstract. Palmprint recognition has become popular and significant in many fields because of its high efficiency and accuracy in personal identification. In this paper, we present a scheme for palmprint features extraction based on deep convolutional neural network (CNN). The CNN, which naturally integrates low/mid/high-level feature, performs excellently in processing images, video and speech. We extract the palmprint features using the CNN-F architecture, and exactly evaluate the convolutional features from different layers in the network for both identification and verification tasks. The experimental results on public PolyU palmprint database illuminate that palmprint features from the CNN-F respectively achieve the optimal identification rate of 100% and verification accuracy of EER = 0.25%, which demonstrate the effectiveness and reliability of the proposed palmprint CNN features.

Keywords: Deep convolutional neural network · Palmprint recognition
Feature extraction

1 Introduction

As a kind of biometric identification technology, palmprint recognition has become a research focus in the field of artificial intelligence, pattern recognition and image processing in recent years. Existing palmprint recognition methods can be divided into several categories including structure-based methods, texture-based methods, subspace-based methods, statistics-based methods. The structure-based methods are to extract the relevant point features and line features [1, 2]. However, the recognition accuracy of the structure-based methods is relatively low, and the features need more storage space. Texture-based methods are to extract rich texture information from palmprint, for instance, PalmCode [3], Competitive Code [4], RLOC [5], BOCV [6] and double half-orientation based method [7]. These methods have stronger classification ability as well as good recognition accuracy. However, they may be affected by the translation and rotation of palmprint image because of the coding of palmprint features. The subspace-based methods means that the palmprint images are regarded as high dimensional vectors or matrices. They are transformed into low dimensional vectors or matrices by mapping or transformation, and make representations and matching for the palmprint in the low dimensional space [8–10]. The subspace methods possess high recognition accuracy and fast recognition speed. The statistics-based methods, Fourier Transform [11] and

© Springer Nature Singapore Pte Ltd. 2018
Y. Wang et al. (Eds.): IGTA 2017, CCIS 757, pp. 12–19, 2018.
https://doi.org/10.1007/978-981-10-7389-2_2

Wavelet Transform [12, 13], employ the center of gravity, mean value and variance of the palmprint image as the features. The features that the statistics-based methods extract are relatively small. All of the above methods indicate a superiority performance in palmprint recognition. Palmprint features extraction is the most basic and important part of palmprint recognition, which is the key to the recognition performance.

Recently, deep neural networks, whose fundamental ingredient is the training of a nonlinear feature extractor at each layer [14, 15], have demonstrated the excellent performance in image representation. A variety of depth convolutional neural networks, such as AlexNet [16], VggNet [17] and ResNet [18], achieve outstanding performance on processing images. Learning from a large-scale ImageNet database [19], they can extract genetic feature representations that generalize well and could be transplanted onto other image applications [20, 21]. Since we do not have enough palmprint images to train deep convolutional neural network from scratch, we employ the pre-trained deep convolutional neural network, CNN-F [22], as a feature extractor for the palmprint image in this paper. The goal is to introduce the pre-trained CNN-F for palmprint features extraction, and extensively evaluate the CNN features for palmprint verification and identification tasks.

The rest of paper is organized as follows. In Sect. 2, we briefly introduce the architecture of CNN-F and palmprint convolutional features. Experimental results for verification and identification tasks are given in Sect. 3, followed by the conclusion in Sect. 4.

2 Palmprint Recognition Based on CNN-F

2.1 Architecture of the CNN-F

The CNN-F ("F" for "fast") network [17] is made by Chatfield et al. [22] and inspired by the success of the CNN of Krizhevsky et al. [16]. It examined in Reference [22]. This network is meant to be architecturally similar to the original AlexNet [16]. The CNN-F configuration is given in Table 1. It has recently achieved state-of-the-art performance on image classification on ImageNet database, and includes 8 learned layers. The first five learned layers are said to be convolutional layers, the last three learned layers on the top of architecture are called Fully Connected (FC). The first convolutional layer ("layer 1") filters the $224 \times 224 \times 3$ size input image with 64 kernels of size $11 \times 11 \times 3$ with a stride of 4 pixels (this is the distance between the receptive field centers of neighboring neurons in a kernel map). The second convolutional layer ("layer 5"), which takes as input the output of the previous layer, filters it with 256 kernels of size $5 \times 5 \times 256$. Different from [17] and similar to [16], the first two convolutional layers include the Local Response Normalization (LRN) [16] operator. As well, the next three convolutional layers ("layer 9", "layer 11" and "layer 13") each has 256 kernels of size $3 \times 3 \times 256$. The first two FC layers ("layer 16" and "layer 17") are regularized using dropout [16], and output 4096 dimensional convolutional features. The output of the last FC layer ("layer 20") are 1000 dimensions. Please consult [22] for further details.

Table 1. The CNN-F configuration (For each convolution layer, the number of convolution filters, receptive field size, the convolution stride and spatial padding are indicated.)

Layer	0	1	2	3	4	5	6	7	8	9	10
Type	input	conv	relu	lrn	mpool	conv	relu	lrn	mpool	conv	relu
Name	-	conv1	relu1	norm1	pool1	conv2	relu2	norm2	pool2	conv3	relu4
Filt dim	-	3	-	-	-	64	-	-	-	256	-
Num filts	-	64	-	-	-	256	-	-	-	256	-
Stride	-	4	1	1	2	1	1	1	2	1	1
Pad	-	1	0	0	1	1	0	0	1	1	0
Layer	11	12	13	14	15	16	17	18	19	20	21
Type	conv	relu	conv	relu	mpool	conv	relu	conv	relu	conv	softmax
Name	conv4	relu4	conv5	relu5	pool5	fc6	relu6	fc7	relu7	fc8	prob
Filt dim	256	-	256	-	-	256	-	4096	-	4096	-
Num filts	256	-	256	-	-	4096	-	4096	-	1000	-
Stride	1	1	1	1	2	1	1	1	1	1	1
Pad	1	0	1	0	1	1	0	1	0	1	0

2.2 Palmprint Convolutional Features

The CNN-F is suitable to images of 224×224 pixels size, which must be colorful. Our image size is 128×128 and gray. So we have made a little pre-processing, which palmprint images are first resized to 224×224 and transferred to be colorful. Each layer has a plurality of feature maps, one of which is extracted by a convolution filter. For example, the input image is convoluted with 64 kernels of size $11 \times 11 \times 3$ to obtain 64 feature maps, which is the extracted convolution feature of the first convolutional layer. The feature maps, as input data, are then processed by the next layers to obtain other different feature maps according to the number of convolution filters and the filter size. Similar processing is done in other layers. Finally, we can capture the features of each layer and extract features of different layers from the network. We measure the recognition rate of the palmprint images according to the features. Then, we use cosine distance to calculate the difference of the inter-class and intra-class palmprint images, according to the cosine distance calculate the value of False Acceptance Rate (FAR), False Reject Rate (FRR), Equal Error Rate (EER) and recognition rate.

3 Experiments and Analysis

The experiments extract the palmprint images features using various layers of the network, and evaluate them on the PolyU palmprint database [23] for both recognition and verification tasks. All of our experiments are carried out on a PC machine with 3.30 GHz CPU, 4G memory and Matlab R2015b.

3.1   The PolyU Palmprint Database

The palmprint database of Hong Kong Polytechnic University (PolyU) is the most authoritative palmprint database in the world. It contains 7752 images of 386 different palms captured from two sessions with the size of each original image being 384 × 284. The experiments use the first session of the database, including 3855 images from 386 palms. The image size of the region of interest (ROI) segmented is 128 × 128 pixels. The partial palmprint images after segmentation are given in Fig. 1.

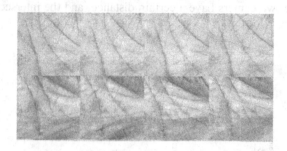

Fig. 1. Typical ROI images in PolyU palmprint database

3.2   The Verification Results

Figure 2 is the receiver operating characteristic (ROC) curve to evaluate the accuracy. Each point on the curve corresponds to the FAR and FRR under a safe threshold. A low value of EER indicates that our algorithm has a high recognition rate. We extract the convolutional features of the layers respectively, and use them to calculate the cosine distance of inter-class and intra-class palmprint images. Among the layers, the best performance is achieved by the features in 13th layer. In the curve, it is illuminated that the proposed method achieves the optimal verification accuracy of EER = 0.25%.

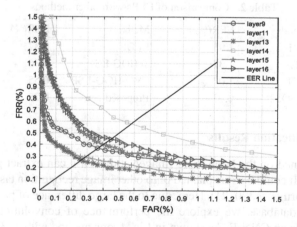

Fig. 2. The comparative ROC curves obtained by using various layers

Figure 3 is the matching degree distribution curve of true matching and false matching. The experiment adopts one to one matching strategy. A total of 91675 feature matching have been performed, in which the times of true matching (feature matching from the same palm) are 17370, the times of false matching (feature matching from different palms) are 78305. On the matching degree distribution curve, the distributions of true matching scores and false matching scores are similar to the Gauss distribution. The center of true matching scores is near 0.91 while the center of false matching scores is near 0.59. As show in Fig. 3, our method can effectively distinguish different palmprint images, which the two centers have a certain distance, and the intersection of the two curves is not much.

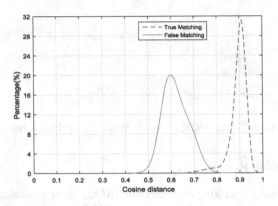

Fig. 3. Matching curves of intra-class and inter-class

Table 2 shows the proposed CNN-based method comparison of EERs with other methods, including WBFF [12], OWE [13], BDCT [24], 2D-DOCT [25], LLDP [26], WHOG-LSP and FVO-HOG-LSP [27].

Table 2. Comparison of EERs with other methods

Methods	EER(%)	Methods	EER(%)
WBFF	1.95	LLDP	0.37
OWE	1.37	WHOG-LSP	0.36
BDCT	1.07	FVO-HOG-LSP	0.55
2D-DOST	0.93	Proposed	**0.25**

3.3 The Identification Results

The CNN-F trained on the large-scale ImageNet database can extract genetic feature representations. It could be transplanted onto other image recognition tasks and achieve impressive performance [20, 21]. Here, due to the large difference of palmprint images with ImageNet database, we explore the performance of convolutional features of different layers from CNN-F. As shown in Fig. 4, our method with 1, 3 and 5 training images of each palm with different convolution layers of CNN-F achieves remarkable performance. Among the layers, the best performance is achieved by the features in 8th–16th layers, which achieves 100% recognition rate on gallery set with 3 and 5 images per palm. Only using a single image per palm as gallery set, our method obtains a high identification accuracy of 99.62%. Then, the comparative recognition rate results with other state-of-the-art methods are shown in Table 3.

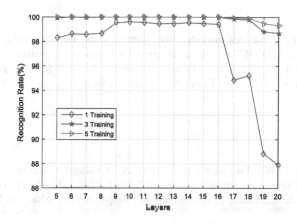

Fig. 4. The recognition rate results obtained by using palmprint features of different layers

Table 3. Recognition rates of different methods on PolyU database

Methods	Total samples	Different palms	Train samples	Recognition rate(%)
RLOC [5]	7752	386	1	98.37
Contourlet transform [28]	7752	386	3	88.91
2D-DOST [25]	900	150	3	97.29
BDCT [24]	2000	100	4	98.93
KPCA+GWR [29]	3860	386	4	99.69
OWE [13]	2000	100	5	98.90
2DGaborwavelets +PCNN [30]	3860	386	5	97.37
Proposed	3855	386	3	**100**

4 Conclusion

In this paper, we introduce deep convolutional features for palmprint recognition. The top layers of CNN-F describe the global features of palmprint images, but they include too much tuned for palmprint classification task. Meanwhile, the intermediate layers describe the local features of palmprint images, and they can serve as good descriptors for the new features of input images. Hence, extracted features from intermediate layers of CNN-F achieve better recognition performance than other layers. Moreover, even without any training operation, the palmprint convolutional features of middle layers outperform most of the other baselines. In future, we mainly have two tasks. Firstly, we will give more pre-processing to the palmprint images on the PolyU database. Secondly, we should use data augmentation approach to obtain more training palmprint images, and then train a network with the palmprint images database to improve the recognition performance.

Acknowledgements.   We acknowledge the support from the National Natural Science Foundation of China (No. 91546123), the Program for Liaoning Innovative Research Team in University (No. LT2015002), the Liaoning Provincial Natural Science Foundation (No. 201602035) and the High-level Talent Innovation Support Program of Dalian City (No. 2016RQ078).

References

1. Zhang, D., Shu, W.: Two novel characteristics in palmprint verification: datum point invariance and line feature matching. Pattern Recogn. **32**(4), 691–702 (1999)
2. Duta, N., Jain, A.K., Mardia, K.V.: Matching of palmprints. Pattern Recogn. Lett. **23**(4), 477–485 (2002)
3. Zhang, D., Kong, W., You, J., Wong, M.: Online palmprint identification. IEEE Trans. Pattern Anal. Mach. Intell. **25**(9), 1041–1050 (2003)
4. Kong, W.K., Zhang, D.: Competitive coding scheme for palmprint verification. In: International Conference on Pattern Recognition, pp. 23–26 (2004)
5. Jia, W., Huang, D.S., Zhang, D.: Palmprint verification based on robust line orientation code. Pattern Recogn. **41**(5), 1504–1513 (2008)
6. Guo, Z., Zhang, D., Zhang, L.: Palmprint verification using binary orientation co-occurrence vector. Pattern Recogn. Lett. **30**(13), 1219–1227 (2009)
7. Fei, L.K., Xu, Y., David, Z.: Half-orientation extraction of palmprint features. Pattern Recogn. Lett. **69**(C), 35–41 (2016)
8. Lu, G., Zhang, D., Wang, K.: Palmprint recognition using eigenpalms features. Pattern Recogn. Lett. **24**(9–10), 1463–1467 (2003)
9. Zhang, S., Lei, Y.K., Wu, Y.H.: Semi-supervised locally discriminant projection for classification and recognition. Knowl.-Based Syst. **24**(2), 341–346 (2011)
10. Yan, Y., Wang, H., Chen, S., et al.: Quadratic projection based feature extraction with its application to biometric recognition. Pattern Recogn. **56**(C), 40–49 (2016)
11. Li, W.X., Zhang, D., Xu, Z.Q.: Palmprint recognition based on Fourier transform. J. Softw. **13**(5), 879–886 (2002)
12. Krishneswari, K., Arumugam, S.: Intramodal feature fusion using wavelet for palmprint authentication. Int. J. Eng. Sci. Technol. **3**(2), 1597–1605 (2011)
13. Prasad, S.M., Govindan, V.K., Sathidevi, P.S.: Palmprint authentication using fusion of wavelet based representations. In: World Congress on Nature & Biologically Inspired Computing, pp. 15–17 (2010)
14. Hinton, G.E., Osindero, S., Teh, Y.W.: A fast learning algorithm for deep belief nets. Neural Comput. **18**(7), 1527–1554 (2006)
15. Vincent, P., Larochelle, H., Lajoie, I., et al.: Stacked denoising autoencoders: learning useful representations in a deep network with a local denoising criterion. J. Mach. Learn. Res. **11**(6), 3371–3408 (2010)

16. Krizhevsky, A., Sutskever, I., Hinton, G.E.: Imagenet classification with deep convolutional neural networks. Adv. Neural. Inf. Process. Syst. 25(2), 1097–1105 (2012)
17. Simonyan, K., Zisserman, A.: Very deep convolutional networks for large-scale image recognition. Comput. Sci. (2014)
18. He, K., Zhang, X., Ren, S., Sun, J.: Deep residual learning for image recognition. Comput. Sci. (2015)
19. Deng, J., Dong, W., Socher, R., et al.: ImageNet: a large-scale hierarchical image database. In: Computer Vision and Pattern Recognition, pp. 248–255 (2009)
20. Donahue, J., Jia, Y., Vinyals, O., et al.: DeCAF: a deep convolutional activation feature for generic visual recognition. Comput. Sci. 50(1), 815–830 (2013)
21. Razavian, A.S., Azizpour, H., Sullivan, J., et al.: CNN features off-the-shelf: an astounding baseline for recognition. In: Computer Vision and Pattern Recognition Workshops, pp. 24–29 (2014)
22. Chatfield, K., Simonyan, K., Vedaldi, A., et al.: Return of the devil in the details: delving deep into convolutional nets. Comput. Sci. (2014)
23. The Hong Kong Polytechnic University. PolyU Palmprint Database. (2004,1,1) [2006,7,15]. http://www.comp.polyt.edu.hk/~biometrics/
24. Meraoumia, A., Chitroub, S., Bouridane, A.: Gaussian modeling and Discrete Cosine Transform for efficient and automatic palmprint identification. In: International Conference on Machine and Web Intelligence, pp. 121–125 (2010)
25. Saedi, S., Charkari, N.M.: Palmprint authentication based on discrete orthonormal S-Transform. Appl. Softw. Comput. 21(8), 341–351 (2014)
26. Luo, Y.T., Zhao, L.Y., Zhang, B., et al.: Local line directional pattern for palmprint recognition. Pattern Recog. 50(C), 26–44 (2016)
27. Hong, D., Liu, W., Wu, X., et al.: Robust palmprint recognition based on the fast variation Vese-Osher model. Neurocomputing 174, 999–1012 (2015)
28. Butt, M.A.A., Masood, H., Mumtaz, M., et al.: Palmprint identification using contourlet transform. In: International Conference on Biometrics: Theory, Applications and Systems, pp. 1–5 (2008)
29. Ekinci, M., Aykut, M.: Gabor-based kernel PCA for palmprint recognition. Electron. Lett. 43(20), 1077–1079 (2007)
30. Wang, X., Lei, L., Wang, M.: Palmprint verification based on 2D-Gabor wavelet and pulse-coupled neural network. Knowl.-Based Syst. 27(3), 451–455 (2012)

Isosurface Algorithm Based on Generalized Three Prism Voxel

Qing Li[1], Qingyuan Li[1,2,4(✉)], Xiaolu Liu[3], Zhubin Wei[4],
and Qianlin Dong[4]

[1] School of Mapping and Geographic Science, Liaoning Technical University,
Fuxin 123000, China
muzigef@163.com
[2] Key Laboratory of Geo-Informatics, Chinese Academy of Surveying and
Mapping, Beijing 100830, China
liqy@casm.ac.cn
[3] Dalian Jin Yuan Survey Technology Co., Ltd, Dalian 116600, China
[4] College of Geoscience and Surveying Engineering,
China University of Mining and Technology, Beijing 100083, China

Abstract. It is an effective method to use isosurface expressing inhomogeneous attribute field of solid objects inside. Due to the shortcomings such as topological ambiguity and segmentation ambiguity of the widely used isosurface algorithms (moving cube and moving tetrahedral), this paper presents an isosurface extraction algorithm based on generalized tri-prism voxel, which is called moving generalized triangular prism (MGTP) algorithm. The triangular patches are extracted from each generalized triangular prism (GTP) to establish the isosurface in this algorithm. In this paper, the linear interpolation algorithm is used to calculate the equivalent points and subdivision points, which can eliminate isosurface cracks. The topological structure of the equivalent patches is determined according to the number of GTP equivalent points. If there is topology ambiguity in GTP, isosurface is extracted after using the subdivision method to eliminate it. The MGTP algorithm can effectively solve the problem of topological ambiguity and segmentation ambiguity.

Keywords: MGTP algorithm · Isosurface · Equivalent point
Topological ambiguity · Subdivision GTP

1 Introduction

In geological body modeling, 3D data model and structures such as grid, irregular blocks, cross-sections and volume data structures were studied in the early 1990s, and the three-dimensional geological modeling theory was established preliminarily [1]. Since then, many scholars had carried out a lot of researches and practical applications in 3D geological modeling and visualization techniques. The focus of three-dimensional geological modeling had been transferred from single geometric

Foundation Support: National Natural Science Foundation of China (41272367).

modeling early to both the shape and expression of non-uniformity attribute in geo-logical body [2]. It is an important method to express attribute information of geologic body by using Isosurface. The most classical isosurface extraction method is MC (Marching Cube) algorithm proposed by Lorensen and Cline [3] in 1987. Because of the simple and easy implementation, MC algorithm has been widely concerned and applied. In recent years, the MC algorithm has been extensively studied and applied in many fields and has made a lot of research results, such as three-dimensional recon-struction of medical image data [4, 5], scalar field analysis in finite element analysis, molecular surface display in molecular chemistry and three-dimensional geomorphol-ogy simulation [6, 7]. However, there are still some problems in the MC algorithm, such as incorrect topology, low extraction efficiency, limited application range and so on. A lot of other improved algorithms have been put forward by scholars to solve those problems. MT (Marching Tetrahedral) algorithm [8, 9] is the most classical algorithm. It can solve the topological ambiguity and has higher approximation accuracy, however, a large number of triangular equivalent patches lead to an increase in computational complexity in MT algorithm. In addition, there is segmentation ambiguity in MT algorithm. In recent years, the method of visualization of geologic body based on triangular prisms has been paid more attention, for example, the three-dimensional data model based on analogical triangular prism and later the gen-eralized triangular prism (GTP) modeling method proposed by Lixin Wu and Penggen Cheng [10–13]. The visualization algorithms based on GTP have many important advantages, and the isosurface construction algorithm based on GTP lacks the research. In this paper, a new algorithm based on moving generalized triangular prism (MGTP) is proposed to extract isosurface, which is inspired by both MC and MT algorithm and the subdivision method used to eliminate ambiguity surface of the square, which is proposed by Yanhong Zou and Jianchun He [14].

2   MC and MT Algorithm Theory

At first, the paper introduces the basic theory about MC and MT algorithm.

The MC algorithm searches for triangular isosurface patches in cubes one by one. The cube consists of eight points, and each of the four points falls on the same plane. For a given threshold I, it is recorded as 0 if the attribute value of the cube vertex is less than I, otherwise, it is recorded as 1. The attribute value of any point P (x, y, z) in the cube can be interpolated by the attribute values of the eight vertices, which can be represented by the following formula (1):

$$F(x, y, z) = a_0 + a_1 x + a_2 y + a_3 z + a_4 xy + a_5 yz + a_6 xz + a_7 xyz \qquad (1)$$

Where a_i ($i = 0, 1, 2, ..., 7$) is a function of the eight vertex attribute values of the cube.

According to the isosurface function, it can be calculated that the point sets sat-isfying $F(x, y, z) = I$ on the outer surface of the cube, and the approximated isosurface in the cube. Durst [15] found that when the four sides of the square have intersections with the isosurface (called equivalent points), the MC algorithm cannot guarantee isosurface patches with the same structure on the common surface of two adjacent cubes, so there will be cracks, the common surface is usually called the ambiguity surface. Natarajan [16] found that even if the cube does not include the ambiguity surface, the cube may also include different topological structure isosurface, which is called the body ambiguity. The surface ambiguity and body ambiguity are collectively called topology ambiguity. In order to eliminate the topological ambiguity of MC algorithm, Nielson [17] and Xiuxia Liang and Caiming Zhang [18] calculated the critical points of the trilinear interpolation function respectively, and calculated the topology structure of the approximated isosurface of the cube according to the number of the cube's critical points. But this method is complicated in both theory and program. Yanhong Zou proposed to use the subdivision method to eliminate surface ambiguity [14], but because the topology structure of the cube intersecting with the isosurface is complex, even if there is not surface ambiguity, there may be body ambiguity. This method cannot eliminate topology ambiguity completely.

MT algorithm is an improved algorithm, which is developed on the basis of the MC algorithm to subdivide the cube into tetrahedrons for eliminating topology ambiguities. The cube is usually subdivided into five tetrahedrons, six tetrahedrons or 24 tetrahedrons. There are two ways to subdivide it into five tetrahedrons, four ways to subdivide it into six tetrahedrons, one way to subdivide it into 24 tetrahedrons [19]. MT algorithm can eliminate the problem of topology ambiguity, but it will produce a large number of triangular isosurface patches. The cube will be subdivided, even though the isosurface has not topology ambiguity in this algorithm. Cignoni [20] found that the topological structure of the isosurface is related to the subdivision mode in MT algorithm, there will be cracks if the adjacent cubes are not subdivided with same way, which is called subdivision ambiguity. In order to make up the shortcomings of MT algorithm, Li Cheng proposed an isosurface extraction algorithm which is based on Delaunay tetrahedron [21]. However, the tetrahedron cannot reflect the structure of stratified geologic body and its attribute field, so it cannot be suitable for isosurface extraction of stratified geologic body.

3 Moving Generalized Triangular Prism Algorithm

The structure of GTP involves six vertices, a top face, a bottom face, and three sides face. For a given threshold I, it is recorded as 0 if the attribute value of the GTP vertex is less than I, otherwise it is recorded as 1. There are 64 intersections of the isosurface and the GTP, decreasing the number of conditions to 8 after removing repeat structures produced by rotational symmetry and the complementary symmetry. There are six structures with no ambiguity, one structure with one ambiguity, and one structure with two ambiguities. Therefore, the structures are $6 + 2^1 \times 1 + 2^2 \times 1 = 12$ after taking the surface ambiguity into account. As shown in Fig. 1.

In the 16 structures of the MC algorithm, there are ten structures without ambiguity, two of them with one ambiguity, two of them with two ambiguities, one with three ambiguities, and one with six ambiguities [22]. Therefore, the structures of MC algorithm are $10 + 2^1 \times 2 + 2^2 \times 2 + 2^3 \times 1 + 2^6 \times 1 = 94$. Comparing the results, it can seen that the MGTP algorithm is much less complexity than the MC algorithm.

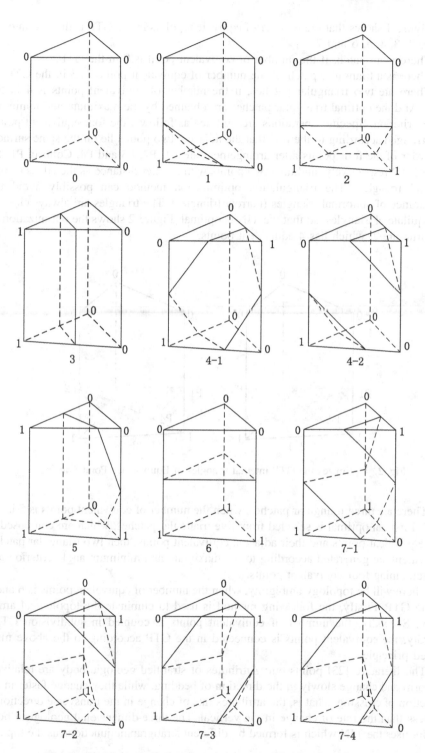

Fig. 1. Topological relations based on generalized triangular prism

Figure 1 shows that the number of equivalent points in the GTP is divided into six types: 0, 3, 4, 5, 6 and 7.

There is no patch, if the number of equivalent point is 0 in the GTP.

There is a triangular patch, if the number of equivalent points is 3 in the GTP.

There are two triangular patches, if the number of equivalent points is 4 in the GTP. And the optimal triangular patches are obtained by the maximum and minimum angle criterion. Specific operations are outlined as follows: the four equivalent points are arranged according to the rule that the adjacent two points lie on the same surface, the order of the four points after arrangement are P1, P2, P3 and P4. Connect P1, P3 and P2, P4 respectively, and take two points with smaller distance as the edges of two internal triangles. The triangulation optimization method can possibly avoid the appearance of abnormal triangles (narrow triangles). The triangles are always close to the equilateral triangles, so that the TIN is optimal. Figure 2 shows the optimization of the structure 2, which has 4 equivalent points.

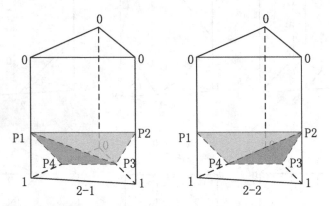

Fig. 2. Optimizes the GTP internal triangles of Equivalence Point 4 in Fig. 1

There are three triangular patches, when the number of equivalent points is 5 in the GTP. First, an optimal is selected from five triangular patches, which are composed of five equivalent points and their adjacent equivalent points; then two triangular patches equivalent are generated according to the maximum and minimum angle criterion and the remaining four equivalent points.

There will be topology ambiguity, when the number of equivalent points is 6 and 7 in the GTP. Firstly, the following method is used to eliminate the topological ambiguity. Secondly, the number of equivalent points is counted in subdivision GTPs. Thirdly, the equivalent points is connected in the GTP according to the above mentioned principle.

The literature [23] points out: Attributes of stratified geologic body are relatively uniform and change slowly in the direction of bedding, while they change faster in the direction of crossing. That is, the attributes rate of change in the transverse direction is far less than the rate of change in the vertical. The three-dimensional geological body model uses the TIN which is formed by different stratigraphic junctions as the top and bottom surfaces of generalized triangular prisms [24], MGTP algorithm can show the bedding and crossing attribute information of stratified geologic body well.

4 The Subdivision Method to Eliminate the Topology Ambiguity of MGTP Algorithm

Figure 1 tells us: there is an ambiguity surface in the fourth structure, there are two ambiguity surfaces in the seventh structure, and there is not ambiguity in other structures. In the first, second, third, fifth, and sixth structures, the polygons formed by the isosurface intersecting the GTP are triangular, quadrilateral and pentagonal. The fourth and seventh structures are not only surface ambiguity, but also 4–2, 7–2, and 7–3 are body ambiguity. The GTPs which have 6 or 7 equivalent points will appear the topological ambiguity. Figure 3 shows the body ambiguity of the structure 4–2:

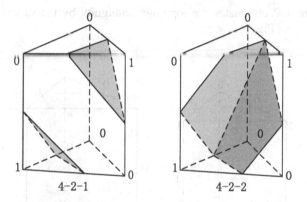

Fig. 3. Body ambiguity

According to the above analysis, there may turn up the body ambiguity, only when the surface ambiguity occurs. That is, as long as there is not surface ambiguity in the GTP, there will be not body ambiguity. The principle of MGTP algorithm to eliminate topology ambiguity is outlined as follows:

1. Firstly, the original GTP is subdivided into GTP-1 and GTP-2 using subdivision triangle, which is generated by connecting the midpoint of the three side edges in the GTP.
2. Secondly, GTP-1 and GTP-2 is subdivided into eight GTPs by the midpoint of the three edges in the top face and bottom face, and the midpoint of that subdivision triangle.
3. Finally, the attribute value of the eight new GTPs is calculated using the linear interpolation algorithm, and then the number of equivalent points for each new GTP is counted. If there is a topology ambiguity, steps 1, 2, and 3 is looped to eliminate it.

The subdivision GTP is shown in Fig. 4:

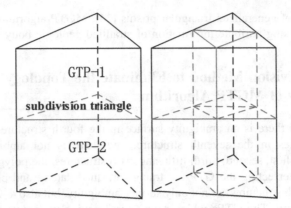

Fig. 4. Subdivision GTP

The structure 4–2 eliminates the topology ambiguity by the subdivision method, which is showing in Fig. 5.

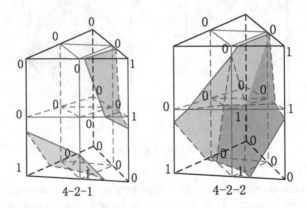

4-2-1   4-2-2

Fig. 5. Example of the subdivision method

MGTP algorithm uses the linear interpolation algorithm to calculate equivalent points and subdivision points in the GTPs, so the resulting isosurface is not cracks. The subdivision method can be used to eliminating the topology ambiguity and improve the accuracy of isosurface extraction, so it has a good expansibility.

5   Implement the MGTP Algorithm

The processes of implementation of the MGTP algorithm can be outlined as follow. Firstly, the non-null GTPs should be searched according to the threshold I before extracting the isosurface. Secondly, a container is set to save non-null GTPs, so that

GTPs can intersect the isosurface more quickly and efficiently. Finally, the isosurface is constructed according to the non-null GTP.

The following method is used to retrieve non-null GTPs:

> // Retrieve the equivalence points in the data network by edge
>
> for i = 0, 1, 2, ..., EdgeNum
>
> {
>
> if there is a IsoVerte   then
>
>   IsoVerte.ID = Edge.ID;
>
>   //Using thelinear interpolation calculate coordinate value
>
>   IsoVerte.x = Edge.x1 $\times$ Scale1 + Edge.x2 $\times$ Scale2;
>
>   IsoVerte.y = Edge.y1 $\times$ Scale1 + Edge.y2 $\times$ Scale2;
>
>   IsoVerte.z = Edge.z1 $\times$ Scale1 + Edge.z2 $\times$ Scale2;
>
>   Store the IsoVerte into IsoVertes;
>
> }
>
> // Retrieve non-empty GTPs
>
> for j = 0, 1, 2, ..., 9;
>
> {
>
>   for k = 0, 1, 2, ..., IsoVertes.size( )
>
>   if (GTPEdge[j].ID == IsoVertes[k].ID)   then
>
>   IsoGTP.isoVertexNum++;
>
> }
>
> if (GTP.isoVertexNum > 0)   then
>
>   Store the GTP into IsoGTPs;

All the equivalent points are stored into the container named IsoVertes, and non-null GTPs are stored into the container named IsoGTPs.

The steps of generating isosurface are outlined as follows:

1. The number of GTP equivalent points is read by retrieving non-null GTP container elements sequentially.
2. There is a triangular patch, if the number of equivalent points is 3 in the GTP. The patch is saved into container named m_IsoTriangle, and the GTP is removed from m_IsoGTP.
3. There are two triangular patches, if the number of equivalent points is 4 in the GTP. And the optimal triangular patches are obtained by the maximum and minimum angle criterion. The patches are saved into container named m_IsoTriangle, and the GTP is removed from m_IsoGTP.

4. There are three triangular patches, when the number of equivalent points is 5 in the GTP. The patches are saved into container named m_IsoTriangle, and the GTP is removed from m_IsoGTP.
5. There will be topology ambiguity, if the number of equivalent points is 6 and 7, the subdivision method is used to eliminate the topology ambiguity. Calculating the number of equivalent points in each subdivision GTP, adding the non-null subdivision GTPs to m_IsoGTP, and then removing the original GTP from the container.
6. Non-null GTP elements were selected successively, repeating steps 2, 3, 4 and 5, until the non-null GTP container is empty.
7. The triangular equivalent patches stored in the m_IsoTriangle are drawn by OpenGL, and the MGTP algorithm ends.

The advantages of the MGTP algorithm are summarized as follows: (1) Equivalent points do not be extracted repeatedly, since edges in the data network are traversed when extracting them. (2)The connection of the equivalent point is judged by the number of the equivalent points of the GTP, so the algorithm is clear and easy to implement. (3) The equivalent points in GTP are stored according to the ID stored in the GTP, at the same time, MGTP algorithm follows the rule of "no ambiguity, not subdivision", all of them can greatly reducing the amount of data storage and improving the speed of operation. (4) Equivalent points of the original non - null GTPs and the subdivision GTPs are calculated by the linear interpolation algorithm, as a result, the isosurface will not be cracked. (5) Triangular patches are obtained by the minimum angle maximization criterion, which avoids the appearance of elongated triangles and obtains optimal triangles.

6 The Result and Analysis of Isosurface Extracted by MGTP Algorithm

In this experiment, the data used is the simulation attribute field of ore grade, the software used is "Geological 3D Engineer Assistant (G3DA)" of China Academy of Surveying and Mapping, on which the MGTP algorithm is implemented in C++. In the attribute field, the minimum attribute value is 85.57 and the maximum attribute value is 187.77. The fence diagram of attribute field is shown in Fig. 6; the isosurface extraction is shown in Fig. 7(a), when the attribute value is 175; the isosurface extraction is shown in Fig. 7(b), when the attribute value is 180. The pink dots in Fig. 7 (a) and (b) are equivalent points. Figure 7(c) and (d) is superposition showing the isosurface with attribute values of 175 and 180 in a translucent pattern. Figure 7(c) is a plan view and Fig. 7(d) is a front view.

The isosurface with attribute values of 175 and 180 is consistent with the fence diagram of attribute field in Fig. 6. The simulated attribute values are reduced from the explosion point to the surroundings, so isosurface with attribute values of 175 and 180 is almost closed. It can be seen from Fig. 7(c) and (d) that the isosurface with an attribute value of 180 is surrounded by an isosurface with an attribute value of 175, and the spatial range of the attribute value in the range of 175 to 180 can be extracted. By comparing Fig. 7(c) and (d), it shows that the attribute values in the bedding direction

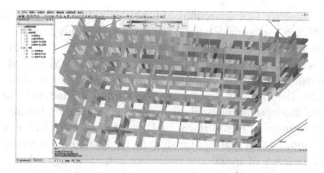

Fig. 6. The fence diagram of attribute field

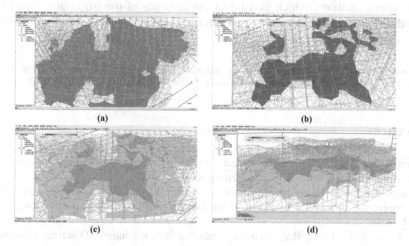

(a)   (b)

(c)   (d)

Fig. 7. Result and analysis of isosurface extracted by MGTP algorithm (a) Isosurface with an attribute value of 175; (b) Isosurface with an attribute value of 180 (c) Top view of the superimposable isosurface with attribute values of 175 and 180; (d) Front view of the superimposable isosurface with attribute values of 175 and 180

change slower than in the crossing direction. MGTP algorithm solves the topological ambiguity in MC and segmentation ambiguity in MT, eliminates isosurface cracks and topology errors of triangular patches. The result of isosurface extraction confirms the correctness of the MGTP algorithm theory, at the same time, shows that the MGTP algorithm is suitable for the isosurface extraction of stratified geologic body.

7 Conclusion

GTP model has expanded the range of applications in the three-dimensional geological modeling and visualization. The paper presents an isosurface extraction algorithm based on GTP, which can take advantage of GTP model. The paper gets the following conclusions: (1) there are 12 intersections of the isosurface and the GTP after taking the topological ambiguity into consideration. The structure of equivalent surface patches is judged from the number of equivalent points in the GTP. (2) The body ambiguity is possible only when the surface ambiguity appears in the MGTP algorithm. The algorithm eliminates the surface ambiguity by the subdivision method, at the same time, it eliminates the topology ambiguity. The subdivision method can not only be used to eliminate the topological ambiguity of MGTP algorithm, but also can be used to improve the accuracy of isosurface, and the expansion of the method is well. (3) The MGTP algorithm is suitable for discrete data based on borehole sampling, it makes up the deficiency of traditional isosurface extraction algorithm, which cannot deal with irregular cube data. It also takes into account that the attributes rate of change is different in the direction of bedding and crossing. (4) The MGTP algorithm has many advantages, but equivalent points are calculated by linear interpolation algorithm, they are just approximations, which may affect the accuracy of the isosurface. Apart from the subdivision method used in this paper, further research is needed for improving the accuracy of isosurface.

Acknowledgments. The authors gratefully acknowledge support from the National Natural Science Foundation of China (41272367).

References

1. Simov, W.: Holding 3D Geoscientific Modeling Computer Technique for Geological Characterization. South Sea in Press, Hong Kong (1994)
2. Royse, K.R.: Combining numerical and cognitive 3D modelling approaches in order to determine the structure of the Chalk in the London Basin. J. Comput. Geosci. **36**(2), 500–511 (2010)
3. Lorensen, W.E., Cline, H.E.: Marching cubes: a high resolution 3D surface construction algorithm. J. Comput. Graph. **21**(4), 163–169 (1987)
4. Liu, S., Yang, X., Chen, K.: Segmentation MC algorithm-based method of ultrasound image 3D reconstruction. J. Tsinghua Univ. Sci. Technol. **50**(8), 1214–1218 (2010). (in Chinese)
5. Liu, H., Wang, S., Lu, X.: The multi-storey medical image reconstruction based on marching cube algorithm. J. South-Central Univ. Nationalities Nat. Sci. Ed. **28**(3), 79–84 (2009). (in Chinese)
6. Li, S., Tang, J., Wu, G.: Algorithm of geology mesh surface reconstruction based on constraints. J. Comput. Eng. **35**(1), 253–254 (2009). (in Chinese)
7. Yang, H., Liu, M., Zhao, Y.: 3D geological modelling based on kriging and marching cube algorithm. J. Image Graph. **13**(3), 531–535 (2008). (in Chinese)
8. Doi, A., Koide, A.: An Efficient method of triangulating qqui-valued surfaces by using tetrahedral cells. J. IEICE Trans. E **74**(1), 214–224 (1991)
9. Nielson, G.M., Hamann, B.: The asymptotic decider: resolving the ambiguity in marching cubes. In: IEEE Visualization, San Diego, CA, pp. 83–91 (1992)
10. Lixin, W., Ruixin, Z., Yixin, Q., et al.: 3D Geoscience modelling and virtual mine system. J. Acta Geodaetica et Cartographica Sinica. **31**(1), 28–33 (2002). (in Chinese)

11. Cheng, P., Gong, J., Shi, W., et al.: Geological object modeling based on quasi tri-prism volume and its application. J. Geomatics Inform. Sci. Wuhan Univ. **29**(7), 607–607 (2004). (in Chinese)
12. Wu, L.: Topological relations embodied in a generalized tri-prism (GTP) model for A 3D geo-science modeling system. J. Comput. Geosci. **30**(4), 405–418 (2005)
13. Cheng, P.G., Shi, W.Z., Gong, J.Y., et al.: QTPV data model and algorithm and its application to geological exploration engineering. J. Geo. Spat. Inform. Sci. **5**(1), 64–71 (2005)
14. Zou, Y., He, J.: A spatial shape simulation method for three-dimensional geological body based on marching cubes algorithm. J. Acta Geodaetica et Cartographica Sinica. **41**(6), 910–917 (2012). (in Chinese)
15. Durst, M.J: Letters: additional reference to "Marching Cubes". J. Comput. Graph. **22**(2), 72–73 (1988)
16. Natarajan, B.K.: On generating topologically consistent isosurfaces from uniform samples. J. Vis. Comput. **11**(1), 52–62 (1994)
17. Nielson, G.M.: On marching cubes. J IEEE Trans. Vis. Comput. Graph. **9**(3), 283–297 (2003)
18. Liang, X., Zhang, C.: A Topology complexity based method to approximate isosurface with trilinear interpolated triangular patch. J. Comput. Res. Dev. **43**(3), 528–535 (2006). (in Chinese)
19. Li, C.: Geological data rendering based on MT algorithm. J. Digital Commun. **41**(4), 35–38 (2014). (in Chinese)
20. Cignoni, P., Ganovelli, F., Montani, C., et al.: Reconstruction of topologically correct and adaptive trilinear surfaces. J Comput. Graph. **24**(3), 399–418 (2000)
21. Cheng, L.: Research on the Surface Rendering Algorithm Based on Delaunay Tetrahedral Subdivision. Chengdu University of Technology, Chengdu (2015). (in Chinese)
22. Zhou, Y., Tang, Z.: Adaptive trilinear approximation to isosurfaces of data sets in 3D space. J. Chinese Comput. **17**, 1–10 (1994). (in Chinese)
23. Li, Q., Cui, Y., Sun, L., Chen, C., Dong, Q.: Interpolation for layered ore considering difference of variation rate in along and through layer directions and application in the description of shale gas reservoir. In: 2015 Conference of Geological Society of China, p. 257 (2015) (in Chinese)
24. Xin, Z.: Research on 3D Geological Modeling and Visualization Use GTP method based on VTK. Liaoning Technical University, Fuxin (2012). (in Chinese)

A Novel Classifier Using Subspace Analysis for Face Recognition

Aihua Yu[1,2(✉)], Gang Li[2(✉)], Beiping Hou[2], and Hongan Wang[2]

[1] College of Information Engineering, Zhejiang University of Technology,
Hangzhou, China
yuaihua_seu@163.com
[2] School of Automation & Electrical Engineering,
Zhejiang University of Science and Technology, Hangzhou, China
ieligang@zjut.edu.cn

Abstract. In this paper, a new classification algorithm based on subspace analysis is proposed. The classifier for each class is designed as a projector so that the samples within the class are projected to a near zero vector, while the samples not belonging to the class are projected far away from zero. Experiments on open and closed universe test of ORL data set show that the proposed subspace analysis-based classifier has a high recognition rate in closed universe test and that it is more robust than other methods in open universe experiments. The proposed algorithm has low computational complexity which is suitable for distributed embedded system applications.

Keywords: Face recognition · Subspace analysis
Sparse representation based classification · Support vector machines
Linear regression classification

1 Introduction

Face recognition (FR) methods have been studied for over 3 decades, and various techniques have been developed to handle different problems in face recognition, such as illumination, pose, occlusion and small sample size, etc. In the subspace based FR methods, often the nearest neighbor (NN) [1, 2] classifier and support vector machines (SVM) [3, 4] are the most widely used for the classification. Recently, a new face classification scheme, i.e., the sparse representation based classification (SRC) became a very hot topic [5–10]. In SRC, a query face image is encoded over the original training set with sparsity constraint imposed on the encoding vector. The training set acts as a dictionary to represent the testing samples as a sparse linear combination of its atoms. The classification is then performed by checking which class leads to the

This work was supported by the Grants of NSFCs 61473262, 61503339 and 61503330; Science & Technology Projection of Zhejiang Province (STPZP) 2017C33119; STPZP Education Department Y201430687.

smallest reconstruction residual of the query sample. The recent study found that it is not the l_1 norm SRC, but the collaborative representation classification(CRC) that leads to the success of the algorithm [11]. Although there are many evaluations with occlusion data set, open-universe face identification remains a little-studied problem in the research community [12].

In this paper, based on subspace analysis, an efficient classification algorithm is derived for the situation, where each class of samples belongs to a subspace. The main contributions are given as follows:

- A subspace classifier is proposed in this paper, which has a high recognition rate in closed and open university with low computer cost.
- A energy ratio decision metric is proposed, which help to improve the recognition rate greatly.

The paper is outlined as follows. Section 2 is devoted to providing some existing works on representation-based recognition, which are closely related to ours. Our main contribution is given in Sect. 3, in which a subspace analysis classifier is proposed. In SAC the test samples belong to the class are projection matching to near zero, while the samples don t belong to the class are project far away from zero. Experiments are carried out in Sect. 4 to examine the performance of the proposed approaches in open and closed universe. To end this paper, some concluding remarks are given in Sect. 5.

2   Related Works and Problem Formulation

In this section, we review briefly some related works on CRC, SVM, and LRC. Suppose that we have J class face samples $\{C_j\}_{j=1}^{J}$ and each class C_j has a set of face samples $\{x_{jl}\}$, each represented by a vector of dimension $N \times 1$ and scaled to unit in l_2-norm.

For each class C_j, we randomly select Q face samples to form the dictionary Ψ_i of the class:

$$\Psi_j = [x_{j1} \cdots x_{jq} \cdots x_{jQ}], \, j = 1, 2 \cdots, J \tag{1}$$

and the overall dictionary is then formed as

$$\Psi \overset{\Delta}{=} [\Psi_1 \ldots \Psi_j \ldots \Psi_J] = \{\Psi_i\} \tag{2}$$

It is assumed in the linear representation model that any face image signals $x \in \Re^{N \times 1}$ within the J classes can be represented as a linear combination of L vectors $\{\psi_i\}$, where $L = JQ$.

2.1   Collaborative Representation Based Classification

The CRC is based on the following:

$$\hat{s} \overset{\Delta}{=} \arg \min_{s} ||s||_{l_p} \quad \text{s.t.} \quad ||x - \Psi s||_2^2 \leq \varepsilon \tag{3}$$

where $\epsilon > 0$ is a constant, and $l_p = 0, 1, 2$. When $l_p = 0$, it is a NP hard problem, we can find sparse approximation with orthogonal matching pursuit (OMP). When $l_p = 1$, the sparse solution $\hat{s}$ can be found by various optimization methods [10, 13]. The amazing discovery due to David Donoho was that under certain conditions on the matrix Ψ and the sparsity of s, both l_0 and l_1 have the same unique solution. When $l_p = 2$ vector s has the close form solution:

$$\hat{s} = (\Psi^T \Psi + \lambda I)^{-1} \Psi^T x \tag{4}$$

where λ is used to prevent denominator equal to zero.

2.2 Support Vector Machines Classification

Given a training set of instance-label pairs $(x_i, y_i), i = 1, \ldots, Q$, where $x_i \in \Re^N$ and $y_i \in \{1, -1\}$, the SVM requires the solution of the following optimization problem:

$$(\hat{\omega}, \hat{v}, \hat{\xi}) = \arg \min_{\omega, v, \xi} \quad \frac{1}{2}\omega^T \omega + c_0 \|\xi\|_1$$
$$\text{s.t.} \qquad y_i(\omega^T x_i + v) \geq 1 - \xi_i \tag{5}$$
$$\xi_i \geq 0$$

where c_0 is a nonnegative constant. The classification of a test vector x as follows:

$$label(x) \triangleq sign(\hat{\omega}^T x + \hat{v}) \tag{6}$$

Multi-class SVM aims to assign labels to instances by using support vector machines, where the labels are drawn from a finite set of several elements. A number of methods have been proposed to implement SVM to produce multi-class classification. The dominant approach for doing so is to reduce the single multi-class problem into multiple binary classification problems [14]. For the jth classifier, let the positive examples be all the points in class j, and let the negative examples be all the points not in class j. Let f_j be the jth classifier. Classify with

$$\hat{j} \triangleq \arg \max_{j \in [1, J]} f_j(x) = \arg \max_{j \in [1, J]} \hat{\omega}_j^T x + \hat{v}_j \tag{7}$$

2.3 Linear Regression Classification

The LRC [15, 16] tries to classify the test samples to the class which has the minimum linear representation residual energy. s_j is evaluated against each class model,

$$\hat{s}_j \triangleq \arg \min_s \|x - \Psi_j s\|_2 \quad s.t. \quad \forall i \in [1, J] \tag{8}$$

which can be solved by least square estimation as:

$$\hat{s}_j = (\Psi_j^T \Psi_j)^{-1} \Psi_j^T x \tag{9}$$

Like the process of CRC, LRC result is determined by the residual energy between test face and predicted response variables.

$$\sigma_j^2 \overset{\Delta}{=} ||(x - \Psi_j \hat{s}_j)||_2^2, \forall j = 1, 2, \ldots, J \tag{10}$$

Decision is made in favor of the class with the minimum residual energy:

$$\hat{j} \overset{\Delta}{=} \arg \min_{j \in \{1, \cdots, J\}} \{\sigma_j^2\} \tag{11}$$

3   Subspace Analysis

Let $X = [x_1 \quad \cdots \quad x_l \quad \cdots \quad x_L] \in \Re^{N \times L}$ be a set of samples for some class of signals. Assume that X has the following SVD:

$$X = V \begin{bmatrix} \Sigma_r & 0 \\ 0 & 0 \end{bmatrix} U^T$$

Denote $\Omega \overset{\Delta}{=} V(:, r+1 : N)^T$, where r is the rank of X and $r < N$ is assumed. Clearly,

$$\Omega x_l = 0, \forall l$$

We call

$$\mathcal{H}_e \overset{\Delta}{=} \mathrm{span}\{V(:, r+1), V(:, r+2), \cdots, V(:, N)\}$$

the noise space of X, which is actually the null-space of the matrix X, while

$$\mathcal{H}_s \overset{\Delta}{=} \mathrm{span}\{V(:, 1), V(:, 2), \cdots, V(:, r)\}$$

is called the signal space of X.

For a given $x \in \Re^{N \times 1}$, it is evident that $x \in \mathcal{H}_s$ if and only

$$\Omega x = 0$$

Practically, the measurements are given by

$$\tilde{x}_1 = x_l + \varepsilon_l, \forall\ l$$

where $x_l \in \mathcal{H}_s$ and $\{\varepsilon_l\}$ is an i.i.d. set with zero-mean and a variance σ_0^2. Therefore,

$$R \overset{\Delta}{=} \frac{1}{L}\tilde{X}\tilde{X}^T = \hat{V}\hat{\Lambda}\hat{V}^T \approx V\begin{bmatrix} \Lambda_r & 0 \\ 0 & 0 \end{bmatrix}V^T + \sigma_0^2 I_N$$

So, when $L \gg N$ one can estimate σ_0^2 and Ω from the SVD of R. The former is the smallest singular value of this matrix, while if σ_0^2 is the repeated eigenvalue of R with a multiplicity of p, then $\hat{r} = N - p$ and

$$\Omega = \hat{V}(:, \hat{r} + 1 : N)^T$$

Assume that we have J different classes of linear signals $\{X_j\}_{j=1}^J$. For each X_j, we can design a transform Ω_j with the method described above. Like the MUSIC algorithm, we can classify a vector x from J classes of signals with

$$j_0 \overset{\Delta}{=} \arg\min_j\{\frac{1}{|\,\|\Omega_j x\|_2^2 - \hat{r}\sigma_0^2\,|}\} \tag{12}$$

3.1 Subspace Analysis Classifier

For a class of face samples, we design a face classifier (12) according to the proposed method. We see that each design is related to a class of signals. In order to improve the recognition performance and anti-interference ability, we propose a new recognition algorithm.

Let $\Omega_j \in \mathfrak{R}^{L_j \times N}$ with $L_j \leq N$ to be decided below and

$$\Omega_j \overset{\Delta}{=} \arg\min_\Omega\{\|\Omega X_j\|_F^2 - \alpha\|\Omega X_j^*\|_F^2 \overset{\Delta}{=} \rho(\Omega, X_j)\}$$
$$\text{s.t. } \text{rank}(\Omega) = L_j, \|\Omega(l, :)\|_2 = 1, \forall l \tag{13}$$

To solve the above, let us define

$$\mathcal{L} \overset{\Delta}{=} \rho(\Omega, X_j) + \sum_{l=1}^L \lambda_l(\|\Omega(l, :)\|_2^2 - 1)\}\}$$

Note

$$\rho(\Omega, X_j) = \text{tr}[\Omega(X_j X_j^T - \alpha X_j^* X_j^{*T})\Omega^T] \overset{\Delta}{=} -\text{tr}[\Omega R_j \Omega^T]$$

and hence

$$\frac{\partial \mathcal{L}}{\partial \Omega(l, :)} = -2\Omega(l, :)R_j^T + 2\lambda_l \Omega(l, :) = 0$$

that is

$$(\lambda_l I_N - R_j)\Omega(l,:)^T = 0, \forall l$$

which implies that $\Omega(l,:)^T$ belongs to one of the N normalized eigenvector sets $\{\pm V_j(:,n)\}$ of the symmetric R_j, where

$$R_j \overset{\Delta}{=} \alpha X_j^* X_j^{*T} - X_j X_j^T = V_j \Gamma_j V_j^T$$

where $\Gamma_j \overset{\Delta}{=} \mathrm{diag}(\gamma_1, \cdots, \cdots, \gamma_N)$ with $\gamma_n \geq \gamma_{n+1}, \forall n$. It follows from the constraint $\mathrm{rank}(\Omega_j) = L_j$ that the solutions to (13) are given by

$$\Omega_j(l,:)^T = \pm V_j(:,l), l = 1, 2, \cdots, L_j$$

One can simply take

$$\Omega_j = V_j(:,1:L)^T, \forall j \Rightarrow \Omega^T = \begin{bmatrix} \Omega_1^T & \cdots & \Omega_j^T & \cdots & \Omega_J^T \end{bmatrix} \tag{14}$$

where L_j is such that $\gamma_{L_j} \geq 0$ and $\gamma_{L_j+1} < 0$.

The classification is executed with

$$j_0 \overset{\Delta}{=} \arg\max_j \left\{ \frac{\|\Omega_j^* x\|_2^2}{\|\Omega_j x\|_2^2 + \varepsilon} \right\} \tag{15}$$

Remark:

- When each Ω_j has L repeated rows, $\frac{\|\Omega_j^* x\|_2}{\|\Omega_j x\|_2}$ is independent of L. If $L = 1$, Ω_j^T is actually a vector belonging to the null-space of X_j. In that case, if the query image x belongs to this null-space but orthogonal to this particular Ω_j^T, then x would be classified into the j th class as $\Omega_j x = 0$. So, Ω_j has to be rich enough to span the entire null-space of X_j with the column vectors of Ω_j^T and therefore, the constraint $\mathrm{rank}(\Omega) = L$ is necessary for efficiently transforming.
- When $\alpha = 0$, $\Omega_j X_j = 0$ and hence the transform is purely based on the null-space of X_j. With a small α (it is suggested that $0 \leq \alpha < 1$), more robust Ω_j is expected.
- The choice of L is very important. Generally speaking, the bigger L is, the better subject to $L \leq N - r_j, \forall j$. Actually, one can set different dimension to different Ω_j, say $\Omega_j \in \Re^{L_j \times N}$ with $L_j \leq N - r_j, \forall j$.
- When $r_j < < N, \forall j$, one can design Ω_j using

$$\Omega_j \overset{\Delta}{=} \arg\min_\Omega \{ \|\Omega X_j^*\|_F^2 - \lambda \|\Omega X_j\|_F^2 \}$$
$$\mathrm{s.t.rank}(\Omega) = L_j \leq N - r_j^*, \|\Omega(l,:)\|_2 = 1, \forall l \tag{16}$$

In a similar way, the classification is executed with

$$j_0 \overset{\Delta}{=} \arg\max_j \{ \frac{\|\Omega_j x\|_2^2}{\|\Omega_j^* x\|_2^2 + \varepsilon} \} \tag{17}$$

Alg$_{SAC}$:

- Step I: Test sample and train sample l_2 normalization. Signal compression with PCA;
- Step II: To find the vector Ω with Eq. (13);
- Step III: Decide the class according to the energy ratio as Eq. (15);

4   Experimental Result

In order to verify the classification performance of subspace classification, we test the algorithm on open and closed universe. The CPU is running at 3.4 Ghz (single thread). In the closed universe test, ORL face database is used, while the Yale_extend data set are added as distractor face in open universe experiment.

The ORL face database is created by ATT laboratory of university of Cambridge, which contains 40 people. For some subjects, the images were taken at different times, varying the lighting, facial expressions (open/closed eyes, smiling/not smiling) and facial details (glasses/no glasses). The size of each image is 92×112 pixels, with 256 grey levels per pixel. While Yale_extend face data set contains 5760 single light source images of 10 human subjects each seen under 576 viewing conditions (9 poses $\times$ 64 illumination conditions). For every subject in a particular pose, an image with ambient (background) illumination is also captured. In the experiment each face image will be transformed to 32×32 matrixs, and be normalized to 1024×1 vector.

4.1   Closed Universe Experiment

As shown in Eq. (13), the parameter α has a great influence on the performance of SAC. The 1024×1 vector is compressed to a 100×1 vector.

Table 1. Parameter α versus recognition rate (%)

Parameter α				
$5e-1$	$5e-3$	$5e-5$	$5e-6$	$5e-7$
93.80	94.35	95.00	95.15	95.15

As shown in Table 1, the recognition rate of SAC has a high recognition rate with α in the vicinity of 0. There is no improvement when the α reach $5e-6$. Therefore we set α to $5e-6$.

The energy ratio of the 1th class is shown in Fig. 1. The energy residual of 1th class is shown in Fig. 2. From these we can see the energy ratio can help to improve the classifier performance by expanding the gap between the target class and others.

The comparisons of dimension N are shown in Table 2. It can be seen that the overall recognition rate increases with the increase of compression dimension. The recognition performance of SAC is generally the best one, and its stability is much higher than other classifiers.

The comparisons of number of train samples Q are depicted in Table 3. It can be seen that the overall recognition rate rise with more train samples. The recognition performance of SAC is the best. The comparisons of computer time are displayed in Table 4.

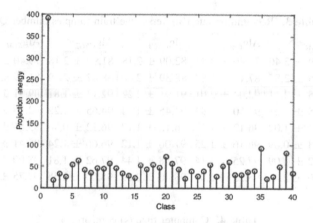

Fig. 1. The energy ratio of the 1st class test sample

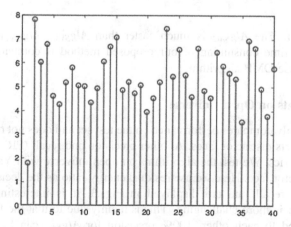

Fig. 2. The energy residual of 1st class test sample

Table 2. Recognition rate (%) versus PCA compression dimension N

N	Alg_{SAC}	Alg_{CRC_0}	Alg_{CRC1}	Alg_{CRC2}	Alg_{SVM}
20	92.15 ± 1.94	91.30 ± 1.26	92.70 ± 1.08	86.65 ± 1.66	92.15 ± 1.81
40	94.00 ± 1.43	93.75 ± 1.68	94.6 ± 1.10	93.35 ± 0.74	92.65 ± 1.70
60	94.85 ± 1.50	94.10 ± 1.07	94.650.52	93.41.24	93.051.89
80	95.35 ± 1.13	94.45 ± 0.86	95.05 ± 0.79	94.3 ± 1.00	92.35 ± 1.74
100	95.25 ± 1.03	94.50 ± 0.94	94.45 ± 1.44	94.65 ± 1.22	92.45 ± 1.72
120	95.3 ± 1.00	94.90 ± 0.93	94.65 ± 1.05	95.00 ± 1.47	92.50 ± 1.54
140	95.95 ± 1.10	94.90 ± 0.80	94.55 ± 0.98	96.45 ± 1.31	91.40 ± 2.66
160	95.20 ± 1.11	94.80 ± 1.00	94.45 ± 0.79	94.25 ± 1.00	91.45 ± 2.96
180	95.20 ± 1.11	94.75 ± 1.00	93.7 ± 0.82	93.90 ± 0.65	91.90 ± 2.03

Table 3. Recognition rate (%) versus the train samples number Q

Q	Alg_{SAC}	Alg_{CRC_0}	Alg_{CRC1}	Alg_{CRC2}	Alg_{SVM}
2	80.80 ± 3.40	79.40 ± 3.44	82.09 ± 2.18	81.90 ± 2.18	79.40 ± 3.72
3	88.35 ± 2.85	87.10 ± 2.87	88.39 ± 2.80	88.42 ± 2.89	81.89 ± 5.70
4	92.75 ± 2.11	92.04 ± 2.01	91.91 ± 2.22	92.12 ± 1.81	89.91 ± 2.81
5	95.25 ± 1.03	94.50 ± 0.94	94.45 ± 1.44	94.65 ± 1.22	92.45 ± 1.72
6	97.12 ± 1.02	96.12 ± 1.17	96.12 ± 1.17	96.12 ± 0.96	95.56 ± 1.23
7	97.83 ± 0.89	96.16 ± 1.25	97.00 ± 1.12	96.66 ± 1.24	96.41 ± 0.88
8	98.62 ± 1.09	97.25 ± 1.14	97.88 ± 1.44	97.62 ± 1.81	98.00 ± 0.64
9	99.00 ± 2.41	98.25 ± 2.05	98.00 ± 2.29	98.00 ± 2.58	97.75 ± 2.18

Table 4. Computer time (s) comparison

	Alg_{SVM}	Alg_{SAC}	Alg_{CRC0}	Alg_{CRC1}	Alg_{CRC2}
time(s)	68.4449	0.3724	0.3670	7.0769	1.5557

From Table 4, The Alg_{SAC} is much faster than Alg_{SVM}, Alg_{CRC1} and Alg_{CRC2}. Meanwhile, The time consuming of our proposed method is comparable to that of Alg_{CRC0}, which use OMP algorithm.

4.2   Experiments on Open Universe

Since accuracy only compares performance on the test set and does not reflect how well an algorithm rejects distractor faces. Another precision and recall (PR) is usually used as evaluation metrics. We test the algorithms on open universe with Yale_extend face data set as distractor face. Here we use residual energy ratio as the decision value. The precision versus recall rate are displayed in Fig. 3. It is interesting to note that open-unverse test is more challenging. This is mainly due to that the face images are structurally closed to each other. 100% precision for Alg_{SAC} can be achieved with 83.0% recall rate, which is the best of all. The Alg_{CRC1} and Alg_{CRC0} are comparable to each other, while the Alg_{SVM} is the worst case of all.

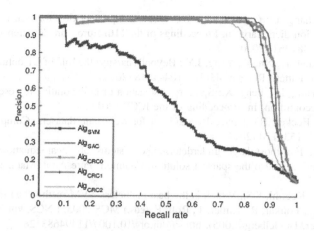

Fig. 3. Precision versus Recall rate

5 Conclusion

A novel SAC has been proposed in this paper, which combines the J classifiers to form a projector. The basic idea of this algorithm is that the test sample that matches the class classifier is projected to near zero, while it is projected far away from zeros by the unmatched classifiers. Experiments on ORL data set in open and closed universe show that the SAC is a very robust and effective method in face recognition. Its overall performance is better than that of the traditional classifiers.

References

1. Altman, N.S.: An introduction to kernel and nearest-neighbor nonparametric regression. Am. Statist. **46**(3), 175–185. https://doi.org/10.1080/00031305.1992.10475879
2. Cover, T.M., Hart, P.E.: Nearest neighbor pattern classification. IEEE Trans. Inf. Theory **13** (1), 21–27 (1967)
3. Cortes, C., Vapnik, V.: Support-vector networks. Mach. Learn. **20**(3), 273–297 (1995)
4. Nie, F., Wang, X., Huang, H.: Multiclass capped lp-norm SVM for robust classifications. In: The 31st AAAI Conference on Artificial Intelligence (AAAI), San Francisco, USA (2017)
5. Wright, J., Yang, A., Ganesh, A., Sastry, S., Ma, Y.: Robust face recognition via sparse representation. IEEE Trans. Pattern Anal. Mach. Intell. **31**, 210–227 (2009)
6. Wagner, A., Wright, J., Ganesh, A., Zhou, Z.H., Ma, Y.: Towards a practical face recognition system: robust registration and illumination by sparse representation. In: IEEE Computer Society Conference on Computer Vision Pattern Recognition Workshops, pp. 597–604 (2009)
7. Feng, Z.Z., Yang, M., Zhang, L., Liu, Y., Zhang, D.: Joint discriminative dimensionality reduction and dictionary learning for face recognition. Pattern Recogn. **46**(8), 2134–2143 (2013)
8. Shi, Q., Eriksson, A., Hengel, A., Shen, C.: Is face recognition really a compressive sensing problem? In: Proceedings of the IEEE Computer Society Conference on Computer Vision Pattern Recognition, pp. 553–560 (2013)

9. Yang, M., Zhang, L.: Gabor feature based sparse representation for face recognition with Gabor occlusion dictionary. In: Proceedings of the 11th European Conference on Computer Vision, pp. 448–461 (2010)
10. Yang, J., Zhang, L., Xu, Y., Yang, J.Y.: Beyond sparsity: the role of L1-optimizer in pattern classification. Pattern Recogn. 45(3), 1104–1118 (2012)
11. Zhang, L., Yang, M., Feng, X.: Spare representation or collaborative representation: which helps face recognition. In: Proceeding of the ICCV (2011)
12. Ortiz, E.G., Becker, B.C.: Face Recognition for web-scale datasets. Comput. Vis. Image Underst. 118, 153–170 (2014)
13. Donoho, D.: For most large underdetermined systems of linear equations the minimal l1-norm solution is also the sparsest solution. Commun. Pure Appl. Math. 56(6), 797–829 (2006)
14. Duan, K.-B., Keerthi, S.S.: Which is the best multiclass SVM method? an empirical study. In: Oza, N.C., Polikar, R., Kittler, J., Roli, F. (eds.) MCS 2005. LNCS, vol. 3541, pp. 278–285. Springer, Heidelberg (2005). https://doi.org/10.1007/11494683_28
15. Naseem, I., Togneri, R., Bennamoun, M.: Linear regression for face recognition. IEEE Trans. Pattern Anal. Mach. Intell. 32(11), 2106–2112 (2010)
16. Zhang, H., Wang, F., Chen, Y., et al.: Combination of linear regression classification and collaborative representation classification. Neural Comput. Appl. 25, 833 (2014). https://doi.org/10.1007/s00521-014-1564-6

Multiplicative Noise Removal Based on Total Generalized Variation

Xinli Xu[1], Huizhu Pan[2], Weibo Wei[1(✉)], Guodong Wang[1],
and Wanquan Liu[3]

[1] College of Computer Science and Technology, Qingdao University, Qingdao,
People's Republic of China
1356793067@qq.com, njustwwb@163.com, allen_wgd@163.com
[2] KingKen Technology Company Ltd., Qingdao, People's Republic of China
1013420734@qq.com
[3] Department of Computing, Curtin University, Perth, Australia
W.Liu@curtin.edu.au

Abstract. When the first order variational models are used for multiplicative noise removal, there always some staircase effect, contract reduction, and corner smearing. In this paper, we will design a new second order variational model based on the total generalized variation (TGV) regularizer to solve these problems. The second order variation model is proposed originally for additive noise removal and we revise it in this paper for multiplicative noise removal. For the sake of computational efficiency, we transform this proposed model into a Split Bregman iterative scheme by introducing some auxiliary variables and iterative parameters, and then solve it via alternating optimization strategy. In order to speed up the computational efficiency, we also apply the fast Fourier transform (FFT), generalized soft threshold formulas and gradient descent method to the related sub-problems in each step. The experimental results show that in comparison with the first order total variation (TV) model, the proposed TGV model can effectively overcome the staircase effect; Also in comparison with the second order bounded Hessian regularization, the TGV model shows the advantage of preserving corners and edges in images.

Keywords: Multiplicative noise · Total variation · Total generalized variation
Hessian model · Split Bregman method

1 Introduction

Various variational models have been extensively employed for image restoration in image processing and computer vision [1, 2]. Many of them were proposed originally for additive noise removal by using the first order regularizers or second order ones to preserve as many image features as possible, such as edges, smoothness, corners, etc. The first order models have been extended to multiplicative noise removal successfully, albeit with a lot of difficulties in modeling and computation for noise removal with multiplicative noises using the second order regularizers.

For an observed scalar image with multiplicative noises $f(x) : \Omega \to R$, its formation equation is given by

© Springer Nature Singapore Pte Ltd. 2018
Y. Wang et al. (Eds.): IGTA 2017, CCIS 757, pp. 43–54, 2018.
https://doi.org/10.1007/978-981-10-7389-2_5

$$f(x) = u(x)\xi(x). \tag{1}$$

where u is the clean image, ξ is the noise. To obtain u and ξ from f is a typical inverse ill-posed problem. The celebrated variational model for solving this problem can be stated as

$$\min\{E(u) = \lambda J(u) + \alpha H(u)\}. \tag{2}$$

where, $J(u)$ is the regularized term to guarantee some preserving features, $H(u)$ is the data term reflecting different noise distributions. λ and α are penalty parameters. For the first order models based on total variation (TV) regularizer [1], Shi and Osher [3] proposed a general formulation for various multiplicative noise distribution

$$\min_{u}\left\{ E(u) = \lambda \int_{\Omega} |\nabla u| dx + \alpha \int_{\Omega} \left(a\frac{f}{u} + \frac{b}{2}\left(\frac{f}{u}\right)^2 + c \log u \right) dx \right\}. \tag{3}$$

where a, b, c are constants. If $c = 0$, $b = 1$, $a = -1$, (3) is reduced to the multiplicative Gaussian noise model [4]; If $a = 1$, $b = 0$, $c = 1$, (3) is the multiplicative Gamma noise model [5]; If $a = 0$, $b = 1$, $c = 1$, (3) is the multiplicative Rayleigh noise model [6]. But in the multiplicative Poisson noise model [7], $H(u) = \int_{\Omega} (u - f \log u) dx$.

The drawbacks of model (3) include: (a) staircase effects, contrast reduction and corner smearing due to first order regularization, which can be overcome by higher order ones as reported in [8] for additive noise removal; (b) the non-convex terms with $\log u$, which can be overcome by introducing auxiliary variable $w = \log u$ to replace it [3]. By using the equivalent form of $w = \log u$, i.e.,

$$u = e^w \tag{4}$$

(3) can be transformed into the following optimization with constraint (4)

$$\min_{w,u}\left\{ E(u) = \lambda \int_{\Omega} |\nabla u| dx + \alpha \int_{\Omega} \left(afe^{-w} + \frac{b}{2}f^2 e^{-2w} + cw \right) dx \right\}. \tag{5}$$

In order to overcome the problems mentioned in (a), [9] designed a second order model based on bounded Hessian regularizer, which was originally proposed by [10].

$$\min_{w,s}\left\{ \begin{array}{l} E(w, s) = \alpha \min_{w,s} \int_{\Omega} \left(afe^{-w} + \frac{b}{2}f^2 e^{-2w} + cw \right) dx \\ \\ + \beta_1 \int_{\Omega} |w - s|^2 dx + \beta_2 \int_{\Omega} |D^2 s| dx \end{array} \right\}, \tag{6}$$

where β_1 and β_2 are positive parameters. Herein, the authors added an extra term $|w - s|^2$ in the new model. And $D^2 s$ denotes the Hessian of s, with $|D^2 s| = \sqrt{s_{xx}^2 + s_{xy}^2 + s_{yx}^2 + s_{yy}^2}$ being the Frobenius norm of the Hessian $D^2 s$. This model overcomes the staircase effects with edge preserving, but it is not an ideal choice to preserve corners and image contrast, which can be improved by the new total generalized variation (TGV) [11] regularizer inspired by its performances in additive noise removal.

The TGV method is based on a higher order symmetry tensor, and its second order version has found successful applications for additive noise removal [12–14]. One of the contributions in this paper is to utilize it for multiplicative noise removal problem. Additionally, we'll investigate how to solve the proposed variational model based on the TGV by using the fast Split Bregman algorithm [15].

The paper includes five sections as follows: In Sect. 2, we mainly introduce the TGV model and present the second order TGV model for multiplicative noise removal problem. In Sect. 3, we apply the split Bregman idea to solve the proposed model. And then we employ an alternating minimization algorithm to minimize the proposed problem. In Sect. 4, we give some numerical experiments. Finally, conclusions are given in the 5th section.

2 The Total Generalized Variation Model

The concept of total generalized variation was proposed in 2010 by Bredies, Kunisch and Pock [10] to approximate arbitrary order polynomial functions using high order variational models in image processing. It integrates tensor information of images to make the smooth regions smoother and edges sharper for an image. The following definition is used in this paper.

Definition 2.1. Let $\Omega \subset R^d$ be a domain, $k \geq 1$ and $\alpha_0, \alpha_1, \cdots \alpha_{k-1} > 0$. Then, the total generalized variation of order k with weight α for $u \in L^1_{loc}(\Omega)$ is defined as the following functional

$$TGV_\alpha^k(u) = \sup\left\{ \int_\Omega u div^k v dx \mid v \in C_c^k(\Omega, Sym^k(R^d)), \left\|div^l v\right\|_\infty \leq \alpha_l, l = 0, \cdots, k-1 \right\}.$$

$$(7)$$

where, $Sym^k(R^d)$ is the space of symmetric tensor. If $k = 1$ and $\alpha > 0$, we can obtain

$$TGV_\alpha^1(u) = \alpha \sup\left\{ \int_\Omega u div(\vec{v})dx \mid \vec{v} \in C_c^1(\Omega, Sym^1(R^2)), \|v\|_\infty \leq 1 \right\} = \alpha TV(u). \quad (8)$$

Equation (8) shows that the TGV can indeed be regarded as a generalization of the TV. By using the Fenchel dual formula, we can change Eq. (8) into the following form:

$$TGV_\alpha^k(u) = \inf_{\substack{u^l \in C^{k-l}(\overline{\Omega}, Sym^l(R^d)) \\ l = l = 1, \cdots, k-1, u_0 = u, u_k = 0}} \sum_{l=1}^k \alpha_{k-l}\|\varepsilon(u_{l-1}) - u_l\|_1, \quad (9)$$

where $\varepsilon(u_{l-1})$ is a symmetric gradient operator with $\varepsilon(u_{l-1}) = \frac{1}{2}\left(\nabla u_{l-1} + (\nabla u_{l-1})^T\right)$. If $k = 2$, the derived second order TGV model can be written as

$$TGV_\alpha^2(u) = \sup\left\{\int_\Omega u\, div^2 v\, dx \mid v \in C_c^2\left(\Omega, Sym^2(R^d)\right), \|v\|_\infty \leq \alpha_0, \|div'v\|_\infty \leq \alpha_l\right\},$$
(10)

with $S^{d\times d}$ denoting the space of symmetric $d \times d$ matrices. The first and second divergences of a symmetric matrix are given by

$$(div(\vec{v}))_i = \sum_{j=1}^d \frac{\partial v_{ij}}{\partial x_j}, \quad (div^2(\vec{v})) = \sum_{i=1}^d \frac{\partial v_{ii}}{\partial x_i^2} + 2\sum_{i=1}^2\sum_{j<i} \frac{\partial v_{ij}}{\partial x_i \partial x_j}. \quad (11a-11b)$$

The definitions of the $\infty-$ norms of $v \in C_c\left(\Omega, S^{d\times d}\right)$ and $\vec{p} \in C_c\left(\Omega, R^d\right)$ are given by

$$\|v\|_\infty = \sup_{x\in\Omega}\left(\sum_{i=1}^d |v_{ii}(x)|^2 + 2\sum_{i<j} |v_{ij}(x)|^2\right)^{1/2}, \quad \|p\|_\infty = \sup_{x\in\Omega}\left(\sum_{i=1}^d |p_i(x)|^2\right)^{1/2}.$$
(12a-12b)

According to the Fenchel formula, TGV formula (10) can be stated as

$$TGV_\alpha^2(u) = \min_{p\in BD(\Omega)}\left\{\alpha_1 \int_\Omega |\nabla u - p|\, dx + \alpha_0 \int_\Omega \varepsilon(p)\, dx\right\}. \quad (13)$$

where $BD(\Omega)$ is the space of vector fields of bounded deformation, $\varepsilon(p)$ denotes the symmetrized tensor with the following definition.

$$\varepsilon(p) = \frac{1}{2}\left(\nabla p + \nabla p^T\right). \quad (14)$$

And the scalar parameters α_0 and α_1 are used to balance the first order and second order partial derivatives.

In this paper, we propose a variational model for multiplicative noise removal based on the TGV regularizer, which is given by

$$E(u) = \beta \int_\Omega \left(a\frac{f}{u} + \frac{b}{2}\left(\frac{f}{u}\right)^2 + c\log u\right)dx + TGV_\alpha^2(u). \quad (15)$$

3 The Split Bregman Method for TGV Model

3.1 Split Bregman Method

There are many numerical algorithms for solving the proposed problem. Here, we employ the split Bregman algorithm [16, 17] to solve the proposed TGV model (15),

$$\min_{u,p}\{E(u,p) = \beta \int_\Omega \left(a\frac{f}{u} + \frac{b}{2}\left(\frac{f}{u}\right)^2 + c\log u \right)dx + \alpha_1 \int_\Omega |\nabla u - p|dx + \alpha_0 \int_\Omega \varepsilon(p)dx\}.$$

(16)

In order to solve this model efficiently, we introduce u as (4) to split the data term, additionally, introduce another two auxiliary variables q and v as

$$q = \nabla u - p, v = \varepsilon(p).$$
(17a − 17b)

Taking into account the constraints (4) and (17a-17b), the minimization problem (16) can be transformed into the following Split Bregman iterative formulation with Bregman parameters (d, e, i)

$$\left(u^{k+1}, w^{k+1}, p^{k+1}, q^{k+1}, v^{k+1}\right) = \arg\min E(u, w, p, q, v)$$

$$= \left\{ \begin{array}{c} \beta \int_\Omega \left(afe^{-w} + \frac{b}{2}f^2 e^{-2w} + cw\right)dx + \frac{\theta_1}{2}\int_\Omega (u - e^w - d^k)^2 dx + \alpha_1 \int_\Omega |q|dx \\ + \frac{\theta_2}{2}\int_\Omega (q - \nabla u + p - e^k)^2 dx + \alpha_0 \int_\Omega |v|dx + \frac{\theta_3}{2}\int_\Omega (v - \varepsilon(p) - i^k)^2 dx \end{array} \right\}.$$

(18)

with

$$d^{k+1} = d^k + e^{w^{k+1}} - u^{k+1}, \ d^0 = 0, w^0 = \log u^0,$$
(19a)

$$e^{k+1} = e^k + \nabla u^{k+1} - q^{k+1} - p^{k+1}, e^0 = 0, q^0 = p^0 = \vec{0},$$
(19b)

$$i^{k+1} = i^k + \varepsilon(p^{k+1}) - v^{k+1}, \ i^0 = \vec{0}, v^0 = p^0 = \vec{0}.$$
(19c)

where, $p = (p_1\, p_2)$, $q = (q_1\, q_2)$, $v = \begin{pmatrix} v_{11} & v_3 \\ v_3 & v_{22} \end{pmatrix}$, $i = \begin{pmatrix} i_{11} & i_3 \\ i_3 & i_{22} \end{pmatrix}$, $e = (e_1\, e_2)$.

The alternative optimization problem (18) can be divided into the following sub-problems on (u, w, p, q, v) successively by using the alternating optimization strategy

$$u^{k+1} = \arg\min_u\{E_1(u) = E(u, w^k, p^k, q^k, v^k)\},$$
(20a)

$$w^{k+1} = \arg\min_{w}\{E_2(w) = E(u^{k+1}, w, p^k, q^k, v^k)\}, \tag{20b}$$

$$p^{k+1} = \arg\min_{p}\{E_3(p) = E(u^{k+1}, w^{k+1}, p, q^k, v^k)\}, \tag{20c}$$

$$q^{k+1} = \arg\min_{q}\{E_4(q) = E(u^{k+1}, w^{k+1}, p^{k+1}, q, v^k)\}, \tag{20d}$$

$$v^{k+1} = \arg\min_{v}\{E_5(v) = E(u^{k+1}, w^{k+1}, p^{k+1}, q^{k+1}, v)\}. \tag{20e}$$

3.2 Solutions for Each Sub-problem

3.2.1 Calculation of u^{k+1} from (20a) Using the FFT [18]

The minimization problem of $E_1(u)$ on u can be solved via a standard variational method, its solution satisfies the following Euler-Lagrangian equation

$$\theta_1\left(u - e^{w^k} - d^k\right) + \theta_2\nabla \cdot (q^k - \nabla u + p^k - e^k) = 0. \tag{21a}$$

Its discretized formulation is as below

$$\theta_1 u - \theta_2\nabla^- \cdot (\nabla^+ u) = \theta_1\left(e^{w^k} + d^k\right) - \theta_2\nabla^- \cdot (q^k + p^k - e^k). \tag{21b}$$

which can be solved using the fast Fourier transform (FFT) method. By introducing the identity operator $Iu_{i,j} = u_{i,j}$ and shifting operators $S_1^{\pm}u_{i,j} = u_{i\pm1,j}$, one can see that the discretized version of (21b) can be rewritten as

$$\theta_1 u_{i,j} - \theta_2(S_1^+ + S_1^- - 2I + S_2^+ + S_2^- - 2I)u_{i,j} = g_{i,j}, \tag{21c}$$

where,

$$g_{i,j} = \theta_1\left(e^{w_{ij}^k} + d_{ij}^k\right) - \theta_2\left(\partial_x^- p_{1i,j}^k + \partial_y^- p_{2i,j}^k + \partial_x^- q_{1i,j}^k + \partial_y^- q_{2i,j}^k\right) + \theta_2\left(\partial_x^- e_{1i,j}^k + \partial_y^- e_{2i,j}^k\right).$$

By using the discrete Fourier transform $\mathcal{F}$, one can obtain the following form,

$$\mathcal{F}S_1^{\pm}u_{i,j} = e^{\pm\sqrt{-1}z_i}\mathcal{F}(u_{i,j}), \quad \mathcal{F}S_2^{\pm}u_{i,j} = e^{\pm\sqrt{-1}z_j}\mathcal{F}(u_{i,j}), \tag{21d}$$

where, $z_i = \frac{2\pi}{N_1}x_i, x_i = 1,\ldots,N_1$ and $z_j = \frac{2\pi}{N_2}y_j, y_j = 1,\ldots,N_2$. So (21c) changes to

$$(\theta_1 - \theta_2(2\cos z_i + 2\cos z_j - 4))\mathcal{F}(u_{i,j}) = \mathcal{F}(g_{i,j}), \quad \mathcal{F}(u_{i,j}) = \frac{\mathcal{F}(g_{i,j})}{D_{i,j}}, \tag{21e}$$

where, $\mathcal{D}_{i,j} = \theta_1 - \theta_2\left(2\cos z_i + 2\cos z_j - 4\right) > 0$. From (21e), we can obtain the discrete inverse Fourier transform $\mathcal{F}^{-1}$ for the updated $u_{i,j}$

$$u_{i,j}^{k+1} = \Re\left(\mathcal{F}^{-1}\left(\frac{\mathcal{F}\left(g_{i,j}\right)}{\mathcal{D}_{i,j}}\right)\right), \tag{21f}$$

where $\Re(\cdot)$ represents the real part of a complex number.

3.2.2 Computing w^{k+1} Based on (20b) and Its Gradient

We can obtain w via the variational method for the problem (20b), it satisfies the following equation,

$$\beta\left(-afe^{-w} - bf^2e^{-2w} + c\right) - \theta_1\left(u^{k+1} - e^w - d^k\right) = 0. \tag{22a}$$

which can be solved via the gradient descent method as

$$w^{k+1} = w^k + \nabla t A^k, \tag{22b}$$

where ∇t represents the time step, and

$$A^k = -\beta\left(-afe^{-w^k} - bf^2e^{-2w^k} + c\right) + \theta_1\left(u^{k+1} - e^{w^k} - d^k\right).$$

3.2.3 Computing p^{k+1} from (20c) Using the FFT

$p = (p_1\,p_2)$ is the solution of (20c) with the following discretized Euler-Lagrangian equations

$$\begin{cases} \left(\theta_2 - \theta_3\partial_x^-\partial_x^+ - \frac{\theta_3}{2}\partial_y^-\partial_y^+\right)p_{1i,j} - \frac{\theta_3}{2}\partial_y^-\partial_x^+p_{2i,j} = h_{1i,j} \\ \left(\theta_2 - \frac{\theta_3}{2}\partial_x^-\partial_x^+ - \theta_3\partial_y^-\partial_y^+\right)p_{2i,j} - \frac{\theta_3}{2}\partial_x^-\partial_y^+p_{1i,j} = h_{2i,j} \end{cases} \tag{23a}$$

where

$$h_1 = \theta_2\left(\partial_x^- u^{k+1} + e_1^k + q_1^k\right) - \theta_3\partial_x^-\left(v_{11}^k - t_{11}^k\right) - \theta_3\partial_y^-\left(v_3^k - t_3^k\right)$$
$$h_2 = \theta_2\left(\partial_y^- u^{k+1} + e_2^k - q_2^k\right) - \theta_3\partial_y^-\left(v_{22}^k - t_{22}^k\right) - \theta_3\partial_x^-\left(v_3^k - t_3^k\right).$$

Similar to Sect. 3.2.1, we can obtain a system of liner equation of discrete FFT,

$$\begin{pmatrix} a_{11} & a_{12} \\ a_{21} & a_{22} \end{pmatrix}\begin{pmatrix} \mathcal{F}\left(p_{1i,j}\right) \\ \mathcal{F}\left(p_{2i,j}\right) \end{pmatrix} = \begin{pmatrix} \mathcal{F}\left(h_{1i,j}\right) \\ \mathcal{F}\left(h_{2i,j}\right) \end{pmatrix}. \tag{23b}$$

where

$$a_{11} = \theta_2 - \theta_3(2\cos z_j - 2) - \frac{\theta_3}{2}(2\cos z_i - 2), a_{22} = \theta_2 - \theta_3(2\cos z_i - 2) - \frac{\theta_3}{2}(\cos z_j - 2),$$

$$a_{12} = -\frac{\theta_3}{2}\left(-1 + \cos z_i + \sqrt{-1}\sin z_i\right)\left(1 - \cos z_j + \sqrt{-1}\sin z_j\right),$$

$$a_{21} = -\frac{\theta_3}{2}\left(-1 + \cos z_j + \sqrt{-1}\sin z_j\right)\left(1 - \cos z_i + \sqrt{-1}\sin z_i\right).$$

By using the inverse Fourier transform, one can get $p_{1_{i,j}}^{k+1}$ and $p_{2_{i,j}}^{k+1}$ as

$$p_{1_{i,j}}^{k+1} = \Re\left(\mathcal{F}^{-1}\left(\frac{a_{22}\mathcal{F}\left(h_{1i,j}\right) - a_{12}\mathcal{F}\left(h_{2i,j}\right)}{\mathcal{D}_{i,j}}\right)\right),$$

$$p_{2_{i,j}}^{k+1} = \Re\left(\mathcal{F}^{-1}\left(\frac{a_{11}\mathcal{F}\left(h_{2i,j}\right) - a_{21}\mathcal{F}\left(h_{1i,j}\right)}{\mathcal{D}_{i,j}}\right)\right). \tag{23c}$$

where $\mathcal{D}_{i,j} = \left(\theta_2 - 2\theta_3\left(\cos z_j + \cos z_i - 2\right)\right)\left(\theta_2 - \theta_3\left(\cos z_j + \cos z_i - 2\right)\right) > 0$.

3.2.4 Computing q^{k+1} from (20d) by Using Generalized Soft Thresholding Formula

Based on the minimization of $E_4(q)$ in Eq. (20d), we can obtain the following Euler equation about q

$$\alpha_1\frac{q}{|q|} + \theta_2(q - \nabla u^{k+1} + p^{k+1} - e^k) = 0, \tag{24a}$$

which can be expressed as generalized soft threshold formula analytically

$$q^{k+1} = \max\left(\left|\nabla u^{k+1} - p^{k+1} + e^k\right| - \frac{\alpha_1}{\theta_2}, 0\right)\frac{\nabla u^{k+1} - p^{k+1} + e^k}{|\nabla u^{k+1} - p^{k+1} + e^k|}. \tag{24b}$$

3.2.5 Computing v^{k+1} from (20e) by Using the Generalized Soft Thresholding Formula

Based on the minimization of $E_5(v)$ in Eq. (20e), we can get the following Euler equation about v

$$\alpha_0\frac{v}{|v|} + \theta_3(v - \varepsilon(p^{k+1}) - i^k) = 0, \tag{25a}$$

We then can apply generalized soft threshold formula to get v^{k+1} as

$$v^{k+1} = \max\left(\left|\varepsilon(p^{k+1}) + i^k\right| - \frac{\alpha_0}{\theta_3}, 0\right)\frac{\varepsilon(p^{k+1}) + i^k}{|\varepsilon(p^{k+1}) + i^k|} \tag{25b}$$

4 Experiments and Analysis

In order to verify the effectiveness of the proposed model and algorithm in this paper, we compare the denoised images processed by TV, Hessian, and TGV models. The images with different multiplicative noises are given as follows: Fig. 1(b) is the Fig. 1 (a) corrupted by Gaussian noise. Figure 2(b) is the Fig. 2(a) corrupted by Gamma noise. Figure 3(b) is the Fig. 3(a) corrupted by Poisson noise. Figure 4(b) is the Fig. 4 (a) corrupted by Rayleigh noise. Figure 1(c), (d), (e) represents the Gaussian noise image, which is restored by the TV regularization, the Hessian regularization, and the TGV regularization. Figure 2(c), (d), (e) represents the Gamma noise image, which is restored by three different regularizations. Figure 3(c), (d), (e) is the restored Poisson noise image and Fig. 4(c), (d), (e) is the restored Rayleigh noise image.

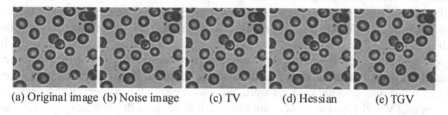

(a) Original image (b) Noise image   (c) TV   (d) Hessian   (e) TGV

Fig. 1. Image corrupted by multiplicative Gaussian noise and restored results

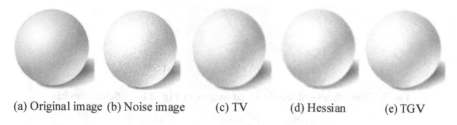

(a) Original image (b) Noise image   (c) TV   (d) Hessian   (e) TGV

Fig. 2. Image corrupted by multiplicative Gamma noise and restored results

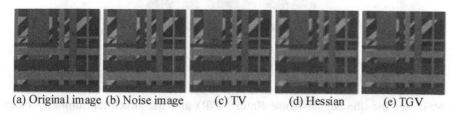

(a) Original image (b) Noise image   (c) TV   (d) Hessian   (e) TGV

Fig. 3. Image corrupted by multiplicative Poisson noise and restored results

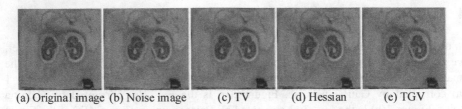

(a) Original image (b) Noise image   (c) TV   (d) Hessian   (e) TGV

Fig. 4. Image corrupted by multiplicative Rayleigh noise and restored results

In Figs. 1, 2, 3 and 4, we can observe the Gaussian, Gamma, Poisson and Rayleigh noised images processed with TV, Hessian and TGV models, respectively. The above different experiments demonstrate that compared with TV and Hessian model, the TGV model has better denoising effect. Using TGV model to deal with the four different multiplicative noise images, the effect is relatively good. Using the TV model to deal with the image can lead to a staircase effect, whereas the TGV model can overcome the staircase effect. The smoothness and corners of the image are maintained well. In Figs. 5 and 6, we test the smoothness and corner preservation ability of the denoised images. The smoothness feature of other model is not ideal. For TGV model's denoised image, the image smooth are kept well. We also observe the corners of the denoised images of TV and Hessian corners are blurred. It is obvious that the image corners are maintained well in TGV.

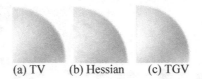

(a) TV   (b) Hessian   (c) TGV

Fig. 5. Smoothness of the denoised images in Fig. 2 by different models

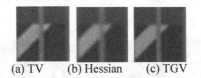

(a) TV   (b) Hessian   (c) TGV

Fig. 6. Corners of the denoised images in Fig. 3 by different models

Next, we use the Signal Noise Ratio (SNR) and the structural similarity index measurement (SSIM) criteria to test the denoised results by using different models

All experiments are performed by using Matlab 2010b on a Windows 7 platform with an Intel Core i5 CPU at 3.30 GHz and 4 GB memory.

Table 1. Comparison of the three regularizations of SNR

Regularization	Figure 1 (Gaussian image)	Figure 2 (Gamma image)	Figure 3 (Poisson image)	Figure 4 (Rayleigh image)
TV	11.2767	3.8557	23.1261	18.7449
Hessian	13.7079	4.0368	23.9886	21.0242
TGV	13.9048	4.2983	24.2343	21.2218

Table 2. Comparison of the three regularizations of SSIM

Regularization	Figure 1 (Gaussian image)	Figure 2 (Gamma image)	Figure 3 (Poisson image)	Figure 4 (Rayleigh image)
TV	0.6912	0.3101	0.4429	0.5402
Hessian	0.6803	0.2677	0.4657	0.5817
TGV	0.7205	0.5688	0.5338	0.6346

As shown in Table 1, the TV regularization model's SNR is lower than the Hessian's and TGV's. The TGV model's SNR is slightly higher than the Hessian model's. As can be seen from the Table 2, the SSIM of the TV model and the Hessian model is uncertain for four different multiplicative noise images. Regarding to Poisson image and Rayleigh image, the TV model's SSIM is higher than the Hessian model's SSIM, and the other two images are just the opposite. The TGV model's SSIM is the highest.

5 Concluding Remarks

In this paper, we mainly revise the TGV model to solve the multiplicative noise removal problem, and compare the performance among the TV regularization, Hessian regularization, and TGV regularization. Then the split Bregman algorithm is used to solve different multiplicative noise models. Experimental results show that in comparisons with other models, the TGV model can obtain better results for different multiplicative noise images. In comparison with other models, the proposed TGV can effectively keep the edges, corners and smoothness.

Acknowledgments. The work has been partially supported by the National Natural Science Foundation of China (61602269), China Postdoctoral Science Foundation (2015M571993, 2017M612204). Authors thank Prof. Xue-Cheng Tai, Department of Mathematics at University of Bergen, Prof. Xianfeng David Gu, Department of Computer Science, State University of New York at Stony Brook for their instructions and discussions, and thank the KingKen Technology Company Ltd. for the cooperative projects in image processing with Qingdao University.

References

1. Rudin, L.I., Osher, S., Fatemi, E.: Nonlinear total variation based noise removal algorithms. Physica D **60**(1–4), 259–268 (1992)
2. Chan, T.F., Shen, J.: Image processing and analysis: variational, PDE, wavelet, and stochastic methods. SIAM **292**(1), 110–115 (2005)
3. Shi, J.N., Osher, S.: A nonlinear inverse scale space method for a convex multiplicative noise model. SIAM J. Imaging Sci. **1**(3), 294–321 (2008)
4. Rudin, L., Lions, P., Osher, S.: Multiplicative denoising and deblurring: theory and algorithms. In: Osher, S., Paragios, N. (eds.) Geometric Level Sets in Imaging, Vision, and Graphics, pp. 103–119. Springer, New York (2003). https://doi.org/10.1007/0-387-21810-6_6
5. Aubert, G., Aujol, J.F.: A variational approach to remove multiplicative noise. SIAM J. Appl. Math. **68**(4), 925–946 (2008)
6. Denis, L., Tupin, F., Darbon, J., Sigelle, M.: SAR image regularization with fast approximate discrete minimization. IEEE Trans. Image Process. **18**(7), 1588–1600 (2009)
7. Setzer, S., Steidl, G., Teuber, T.: Deblurring poissonian images by split Bregman techniques. J. Vis. Commun. Image Representation **21**, 193–199 (2010)
8. Huang, Y.M., Ng, M.K., Wen, Y.W.: A new total variation method for multiplicative noise removal. SIAM J. Imaging Sci. **2**(1), 20–40 (2009)
9. Lv, X.G., Le, J., Huang, J., et al.: A fast high-order total variation minimization method for multiplicative noise removal. Math. Probl. Eng. **87**(1–4), 87–118 (2013)
10. Lysaker, M., Lundervold, A., Tai, X.-C.: Noise removal using fourth-order partial differential equation with applications to medical magnetic resonance images in space and time. IEEE Trans. Image Process. **12**(12), 1579–1590 (2003)
11. Bredies, K., Kunisch, K., Pock, T.: Total generalized variation. SIAM J. Imaging Sci. **3**(3), 492–526 (2010)
12. Valkonen, T., Bredies, K., Knoll, F.: Total generalised variation in diffusion tensor imaging. SIAM J. Imaging Sci. **6**(6), 487–525 (2013)
13. Ono, S., Yamada, I.: Second-order total generalized variation constraint. In: IEEE International Conference on Acoustics, Speech and Signal Processing, pp. 4938–4942 (2014)
14. Bredies, K.: Recovering piecewise smooth multichannel images by minimization of convex functionals with total generalized variation penalty. In: Bruhn, A., Pock, T., Tai, X.-C. (eds.) Efficient Algorithms for Global Optimization Methods in Computer Vision. LNCS, vol. 8293, pp. 44–77. Springer, Heidelberg (2014). https://doi.org/10.1007/978-3-642-54774-4_3
15. Lu, W.Q., Duan, J.M., Qiu, Z.W., et al.: Implementation of high-order variational models made easy for image processing. Math. Methods Appl. Sci. **39**(14), 4208–4233 (2016)
16. Goldstein, T., Osher, S.: The split Bregman method for l1-regularized problems. SIAM J. Imaging Sci. **2**(2), 323–343 (2009)
17. Duan, J.M., Pan, Z.K., Zhang, B.C., Liu, W.Q., Tai, X.-C.: Fast algorithm for color texture image inpainting using the non-local ctv model. J. Global Optim. **62**(4), 853–876 (2015)
18. Zhu, W., Tai, X.-C., Chan, T.F.: Augmented Lagrangian method for a mean curvature based image denoising model. Inverse Probl. Imaging **7**(4), 1409–1432 (2013)

An Improved Superpixel Method for Color Image Segmentation Based on SEEDS

Rongguo Zhang[1](✉), Gaoyang Pei[1], Lifang Wang[1], Xiaojun Liu[2], and Xiaoming Li[1]

[1] School of Computer Science and Technology, Taiyuan University of Science and Technology,
Taiyuan 030024, Shanxi, China
rg_zh@163.com

[2] School of Mechanical Engineering, Hefei University of Technology, Hefei 230009, China
liuxjunhf@163.com

Abstract. There's a precision problem in the boundary segmentation process for color image. Combined bilateral filter with SEEDS method, an improved superpixel method for color image segmentation is proposed here. Firstly, we process the image with bilateral filter method, this procedure can reduce the influence of texture and noise on the boundary and filter the noise without missing the information of boundary. Then, the image is smoother, and we deal the superpixel segmentation of color image with hill-climbing algorithm based on SEEDS method. Experimental results show that the proposed method is better than the SEEDS method on color image segmentation. And also, the boundary recall rate and under-segmentation error rate are advantageous to that of traditional method.

Keywords: SEEDS method · Superpixel · Color image segmentation
Bilateral filter · Hill-climbing algorithm

1 Introduction

Image segmentation, as basic problem in computer vision and digital image process, is an important and difficult research point. Image segmentation means segmenting the different areas in a image and making sure these areas are not crossed [1]. Every single area should have some same conditions. In traditional method, the segmentation treat the pixel as basic processing unit, without taking into account the space and group relationships between pixels. This method will reduce the processing efficiency of algorithm when the size of target image is getting bigger and bigger. So, the concept of superpixel is introduced here [2]. Superpixels are of special interest for semantic segmentation, in which they are reported to bring major advantages. Through this method, we can effectively reduce the scale of the information that need to be processed and the complexity of the subsequent processes.

Through the research on image processing these years, the superpixel has been applied in many areas, like the pretreatment in image segmentation, the skeleton extraction, the estimation of human body pose and the target tracking and recognition, etc. [3]. For example, in literature [4], level set algorithm for tracking driven by superpixel is presented. This algorithm's robustness and efficiency are all excellent. In literature [5],

Y. Wang et al. (Eds.): IGTA 2017, CCIS 757, pp. 55–64, 2018.
https://doi.org/10.1007/978-981-10-7389-2_6

Liu introduced the semantic information to superpixel, and solved the problem of shading that each car will meet. In literature [6], there raised a method of localization based on superpixel. After treating the image with superpixel method by Quick Shift, one can get the feature information of histogram distribution, and then, the CRF optimization will be followed. In literature [7], a method of outline extraction using superpixel is presented.

Most of current superpixel segmentation algorithms are based on gradual addition of cuts or growth of superpixels from assigned centers, these algorithms need to calculate the distance between superpixel module and their surrounding pixels in the process of iteration. So some running costs are inevitable [8]. The emphasized point of superpixel segmentation method is to improve the efficiency [9, 10]. But running times of these methods are not real-time. So the literature [9] proposed a new superpixel segmentation method named SEEDS (Superpixels Extracted via Energy-Driven Sampling).

First of all, we take a regular superpixel partition, and then move the boundary of superpixel to make an optimization. A target function has been introduced to maximize the efficiency, and it is distributed by the color of superpixel, and has added the item of boundary smooth. This optimization is based on the Hill-climbing algorithm, the boundary of superpixel will move when the target function is increasing, so the optimization happened. We update the boundary by using those blocks defined as hierarchy structures. And starting with bigger ones, the blocks are reduced to pixel level with the process of iteration. In literature [11], there came out an contrast experiment referring to the current superpixel methods. The result shows that, comparing with other methods, SEEDS segmentation result is more perfect. SEEDS is faster than the current methods too. Especially, it only needs to find one storage space when only one boundary pixel is been moved. But this method has a problem. It is easy to produce imprecise boundary segmentation if we treat the image with superpixel segmentation directly.

This paper presents an improved surperpixel method called BF-SEEDS (Bilateral Filtering SEEDS), through this method, the influence of noise, texture and something else in segmentation will be reduced. The noise of image can be filtered and the image can be smoother without lost the boundary information. The rest paper is organized as follows. Section 2 is a simple introduction to the SEED method. Section 3 is our improved surperpixel method. In Sect. 4, we provide some experimental results, discuss the proposed method and compare it with existing methods. Finally we conclude in Sect. 5.

2   SEEDS Method

The core theory of SEEDS is hill climbing algorithm which is a local selection algorithm. Starting with the current node, and comparing with the surrounding nodes, it returns the current node if the current node has the maximum value and set the current node as the summit value. If not, it changes the current node with the maximum neighbor node, it circulates several times to reach the summit value. We denote $s \in S$ as the proposed partition, and $s_t \in S$ the lowest energy partition found at the instant t. A new partition is proposed by introducing local changes at s_t. Moving s to s_t can be pixel-level updates or block-level updates. We denote A_k^1 as a candidate set of one or more pixels to be exchanged from the superpixel A_k to its neighbor An. In the case of pixel-level updates A_k^1 contains one pixel, and in the case of block-level updates A_k^1 contains a small set of pixels.

The energy function used to compare:

$$E(s) = H(s) + rG(s) \tag{1}$$

$H(s)$ is color distribution item of superpixel, $H(s)$ estimates the performance of every superpixel.

$$H(s) = \sum_k \psi\left(C_{A_k}\right) \tag{2}$$

$\psi(C_{A_k})$ is the structure measurement of color distribution. We denote $C_{A_k}(j)$ as the color histogram of the set of pixels in A_k, and it is

$$C_{A_k}(j) = \frac{1}{Z} \sum_{i \in A_k} \delta\left(I(i) \in H_j\right) \tag{3}$$

$I(i)$ is the color of pixel i, Z is the normalizing factor of the Histogram and $\delta(.)$ is the indicating function.

$G(s)$ is a boundary item to evaluate the shape of superpixel. It punishes the local irregular nature between superpixel boundaries. It can chose the shape type of superpixel subjectively. So it is helpful to smooth the boundary of superpixel. First of all, we segment the image into square blocks, N_i is the block containing pixel i, the histogram of superpixel label in N_i:

$$b_{N_i}(k) = \frac{1}{Z} \sum_{j \in N_i} \delta\left(j \in A_k\right) \tag{4}$$

The histogram is used to estimate the statistics number of pixels in superpixel K. When the superpixel number in each square N is 1, $G(s)$ is the maximum value. Of course, because the boundary contains more than one superpixel, $G(s)$ cannot reach the maximum value. By reducing the number of superpixel at the boundary, we can strengthen the regularity. r is weight value to make a balance between shape and color of superpixel.

3   Our Improved Superpixel Method

When a image is segmented by SEEDS method, due to the limit of this method, some small areas will be generated in the details of this image that will influence the effect of segmentation. So some filter processes should be done before an image is been initially segmented. The image will be more smoother and the noise will be reduced without lost the boundary information. Our improved superpixel method uses the bilateral filter whose boundary preserving is better [12]. Bilateral filter is a kind of nonlinear filter, it is non-iterative, local and simple, it determines the weight value of the filter through the similarity between individual pixels. Since bilateral filter is a process that using pixel as target but not block, it can holding the boundary structure and increasing the time efficiency.

The image module with noise can be expressed as:

$$f(x, y) = g(x, y) + n(x, y) \tag{5}$$

g is the image without noise; f is image with noise; n is the noise; $f(x, y)$ represents the pixel value information of image f in space of (x, y).

Image filter is a process that filtering the noise n in image f and rebuild the image g. In bilateral filter, the pixel value of recovered Image is been determined by the combination of weight values of neighbor pixels:

$$\widehat{g}(x, y) = \frac{\sum_{(i,j) \in S_{x,y}} w(i, j) f(i, j)}{\sum_{(i,j) \in S_{x,y}} w(i, j)} \tag{6}$$

$w(i, j)$ is the weight ratio; $S_{x,y}$ represents the neighbourhood with the size of $(2N + 1) \times (2N + 1)$ and the center pixel of (x, y). In fact, the right side of formula (6) represents weight average of brightness values of the central pixel's neighbor areas. $w(i, j)$ is the weight ratio. Its value depends on the multiplication of spatial proximity factor w_s and brightness similarity factor w_r:

$$w_s(i, j) = \exp\left(-\frac{(i - x)^2 + (j - y)^2}{2\sigma_s^2}\right) \tag{7}$$

$$w_r(i, j) = \exp\left(-\frac{||f(i, j) - f(x, y)||^2}{2\sigma_r^2}\right) \tag{8}$$

$$w(i, j) = w_s(i, j) w_r(i, j) \tag{9}$$

w_s is getting smaller with the increasing of distance between pixel and center pixel. w_r is getting smaller with the increasing of brightness values between pixel and center pixel. Because, in the area where the image changes slowly, the brightness difference between neighbor pixels is small, so bilateral filter converts to Gaussian low-pass filter. But in the more areas that have dramatic changed. It replaces the original brightness values with the average brightness value of pixels that near the edge points that have similar brightness values. So the image will be more smoothly and the noise will be reduced without lost the boundary information.

In our improved method, N is the pixel number of image; K is the superpixel number of image; the formula (10) is the mapping relation from pixel to superpixel:

$$s:\{1, \dots, N\} \rightarrow \{1, \dots, K\} \tag{10}$$

s(i) is the superpixel partition where the pixel i located. At the same time, we use A_k as the representation of pixel collection in a superpixel:

$$A_k = \{i:s(i) = k\} \qquad (11)$$

The $\{A_k\}$ is the whole partition of image. One pixel can be allocated to one super-pixel, so the intersection of two superpixel set is empty set, as $A_k \cap A'_k = \emptyset$. Confirming the maximum energy function E(s) is the target of superpixel segmentation. The maximum energy function is been represented as S^*:

$$S^* = \arg \max_{s \in S} E(s) \qquad (12)$$

Our improved superpixel method is simply called BF-SEEDS (Bilateral filter Super-pixels Extracted via Energy-Driven Sampling) method. The steps of BF-SEEDS method can be summarized as follows:

Step 1. Input original image f and initialize it;
Step2. Get the bilateral filter result of image with formula (6);
Step 3. Optimize the image with hill-climbing algorithm using energy function in formula (12);
Step 4. Do not stop until the pixel level update is reached.

After the initialization of algorithm, the pixel-level updates and block-level updates have been given. The process of pixel-level updates is moving one pixel from a super-pixel boundary to another superpixel area. The other one is moving a whole block in a superpixel to another superpixel. The algorithm will update the bigger block firstly and smaller ones followed, it will not stop until to the pixel level update.

4 Experimental Results and Analysis

In order to verify the accuracy and efficiency of this algorithm, we use images from the library of Berkeley Computer Vision research group and take experiments on group of these pictures [13]. For the realization of algorithm we use the platform of windows7 64-bit, processor up to 1.90 GHz, system memory for 4G and Visual C++ software.

Bilateral filtering is a nonlinear filtering method which combines the information of the spatial proximity and the similarity of pixels. Its used to combine the spatial function and the kernel function to achieve the characteristic of preserving the boundary infor-mation. Figure 1 shows the contrast results of a variety of filtering methods. We can see that, Because bilateral filtering method considers both the spatial and gray information of the image, it can remove the unnecessary noise information while preserving the image boundary information.

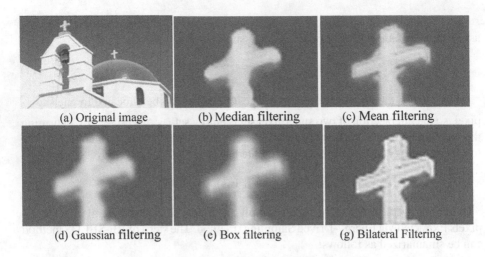

(a) Original image   (b) Median filtering   (c) Mean filtering

(d) Gaussian filtering   (e) Box filtering   (g) Bilateral Filtering

Fig. 1. A variety of filtering methods contrast

The following are the results of 6 group images. Figure 2 shows the contrast result of BSD-118035 segmentation. As shown in Fig. 2(a) is the original image. The redundant texture in Fig. 2(b) has been eliminated after smoothing the cross edge, and the boundary is been well preserved. In Fig. 2(c), the original method could not segment the shadow and background of the cross well. In Fig. 2(d), using the BF-SEEDS method proposed in this paper, the cross and shadow of church are all been segmented well.

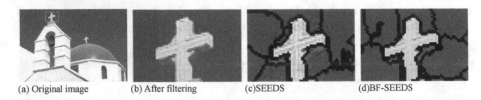

(a) Original image   (b) After filtering   (c)SEEDS   (d)BF-SEEDS

Fig. 2. BSD-118035 segmentation result contrast

Figure 3 shows the contrast result of BSD-317080 image segmentation. In Fig. 3(b), the legs of the deer are clearer after bilateral filtering. In Fig. 3(c), the dark area of the deer legs and the background leaves were not well segmented by the original method.

(a) Original image   (b) After filtering   (c)SEEDS   (d)BF-SEEDS

Fig. 3. BSD-317080 segmentation result contrast

In Fig. 3(d), using the BF-SEEDS method, the legs of the deer are separated from the background leaves.

Figure 4 shows the contrast result of BSD-189011 image segmentation. In Fig. 4(b), after the bilateral filtering the redundant texture of the hat edge is eliminated. In Fig. 4(c), the edge of the hat is not satisfactory using the original method. In Fig. 4(d), using the BF-SEEDS method, the edge portion of the cap is separated from the background.

(a) Original image   (b) After filtering   (c)SEEDS   (d)BF-SEEDS

Fig. 4. BSD-189011 segmentation result contrast

Figure 5 shows the contrast result of BSD-12003 image segmentation. Compared Fig. 5(c) and (d), we can see that the boundary information and shadow part of target image are better segmented using proposed method.

(a) Original image   (b) After filter   (c)SEEDS   (d)BF-SEEDS

Fig. 5. BSD-12003 segmentation result contrast

Figure 6 shows the contrast result of BSD-385028 image segmentation. Compared Fig. 6(c) and (d), we can see that leaves and background images are better segmented using proposed method.

(a) Original image   (b) After filter   (c)SEEDS   (d)BF-SEEDS

Fig. 6. BSD-385028 segmentation result contrast

Figure 7 shows the contrast result of BSD-67079 image segmentation. Compared Fig. 7(c) and (d), we can see a satisfactory segmentation result is obtained between the boundary and the background of the stone column using proposed method.

(a) Original image   (b) After filter   (c)SEEDS   (d)BF-SEEDS

Fig. 7. BSD-67079 segmentation result contrast

More images are tested using two methods, as shown in Table 1. The running time of BF-SEEDS method is longer than that of SEEDS, but its boundary recall (BR) is higher, and what's more, the under-segmentation error (UE) of BF-SEEDS is lower.

Table 1. Comparition results of two methods

Test image	Image size	Superpixel number	SEEDS method			BF-SEEDS method		
			Time(s)	BR	UE	Time(s)	BR	UE
035	481 × 321	400	4.399	0.846	0.084	6.146	0.863	0.079
080	481 × 321	400	5.867	0.835	0.081	7.062	0.857	0.073
011	481 × 321	400	5.018	0.852	0.089	6.980	0.869	0.081
003	481 × 321	400	4.735	0.824	0.087	6.597	0.848	0.076
028	481 × 321	400	5.103	0.849	0.083	6.899	0.851	0.076
079	481 × 321	400	4.908	0.837	0.088	6.695	0.859	0.075

In the boundary of the recall, compared with the SEED method, with the gradual increase over the number of pixels, the BF-SEEDS method of boundary recall slope increases, the boundary recall rate is higher, when the super pixel number reaches a certain value, the two methods of boundary recall are stable, just like shown in Fig. 8(a). In the under segmentation error rate, compared with the SEED method, with the gradual increase over the number of pixels, the BF-SEEDS method under segmentation error rate gradually decreased, when the super pixel number reaches a certain size, the two methods under segmentation rates are tending to steady state, we can see that in Fig. 8(b).

In Fig. 8(a), the horizontal axis represents superpixel number, the vertical axis represents boundary recall rate. In Fig. 8(b), the horizontal axis represents superpixel number, the vertical axis represents under-segmentation error rate. The BF-SEEDS method uses the bilateral filter to remove the excess texture information of the image, and enables the image to maintain better boundary information. Since bilateral filtering is necessary before image segmentation, the time consumption of our improved superpixel method is increased.

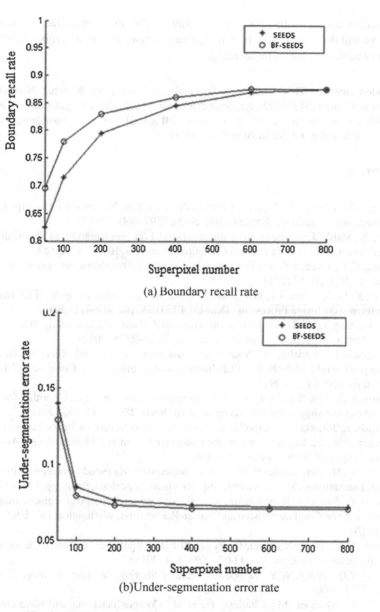

(a) Boundary recall rate

(b)Under-segmentation error rate

Fig. 8. Performance comparison of image segmentation result

5 Conclusions

This paper presents an improved superpixel method for color image segmentation with BF-SEEDS. Using the bilateral filter, we can eliminate the redundant texture information but with preserving the boundary information. Verified by the experiment, compared with original one, BF-SEEDS method in this paper can improve the quality of image segmentation and has some practical meaning for the subsequent image process. In the future, we will do some research on image merge based on the superpixel segmentation to get more information of target image.

Acknowledgement. This work was financially supported by National Natural Science Foundation of China (51375132), Jincheng Science and Technology Foundation (201501004-5), Shanxi Provincial Natural Science Foundation (2013011017-1), Ph.D Foundation of Taiyuan University of Science and Technology (20122025).

References

1. Song, X.Y., Zhou, L.L., Li, Z.G., Chen, J., Zeng, L., Yan, B.: Review on superpixel methods in image segmentation. J. Image Graph. **20**(5), 0599–0608 (2015)
2. Ren, X., Malik, J.: Learning a classification model for segmentation. In: Proceedings of the IEEE International Conference on Computer Vision, pp. 10–17. IEEE (2003)
3. Wang, C.Y., Chen, J.Z., Li, W.: Superpixel segmentation algorithms review. J. Appl. Res. Comput. **31**(1), 6–12 (2014)
4. Zhou, X., Li, X., Chin, T.J., et al.: Superpixel-driven level set tracking. In: IEEE International Conference on Image Processing, Orlando, FL, USA, pp. 409–412 (2012)
5. Liu, L., Xing, J., Ai, H., et al.: Semantic superpixel based vehicle tracking. IEEE Conference on Pattern Recognization, Tsukuba, Japan, pp. 2222–2225 (2012)
6. Fulkerson, B., Vedaldi, A., Soatto, S.: Class segmentation and object localization with superpixel neighborhoods. In: IEEE International Conference on Computer Vision, Kyoto, Japan, pp. 670–677 (2009)
7. Zhang, R.G., Liu, X.J., Dong, L., et al.: Superpixel graph cuts rapid algorithm for extracting object contour shapes. Pattern Recognit. Artif. Intell. **28**(4), 344–353 (2015)
8. Shotton, J., Johnson, M., Cipolla, R.: Semantic texton forests for image categorization and segmentation. In: Decision Forests for Computer Vision and Medical Image Analysis, vol. 5, no. 7, pp. 1–8. Springer London (2008)
9. Zhang, Y., Hartlet, R., Mashford, J., et al.: Superpixels via pseudo-boolean optimization. In: IEEE International Conference on Computer Vision, Barcelona, Spain, pp. 1387–1394 (2011)
10. Liu, M.Y., Tuzel, O., Ramalingam, S., et al.: Entropy rate superpixel segmentation. In: IEEE Conference on Computer Vision and Pattern Recognition, Washington, DC, USA, pp. 2097–2104 (2011)
11. Bergh, M.V., Boix, X., Roig, G., et al.: SEEDS: superpixels extracted via energy-driven sampling. Int. J. Comput. Vis. **111**(3), 298–314 (2015)
12. Zhang, Z.Q., Wang, W.Y.: A modified bilateral filtering algorithm. J. Image Graph. **14**(3), 443–447 (2009)
13. Pablo, A., Michael, M., Charless, F., et al.: Contour detection and hierarchical image segmentation. IEEE Trans. Pattern Anal. Mach. Intell. **33**(5), 898–916 (2010)

Global Perception Feedback Convolutional Neural Networks

Chaoyou Fu[✉], Xiang Wu, Jing Dong, and Ran He

Institution of Automation, Chinese Academy of Sciences, Beijing, China
fuchaoyou2017@ia.ac.cn

Abstract. Top-down feedback mechanism is an important module of visual attention for weakly supervised learning. Previous top-down feedback convolutional neural networks often perform local perception during feedback. Inspired by the fact that the visual system is sensitive to global topological properties [1], we propose a global perception feedback convolutional neural network that considers the global structure of visual response during feedback inference. The global perception eliminates "Visual illusions" that are produced in the process of visual attention. It is achieved by simply imposing the trace norm on hidden neuron activations. Particularly, when updating the status of hidden neuron activations during gradient backpropagation, we get rid of some minor constituent in the SVD decomposition, which both ensures the global low-rank structure of feedback information and the elimination of local noise. Experimental results on the ImageNet dataset corroborate our claims and demonstrate the effectiveness of our global perception model.

Keywords: Feedback · Global perception · Weakly supervised learning

1 Introduction

In recent years, although deep convolutional neural networks (CNNs) have achieved great performance in computer vision and pattern recognition, these successful algorithms are mainly based on feedforward neural networks and neglect the top-down feedback mechanism that is important for the visual processing [2–5], especially for weakly-supervised or semi-supervised learning.

The top-down feedback mechanism of CNNs has attracted some research attentions recently, which focus on utilizing the top-down feedback mechanism to further increase generalization ability of CNNs. Zeiler et al. [6] proposed a deconvolution technique that projects feature responses back to the input pixel space for visualizing and understanding CNNs. Simonyan et al. [7] obtained a class saliency map by a single back-propagation pass with a given label. Springenberg et al. [8] got a clearer class saliency map by preventing the forward and backward pass of negative gradients. Cao et al. [9] inspired by "Biased Competition Theory" [10–12] and proposed an original feedback model to simulate visual attention by inferring the status of hidden neuron activations. Other top-down feedback methods that realize visualization or localization include [13–15].

© Springer Nature Singapore Pte Ltd. 2018
Y. Wang et al. (Eds.): IGTA 2017, CCIS 757, pp. 65–73, 2018.
https://doi.org/10.1007/978-981-10-7389-2_7

Although these top-down feedback methods have got encouraging achievements, current methods only perform local perception and ignore the global structure during feedback. In the process of top-down local perception, neurons cannot be completely suppressed or activated because of the complex relationship between neurons. The status of a neuron is not only decided by external stimuli but also influenced by surrounding neurons. Cognitive neuroscientists explain this phenomenon as the "Visual illusions" [16], which increases the chance of recognition and detection being interfered with distractive patterns.

Considering the global topological properties of human visual system [1] and some works of global view [17, 18] or structural constraint [19–21], we present a novel framework towards a feedback CNNs to eliminate "Visual illusions" in this paper. Our key innovation lies in introducing a Global Perception (GP) algorithm, which explicitly constrains the structure of inter-layers in a global way. By combining the global perception with local perception, the distribution of active neurons in hidden layers is compulsively constrained and the phenomenon of "Visual illusions" almost disappeared, as shown in Fig. 1.

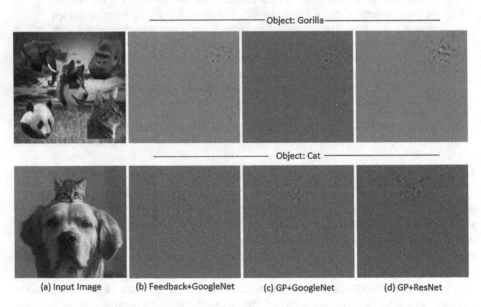

    (a) Input Image   (b) Feedback+GoogleNet   (c) GP+GoogleNet   (d) GP+ResNet

Fig. 1. An illustration of global perception feedback convolutional neural networks. First, we compare the image gradient after the GP process against the Feedback [9], by using the same pre-trained GoogleNet trained on ImageNet 2012 classification dataset. Column (a) shows the input images. Column (b) and (c) show the Feedback results and GP results, respectively. Comparing against Feedback, the GP method filters out more local noise. Then, we demonstrate the more powerful discrimination of ResNet. Column (d) shows the GP results based on pre-trained ResNet. Comparing to GoogleNet, the ResNet has better results.

In practice, we maximize the score of the target class to suppress non-relevant neurons and minimize the trace norm of hidden neuron activations to maintain the low-rank structure of hidden layers. Subsequently, we use the gradient algorithm via back-propagation to update the status of hidden neuron activations.

The proposed method is evaluated on the ImageNet object localization dataset, with two widely used CNNs, i.e., GoogleNet [22] and ResNet [23]. We have demonstrated that our model can get better performance compared with previous feedback models.

2   Model

Current feedforward CNNs [24] mainly consist of convolutional layers, activation functions (such as ReLU) and pooling layers. Among them, ReLU and pooling layers play the role of "gates" [9], which filter out signals with minor contributions to final classification during the bottom-up propagation of input images. However, because these gates serve for all classes in the final fully-connected classification layer instead of a specific category, the activated neurons involve too many noises for a specific category.

In order to merely let the information of the target class pass through, [9] introduced a "feedback layer", which is stacked upon each ReLU layer and consists of binary neuron activation variables $z \in \{0, 1\}$. The output of the feedback layer y is equal to the Hadamard product of the input x and binary variables z. The activation of these variables z are decided by top-down information passed from the target class label. However, this method just performs local perception during feedback and ignores the global properties. Our model adds an extra global perception on the foundation of [9], as shown in Fig. 2.

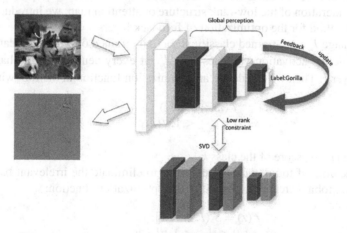

Fig. 2. Framework of our global perception feedback convolutional neural networks. First, given an input image with cluttered background and multiple objects, our networks perform in a bottom-up manner. Then, via a global perception, our networks inversely propagate the given label information and updates the status of hidden neuron activations in a top-down manner. Finally, we get a saliency map that includes class and location information corresponding to the given label.

2.1   Image-Specific Class Saliency Visualization

Given an image I, a class k and the hidden neuron activation status z, the class score of final fully-connected layer $S_k(I, Z)$ is a highly non-linear function of I. Yet, by computing the first-order Taylor expansion, we can approximate $S_k(I, z)$ in the neighborhood of I_0:

$$S_k(I, z) \approx G_k(z)^T I + b \tag{1}$$

where b is the bias term and $G_k(z)$ is the derivative of $S_k(I, z)$ with respect to the image at the point of I_0 and z:

$$G_k(z) = \left. \frac{\partial S_k(I, z)}{\alpha I} \right|_{I_0, z} \tag{2}$$

The size of $G_k(z)$ represents the relevancy between input pixels and relevant categories. Meanwhile, by the backpropagation method, the $G_k(z)$ can be calculated and passed to pixel space to realize the visualization of $G_k(z)$. We also adopt the guided backpropagation method, which was proposed in [8]. The guided backpropagation method makes the visual images clearer by masking out the values corresponding to negative entries of the top gradient that prevents backward pass of negative gradients.

2.2   Optimization of Feedback Layers

The phenomenon of "Visual illusions" seriously affects the effect of top-down suppression. In consideration of the low-rank structure of attention map, we introduce a global perception method for the optimization of feedback layers.

Given image I, a pre-trained classification CNN trained on ImageNet dataset and a class k, we define activation variables z as $z_{i,j,c}^l$ at every neuron (i, j) of channel c, on feedback layer l. Then we can define an optimization function in the following form:

$$\ell(z) = S_k(I, z)$$
$$s.t.\, 0 < z_{i,j,c}^l < 1, \forall l, i, c \tag{3}$$

where $S_k(I, z)$ is the score of the class k.

Since the core of top-down suppression is to eliminate the irrelevant background, we impose a global perception method to the optimization function:

$$\ell(z) = S_k(I, z) - \lambda \|z\|_*$$
$$s.t.\, 0 < z_{i,j,c}^l < 1, \forall l, i, c \tag{4}$$

where $\|z\|_*$ is the trace norm of z, which is used to enforce the low-rank of the feedback information.

Since the trace norm is difficult to directly optimize, we introduce an iterative minimization method for the trace norm [25].

Let $z \in R^{i \times j}$ in the channel c of feedback layer l. The trace norm of z can be shown as

$$\|z\|_* = \sum_{n=1}^{\min(i,j)} \sigma_n \tag{5}$$

Where σ_n denotes the n-th singular value of z. The trace norm can also be represented as

$$\|z\|_* = \frac{1}{2} \inf_{g \geq 0} tr\left(z^T g^{-1} z\right) + tr(g) \tag{6}$$

The infimum is attained for $g = \left(zz^T\right)^{1/2}$.

By using this lemma, the previous optimization function Eq. (4) can be reformulated as

$$\ell(z) = S_k(I, z) - \frac{1}{2} \lambda tr\left(z^T g^{-1} z\right) - \frac{1}{2} \lambda tr(g)$$
$$s.t.\ 0 < z_{i,j,c}^l < 1, \forall l, i, c \tag{7}$$

According to [25], the infimum over g is then attained for

$$g = \left(zz^T + \mu I\right)^{1/2} \tag{8}$$

In order to optimize the Eq. (7) in CNN, we use an alternating optimization method to update the parameters z and g. For the $S_k(I, z)$, we can calculate $\partial S_k / \partial z$ by pre-trained CNN and back-propagation method, while the weights are fixed and parameters z are updated. For the matrix g, we update it via Eq. (8). For the trace norm, according to the Eq. (6), the derivation of z is equal to

$$\frac{\partial \|z\|_*}{\partial z} = g^{-1} z + \left(g^{-1}\right)^T z \tag{9}$$

Hence, the gradient of the Eq. (4) is

$$\frac{\partial \ell(z)}{\partial z} = \frac{\partial S_k}{\partial z} - \frac{1}{2} \lambda g^{-1} z - \frac{1}{2} \lambda \left(g^{-1}\right)^T z \tag{10}$$

The singular value decomposition of z is $UDiag(\gamma_k)V^T$. We get rid of minor constituent of γ_k and get γ_k'. Hence, the inverse of matrix g is

$$S^{-1} = VDiag\left(\frac{1}{\sqrt{\gamma_k' + \mu}}\right)U^T \tag{11}$$

We use the gradient ascent algorithm to update parameters z with the learning rate α:

$$z^{t+1} = z^t + \alpha \left. \frac{\partial \ell(z)}{\partial z} \right|_{z^t} \tag{12}$$

3   Experiment

In this section, we evaluate the effectiveness of our GP feedback model. First, we compare the visualization results against the previous one [9] from qualitative perspective. Then, we conducted experiments of weakly supervised object localization on the ImageNet 2014 validation dataset from quantitative perspective. Every picture needs 10–50 iterations of suppression process, which is the same as [9]. Implementation details are included in our subsequent introduction.

3.1   Qualitative Experiments

In this section, we compare the image gradient after the GP process against the previous one [9] on a set of images with multiple objects. Both of methods are given the same pre-trained GoogleNet with ground truth class labels. We also compare different visualization results between GoogleNet and ResNet. All results are shown in Fig. 1.

Comparison of visualization methods. We compare our global perception feedback method with the local perception feedback method [9] on a set of images with multiple objects. Both of methods are given the same pre-trained GoogleNet [22] with ground truth class labels. Without global perception, the status of hidden neurons are only suppressed by local perception and the visualization results are seriously disturbed by irrelevant background or objects, as shown in Fig. 1, column (b). Compared with local perception approach, our global perception effectively eliminates local noise, as shown in Fig. 1, column (c).

Comparison of CNN classifiers. Since [9] has demonstrated that GoogleNet has better feature extraction ability than AlexNet [26] and VggNet [24], we just consider these two popular CNN architectures: GoogleNet [22] and ResNet [23]. Both of them are downloaded from the Caffe Model Zoo [27]. We evaluate our GP feedback method on GoogleNet and ResNet respectively. The visualizing results are shown in Fig. 1. From visualizations, we find that ResNet better captures the salient map of target label than GoogleNet, suggesting that deeper networks have more powerful discrimination.

3.2   Quantitative Experiments

In this section, we demonstrate the effectiveness of our GP feedback model on the ImageNet 2014 validation dataset, which contains ~50,000 images and corresponding class and position information. As shown in Fig. 1, given an image, our GP feedback model has the ability to determine the positions of the target objects. In the localization task, we get the category of an input image by bottom-up manner and get the bounding boxes of the identified category by top-down manner. A bounding box is considered as correct if its overlap with the ground truth bounding box is over 50%.

Given an image and its corresponding salience map, [9] merely calculates a tightest bounding box by simply thresholding to let the foreground area cover 95% energy out of the whole salience map. This localization method will fail when there are multiple same objects, as shown in Fig. 3, column (c). Different from [9], we get every target object position by external contour detection and calculate every accurate bounding box, as shown in Fig. 3, column (d), which respectively identifies the position of two pandas.

(a) Input Image   (b) GP Image   (c) Feedback   (d) GP

Fig. 3. We select an example to demonstrate the effectiveness of our localization method. Column (a) shows the original image with two pandas. Column (b) shows the visualization result of GP. Because Feedback [9] merely calculates a tightest bounding box by simply thresholding to let the foreground area cover 95% energy out of the whole salience map, the bounding box covers all pandas, as shown in column (c). We get every target object position by external contour detection and respectively calculate every accurate bounding box, as shown in column (d).

Comparison of visualization methods. We compare our global perception feedback method against the original gradient (GT) [7] and the guided backpropagation (GB) [8] and the local perception feedback method (FB) [9] on the ImageNet 2014 validation dataset. We first respectively use our external contour detection method and the localization method of [9] to conduct FB experiment. Our localization method obtains 61.2% localization error and outperforms the localization method of [9] (62.6%), suggesting that our localization method is better. Hence, all methods in Table 1 use our localization method instead of localization method of [9]. The results in Table 1 show that our global perception feedback method significantly outperforms other visualization methods, all on the GoogleNet architecture.

Table 1. Comparison of visualization methods.

	GT [7]	GB [8]	FB [9]	GP
Localization error (%)	65.9	64.8	61.2	59.6

Comparison of CNN classifiers. We also compare the weakly supervised localization accuracies of GoogleNet and ResNet in Table 2, based on our localization method. The results suggest that ResNet significantly outperforms GoogleNet, which agrees with the visualization results in Fig. 1.

Table 2. Comparison of CNN models.

	GoogleNet [22]	ResNet [23]
Localization error (%)	59.6	58.8

4 Conclusion

In this paper, we proposed a global perception model for feedback convolutional neural networks, which further eliminates irrelevant information by forcing the low-rank structure of the responses for hidden layer neurons during the feedback inference. Using GP, we get more discriminative saliency maps correspond to high level semantic labels. Good performance of the method has been demonstrated experimentally on the ImageNet 2014 object localization challenge with weakly supervised information.

References

1. Chen, L.: Topological structure in visual perception. Science **218**(4573), 699–700 (1982)
2. Koch, C., Ullman, S.: Shifts in selective visual attention: towards the underlying neural circuitry. In: Vaina, L.M. (ed.) Matters of Intelligence. Synthese Library (Studies in Epistemology, Logic, Methodology, and Philosophy of Science), vol. 188, pp. 115–141. Springer, Dordrecht (1987). https://doi.org/10.1007/978-94-009-3833-5_5
3. Anderson, C.H., Van Essen, D.C.: Shifter circuits: a computational strategy for dynamic aspects of visual processing. Proc. Natl. Acad. Sci. **84**(17), 6297–6301 (1987)
4. Tsotsos, J.K., Culhane, S.M., Wai, W.Y.K., Lai, Y., Davis, N., Nuflo, F.: Modeling visual attention via selective tuning. Artif. Intell. **78**(1–2), 507–545 (1995)
5. Wolfe, J.M.: Guided search 2.0 a revised model of visual search. Psychon. Bull. Rev. **1**(2), 202–238 (1994)
6. Zeiler, M.D., Fergus, R.: Visualizing and understanding convolutional networks. In: Fleet, D., Pajdla, T., Schiele, B., Tuytelaars, T. (eds.) ECCV 2014. LNCS, vol. 8689, pp. 818–833. Springer, Cham (2014). https://doi.org/10.1007/978-3-319-10590-1_53
7. Simonyan, K., Vedaldi, A., Zisserman, A.: Deep inside convolutional networks: visualising image classification models and saliency maps. arXiv preprint arXiv:1312.6034 (2013)
8. Springenberg, J.T., Dosovitskiy, A., Brox, T., Riedmiller, M.: Striving for simplicity: the all convolutional net. arXiv preprint arXiv:1412.6806 (2014)
9. Cao, C., Liu, X., Yang, Y., Yu, Y., Wang, J., Wang, Z., Huang, Y., Wang, L., Huang, C., Xu, W., et al.: Look and think twice: capturing top-down visual attention with feedback convolutional neural networks. In: Proceedings of the IEEE International Conference on Computer Vision, pp. 2956–2964 (2015)
10. Desimone, R., Duncan, J.: Neural mechanisms of selective visual attention. Annu. Rev. Neurosci. **18**(1), 193–222 (1995)
11. Desimone, R.: Visual attention mediated by biased competition in extrastriate visual cortex. Philos. Trans. R. Soc. B Biol. Sci. **353**(1373), 1245 (1998)
12. Beck, D.M., Kastner, S.: Top-down and bottom-up mechanisms in biasing competition in the human brain. Vis. Res. **49**(10), 1154–1165 (2009)
13. Zhang, J., Lin, Z., Brandt, J., Shen, X., Sclaroff, S.: Top-down neural attention by excitation backprop. In: Leibe, B., Matas, J., Sebe, N., Welling, M. (eds.) ECCV 2016. LNCS, vol. 9908, pp. 543–559. Springer, Cham (2016). https://doi.org/10.1007/978-3-319-46493-0_33

14. Zhou, B., Khosla, A., Lapedriza, A., Oliva, A., Torralba, A.: Learning deep features for discriminative localization. In: Proceedings of the IEEE Conference on Computer Vision and Pattern Recognition, pp. 2921–2929 (2016)
15. Hu, P., Ramanan, D.: Bottom-up and top-down reasoning with hierarchical rectified Gaussians. In: Proceedings of the IEEE Conference on Computer Vision and Pattern Recognition, pp. 5600–5609 (2016)
16. Coren, S., Girgus, J.S.: Visual illusions. In: Held, R., Leibowitz, H.W., Teuber, H.L. (eds.) Perception. Handbook of Sensory Physiology, vol. 8, pp. 549–568. Springer, Heidelberg (1978). https://doi.org/10.1007/978-3-642-46354-9_16
17. Lin, S., Ji, R., Guo, X., Li, X., et al.: Towards convolutional neural networks compression via global error reconstruction. In: International Joint Conferences on Artificial Intelligence (2016)
18. Huang, R., Zhang, S., Li, T., He, R.: Beyond face rotation: global and local perception GAN for photorealistic and identity preserving frontal view synthesis. arXiv preprint arXiv: 1704.04086 (2017)
19. Wu, X., Song, L., He, R., Tan, T.: Coupled deep learning for heterogeneous face recognition. arXiv preprint arXiv:1704.02450 (2017)
20. He, R., Tan, T., Wang, L.: Robust recovery of corrupted low-rank matrix by implicit regularizers. IEEE Trans. Pattern Anal. Mach. Intell. 36(4), 770–783 (2014)
21. He, R., Sun, Z., Tan, T., Zheng, W.S.: Recovery of corrupted low-rank matrices via half-quadratic based nonconvex minimization. In: 2011 IEEE Conference on Computer Vision and Pattern Recognition (CVPR), pp. 2889–2896. IEEE (2011)
22. Szegedy, C., Liu, W., Jia, Y., Sermanet, P., Reed, S., Anguelov, D., Erhan, D., Vanhoucke, V., Rabinovich, A.: Going deeper with convolutions. In: Proceedings of the IEEE Conference on Computer Vision and Pattern Recognition, pp. 1–9 (2015)
23. He, K., Zhang, X., Ren, S., Sun, J.: Deep residual learning for image recognition. In: Proceedings of the IEEE Conference on Computer Vision and Pattern Recognition, pp. 770–778 (2016)
24. Simonyan, K., Zisserman, A.: Very deep convolutional networks for large-scale image recognition. arXiv preprint arXiv:1409.1556 (2014)
25. Grave, E., Obozinski, G.R., Bach, F.R.: Trace lasso: a trace norm regularization for correlated designs. In: Advances in Neural Information Processing Systems, pp. 2187–2195 (2011)
26. Krizhevsky, A., Sutskever, I., Hinton, G.E.: Imagenet classification with deep convolutional neural networks. In: Advances in Neural Information Processing Systems, pp. 1097–1105 (2012)
27. Caffe Model Zoo. https://github.com/BVLC/caffe/wiki/Model-Zoo

Single Image Defogging Based on Step Estimation of Transmissivity

Jialin Tang, Zebin Chen$^{(\boxtimes)}$, Binghua Su, and Jiefeng Zheng

School of Information Technology, Beijing Institute of Technology, Zhuhai 519088, China
thong03@163.com, bhsu@263.net, 496038259@qq.com,
1210423695@qq.com

Abstract. Some advanced defogging algorithms can reconstruct most details of the image, but cause color anomaly, which is too saturated or seriously distorted in some local areas in the restored image. In this paper, we present a new framework for image defogging using step estimation of transmissivity. Firstly, we capitalize a binary tree algorithm to segment image successively and utilize the small image blocks after every iteration as the effective area to estimate the atmospheric light. Second, we set a threshold to separate the image into two parts: bright and dark region. For the dark region of the image, we calculated transmissivity on the basis of the dark channel prior and obtain adaptive transmissivity estimation in the bright region. The experimental results show that the algorithm can effectively solve halo and color distortion after defogging.

Keywords: Image defogging · Step · Binary tree · Dark channel prior
Adaptively

1 Introduction

In the fog environment, the picture captured by camera often has low contrast and high noise, which makes it difficult for people and computer systems to perceive specific environment information and make judgement. Therefore, how to reconstruct more details for the true scene and achieve high quality defogging performance is quite significant for many computer vision applications [1].

Generally, in the field of image processing and computer vision, the image defogging algorithms can be categorized into single image defogging and multiple images defogging. The multiple images defogging methods often take a series of images in the same scene under different weather conditions, and obtain a clear defogging image based on polarization analysis and target depth [2, 3]. However, this methods are not only high cost in time and labor consuming for the difficulty to get multiple images in the same scene, but also the restriction which comes from the weather conditions that make it impractical to carry out.

The single image defogging techniques have made significant progress in the past decades. This kind of methods not only avoided the problems appeared in multiple images defogging algorithms, but also achieved better image reconstruction quality [1]. Tan [4] improved the image resolution by the usage of maximum local contrast. Although this approach obtained good the image visibility, however the image color often too saturated

© Springer Nature Singapore Pte Ltd. 2018
Y. Wang et al. (Eds.): IGTA 2017, CCIS 757, pp. 74–84, 2018.
https://doi.org/10.1007/978-981-10-7389-2_8

which leads to heavy Halo effect around the edge for the large change in depth of field [10, 12]. Assuming that the surface reflectance and transmission values are not statistically correlated, Fattal [5] used independent component analysis (ICA) to estimate the scene reflectance, and then combined with the atmospheric light to defog for an image. Since this method utilized statistical features of the input data, namely, when thick fog exists in an image or the signal-noise ratio was low, which make statistical features invalid [1, 12, 14]. Kopf's [8] approach also achieved better image defogging performance, but this algorithm dependent heavily on the prior geographic information.

In order to address the above issues, Fattal and He [6, 7] analyzed characteristics of outdoor images without fog, and introduced the concept of dark channel prior, and eventually integrated into the degradation model of fog image, which made it a groundbreaking at that time. Since this approach utilized the dark channel prior for image defogging, that is, when there is a large sky area with white cloud and other bright area, eventually the dark channel would disappear, and the defogged images usually have strong color distortion [11]. In order to solve these problems, Li [18] proposed a more powerful but faster defogging algorithm based on image segmentation.

In this paper, we capitalize a binary tree decomposition first in order to find effective area of atmospheric light from the gray scale image, and then take mean value of all pixels in that region as the accurate value of estimated atmospheric light. Furthermore, the estimation of transmissivity ratio can be divided into two steps. The first step is to estimate the transmissivity of dark region on the basis of dark channel prior, and the second step is to obtain the transmissivity of the bright region adaptively using the transmissivity of the dark region. In order to avoid residual fog appears in the image after defogging for the large gradient variations at the edge of depth of field, we refine the estimation of transmissivity by using the guided filter. Finally, we set up a series of experiments to verify the effectiveness of our algorithm. The quantitative and qualitative experimental results show that our step estimation of transmissivity approach has the best performance and strong robustness, therefore can be applied to practical applications in various scenes.

2   Image Defogging Model

2.1   Physical Model of Fog Imaging

Currently, a very widely used physical model of fog imaging is the atmospheric scattering model [1, 5], namely

$$I(x) = J(x)t(x) + A(1 - t(x)) \tag{1}$$

In the equation, $I(x)$ is intensity of the observed image, $J(x)$ for the scene light intensity, and A shows the overall atmospheric light intensity. Furthermore, $t(x)$ is the medium transmission function, which describes the percentage of light emitted from an object or scene to the camera, called transmissivity. The goal of defogging is to estimate the atmospheric light intensity A and transmissivity $t(x)$ in order to recover $J(x)$ from $I(x)$. Therefore the Eq. (1) can also be written as

$$J(x) = \frac{I(x) - A(1 - t(x))}{t(x)} \tag{2}$$

The difficulty to defog image based on the physical model is that if only one foggy image is inputted, the image defogging could be an ill-conditioned problem that lack of constraints as there are infinite fogless images $J(x)$ can satisfy Eq. (1). Therefore, it is difficult to solve Eq. (1) directly, and we need to estimate the atmospheric light intensity A and transmissivity $t(x)$ first by combining some assumptions or prior information related to the input image.

2.2 Dark Channel Prior

From the fog imaging model, some reliable physical assumptions can effectively solve A and $t(x)$. Based on the assumption of statistical independence, Fattal assumed local block albedo is a constant vector, and all the $J(x)$ in local blocks had the same direction in the vector [5, 6]. Under this assumption, although it is possible to get rid of most fog on the image, when there is no significant change in the independent component of the image or the noise-signal ratio is low, which leads to poor defogging performance for the lack of statistical information [11, 14].

In order to address this issue, He introduced the dark channel prior [5]. The dark channel prior is obtained through statistical analysis of a large number of outdoor images without fog. For most natural images, there exists at least one color channel in the local region with low luminance value and most of the pixel brightness value is close to zero in the non-sky area. Therefore, for any natural image J, the dark channel can be defined as

$$J^{dark}(x) = \min_{y \in \Omega(x)} \left(\min_{c \in \{R,G,B\}} J^c(y) \right) \tag{3}$$

In this formula, J^c is one of the three color channels R, G and B in a natural image J, $\Omega(x)$ is a 15×15 square area centered on the pixel x. $\min_{c \in \{R,G,B\}}$ is used to obtain the minimum color channel map of J, and $\min_{y \in \Omega(x)}$ term makes minimum filtering on the minimum color channel map obtained. According to the concept of dark channel prior,

$$J^{dark} \to 0 \tag{4}$$

3 Rough Estimation of Transmissivity and Solution of Atmospheric Light

3.1 Rough Estimation of Transmissivity

Through the fog imaging model and dark channel prior [5, 17], a transmissivity model can be derived, like the following equation depicts

$$t(x) = 1 - \min_{y \in \Omega(x)} \left(\min_{c \in \{R,G,B\}} \frac{I^c(y)}{A^c} \right) \tag{5}$$

However, in real life, there are some particles in the air, even if the weather is sunny and white cloud. When you look at a object far away from you, the impact of fog can also be detected, which makes it possible for human eye to feel the parallax. Therefore, in order to make the image nature and vivid, it is necessary to keep a certain degree of fog when the fog is removed and a constant ω is introduced in Eq. (5), namely

$$t(x) = 1 - \omega \min_{y \in \Omega(x)} \left(\min_{c \in \{R,G,B\}} \frac{I^c(y)}{A^c} \right) \tag{6}$$

Where $\omega \in (0, 1]$, the size of ω affects the residual fog on the defogged image.

3.2   Estimation of Atmospheric Light by Binary Tree

In the processing of image defogging, the key point is to estimate the value of atmospheric light A. To estimate A correctly is not an easy task in image defogging field, which attract a lot of attentions now a days. The estimation of A is related to the final image restoration to a great extent.

Tan [4] directly used the brightest pixel values on the fog image to estimate the size of A. He [5] selected the 0.1% of the total pixels from the dark channel map of the input image, and then mapped the pixels back to the original image in order to find A, which is the maximum luminance value in the original image. These approaches take the pixel value in the original image as an estimation value of the atmospheric light intensity A. When other objects with higher brightness appear in foreground (for example in a complex traffic scene), this kind of pixels often come from foreground rather than sky. Therefore, the approaches of Tan and He is not reasonable in getting the atmospheric light intensity [17, 18]. On the contrary, we use the binary tree algorithm to get a more accurate candidate region of atmospheric light.

The detailed processing approach of estimating atmospheric light using binary tree algorithm is: first, the gray level image of a fog image is obtained (Fig. 1(b)), and separate the image into two equal parts, the next is to compare the averages of all gray values of two parts while keep the area with larger average value. Furthermore, the area is divided into left and right equal parts horizontally and keep the area with larger average similarly. In order to get more accurate sky areas, we repeat it eight times and finally the small area is utilized as the effective area to solve the atmospheric light. The effective area of atmospheric light worked out by this approach is in Fig. 1(c).

We assume that the values of the three color channels of atmospheric light are the same, the effective area based on binary tree algorithm after iterations is $\Phi(x)$. The average gray value of the region is taken as the value of three channels of atmospheric light,

$$A^c = mean[\Phi(x)], \ c \in \{R, G, B\} \tag{7}$$

Where $mean[\bullet]$ is the average value of all the pixels in $\Phi(x)$.

(a)   (b)   (c)

Fig. 1. (a) Original input image; (b) Gray image; (c) Search valid area.

4   Correction and Optimization of Transmissivity

After getting the atmospheric light value by use of binary tree, the transmissivity can be roughly estimated (Fig. 2(a)) by using Eq. (6). However, there are two problems to directly use transmissivity in order to reconstruct the image: first, a large number of spots will appear in the sky of the image after defogging when there is a large area of sky on the image, (Fig. 2(c)); second, the transmissivity of apparent blocky phenomenon will lead to a small amount of fog around the object edge in the restored image (Fig. 2(d)). For the visual effect of local image after defogging can be affected by the above two problems, we adopt two approaches to avoid this. One is the adaptive correction of transmissivity and the other is the refinement of transmissivity.

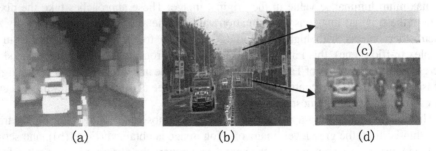

(a)   (b)   (d)

Fig. 2. (a) Estimated transmission map; (b) Final haze-free image; (c) Sky area; (d) Traffic scene.

4.1   Adaptive Correction of Transmissivity

There would exist serious distortion in the defogged sky image. Because the pixel value of the region is usually large and has no dark channel, which leads to low sky transmissivity and over enhanced in the sky part of the final defogged image [12, 13]. A simple way to solve this problem is to find out the high brightness of the input image, in this case, a constant is uniformly set to the corresponding transmissivity of this region [11]. However, this approach is lack of robustness since it may cause the whole image overexposed after defogging if a large constant is given; On the contrary, if the constant is too small, the sky would leads to a certain degree of distortion.

In order to make the constant can be adapted to different images, we assume that the constant is closely related to a pixel in the image, and the pixels in the grade image are divided into two regions according to the threshold δ: bright and dark region. $I(x) \geq \delta$ is defined as bright region, represented by B; and $I(x) < \delta$ as dark region, which is represented by D. Otsu algorithm and then to use for selection of threshold δ.

In the dark region with low brightness, the dark channel prior is established first. We directly use (6) to calculate transmissivity and mark as t(u). For the other region that the dark channel is not established, namely, the region with higher brightness, we uniformly set transmissivity as a constant, which is $\varepsilon \max[t(u)]$.

Define $I^{dark}(x) = \min\limits_{y \in \Omega(x)} \left(\min\limits_{c \in \{R,G,B\}} \dfrac{I^c(y)}{A^c} \right)$, the adaptive correction of transmissivity formula is shown as (8)

$$t(x) = \begin{cases} 1 - \omega I^{drak}(x), & x \in B \\ \varepsilon \max[t(u)], & x \in D, u \in B \end{cases} \tag{8}$$

Where $\max[\bullet]$ is the maximum value of $t(u)$, ε is a constant of $(0,1]$, which is generally set to 0.5.

4.2 Transmissivity Refinement by Guided Filter

When solving the dark channel of fog image, an image filter is set up using the minimum value of 15×15. Therefore an obvious large block phenomenon (Fig. 3(a)) may appear after the transmissivity $t(x)$ is obtained, which will further lead to some residual fog at the image edge after defogging [17]. In order to avoid such problem, an image matting approach is utilized to optimize the transmissivity [6], which can achieve good refinement effect. However this approach cannot be used in real time because of its high time complexity [11, 17]. Under the premise of reducing the precision and without affecting the defogging effect, a higher efficiency guided filter is used to refine the transmissivity [7, 10].

The guide map is based on the gray image of fog traffic image, marked as I_g. According to the local linear model of guided filter, the transmissivity $t(x)$ can be expressed as

(a)   (b)   (c)

Fig. 3. (a) Corrected transmission map; (b) refined transmission map; (c) image after haze removal by our approach.

$$t(x) = a_k I_{g_i} + b_k, \quad \forall i \in w_k \tag{9}$$

Where w_k is the area centered on the pixel k in the guided map I_g with window radius of r and (a_k, b_k) is constant in w_k.

In order to keep whole similarity between transmissivity $t(x)$ with gray image I_g, we minimize the object function of (10) in w_k,

$$E(a_k, b_k) = \sum_{i \in w_k} [(a_k I_{g_i} + b_k - t(x))^2 + \rho a_k^2] \tag{10}$$

Where ρ is a regularization parameter and is insensitive to the optimized result.

The transmissivity of the sky can be derived using above method. The fully optimized transmissivity using the guided filter is shown in Fig. 3(b) and the defogging result using our transmissivity estimation algorithm is shown in Fig. 3(c).

5   Experimental Result and Analysis

In this section, a series of experiments in order to verify effectiveness of the algorithm are built. The experimental images are from Baidu, Google and other sites. In the experiment, we set ω affecting defogging to 0.85, regularization parameter ρ to 10^{-6}, window radius r of guided filter to 4 times of minimum filtering radius, namely r = 60. The computer used in the lab is equipped with 2.6 GHz Intel Core(TM) i5-3230M and 4 GB memory.

5.1   Defogging in Traffic Environment

In the traffic scene, the driver need to concentrate on the road ahead during the driving. In the fog and haze day, the foggy environment around the road may cause the distraction of the drivers and decreased atmospheric visibility. Therefore, traffic image defogging technique should avoid serious distortion on the image after defogging and to ensure maximum defogging effect on the road, which is of great significance for the driver to quickly and correctly judge the road ahead.

Figure 4 shows local effect of the defogging image. From Fig. 4(a), we can see the road visibility is low due to the fog and haze day, which makes it difficult to see clearly words on the road signs ahead and the driving motor vehicles. He's [7] approach has a better defogging effect for traffic road, but there are a lot of spots in the sky and exists obvious color distortion (Fig. 4(b)) at the junction of the close range and sky. This is due to the dark channel prior disappears when there is a large sky area, white cloud and other bright areas in the image, So in this case, we cannot estimate directly transmissivity of this area.

Figure 4(c) shows Cai's [10] approach, in this work, they utilize deep learning based algorithm, which can avoid sky distortion and get a good defogging effect on the whole. However, in some local areas, their method shows weak performance, like road signs that drivers have interests in the traffic, and the visibility is not clear enough due to a little fog.

Fig. 4. (a) Original input image; (b) He [7]; (c) Cai [10]; (d) Result of our approach.

Fig. 5. (a) Original input image; (b) He [7]; (c) Cai [10]; (d) Result of our approach.

As a comparison, our approach (Fig. 4(c)) can not only clearly show details of the roadside trees, but also make the words on the road signs in front understandable and the clear driving motor vehicles as well. The defogged image is natural and clear. Figure 5 shows another comparison experiment, we can see that our approach can also achieve a good defogging effect. In addition, the time comparison of algorithm in Table 1 shows that our approach can achieve defogging image faster than He [7] and Cai [10].

Table 1. Time comparison of different algorithms

Image	Size	He/s	Cai/s	Our/s
Figure 4	510×450	1.37	2.83	**0.95**
Figure 5	450×600	2.48	3.31	**1.12**
Average	–	1.93	3.07	**1.03**

5.2 Comparison with Other Mainstream Defogging Algorithms

Figures 6 and 7 show comparison results of our algorithm with other four mainstream defogging algorithms. Figure 6(c) is the defogging result of Tan [4]. Obviously, this approach uses maximum local contrast to defog, which can easily lead to saturated color of the restored image like an oil painting. Figure 6(d) is the defogging result of Tarel [9]. There is a certain color difference in the image obtained by this approach, and it is easy

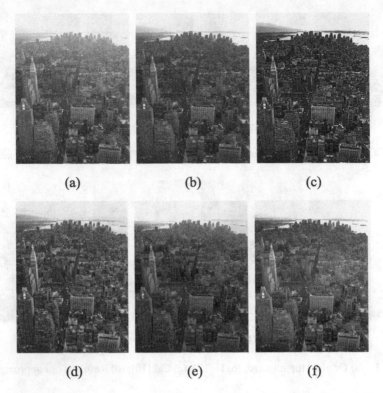

Fig. 6. (a) Original input image; (b) Result of our approach; (c) Tan [4]; (d) Tarel [9]; (e) Fattal [5]; (f) Kopf [8].

to cause Halo effect at the edge of depth of field with uneven variations. Fattal's [5] algorithm capitalizes independent component analysis (ICA) which leads to weak defogged performance for the lack of statistical information in the thick fog and low signal-to-noise ratio area, as shown in Figs. 6(e) and 7(e).

Kopf's [8] approach achieves better visual effects than Fattal's, as shown in Figs. 6(f) and 7(f). However, this approach relies on some geographic information in the region of the image, the effectiveness of the information will affect the final defogging effect [6, 10]. In addition, from Fig. 6(f) we can see there is still a few fog not removed in the close range of some buildings. The defogging result of our approach is demonstrated in Figs. 6(b) and 7(b). We can see that our approach can not only have a good defogging effect on the image, but also avoid excessive distortion of sky and achieve a good overall defogging effect. The problem is that some areas of the image after defogging appear dark, which is a common point of using the dark channel prior to realize defogging.

The above contents are display and evaluation of the visual effect. Next, we use the structural similarity index SSIM to evaluate the performance of various algorithms, we can determine the quality of restored image by comparing SSIM size of algorithms. In general, the greater SSIM is, the better the effect of restored image is [19]. Table 2 shows

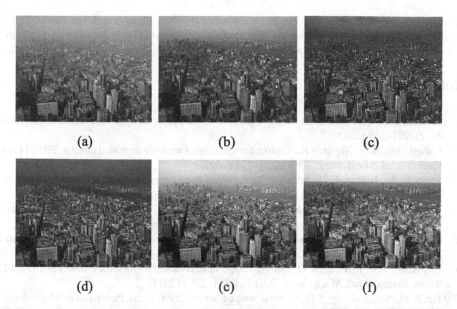

Fig. 7. (a) Original input image; (b) Result of our approach; (c) Tan [4]; (d) Tarel [9]; (e) Fattal [5]; (f) Kopf [8].

SSIM of all the algorithms, we can see that our algorithm has a higher recovery quality than other algorithms.

Table 2. SSIM comparison of different algorithms

Image	Our/SSIM	Tan/SSIM	Tarel/SSIM	Fattal/SSIM	Kopf/SSIM
Figure 6	**0.9417**	0.6268	0.8427	0.8719	0.9128
Figure 7	**0.9385**	0.7379	0.8281	0.8982	0.8898
Average	**0.9401**	0.6824	0.8354	0.8851	0.9013

6 Conclusion

In this paper, a framework of step estimation of transmissivity for image defogging is introduced. This approach does not depend on the initial estimation of depth information in the scene, but only just use a single image to complete the image defogging task. The experimental results show that our method is close to or even exceeds other most state-of-art approaches. In addition, our method achieve very good performance and can be applied to all kinds of scenes. For example, when there is a large sky area in the image, the direct usage of dark channel prior for defogging will lead to excessive distortion of sky, but our approach can overcome this shortcoming.

Although the step estimation of transmissivity approach can effectively reconstruct the foggy images the defogging efficiency still cannot satisfy the requirements of real-time processing for some practical scenes. Therefore, we will further refine our approach in order to reduce the time complexity in the next stage.

Acknowledgements. This work has been supported by Guangdong Youth Innovation Talent Project (2016KQNCY204) and Special Funds for the Cultivation of Guangdong College Students' Scientific and Technological Innovation (pdjh2017b0927).

References

1. Wu, D., Zhu, Q.S.: The latest research progress of image dehazing. Acta Automatica Sinica **41**(2), 221–239 (2015)
2. Narasimhan, S.G., Nayar, S.K.: Contrast restoration of weather degraded images. IEEE Trans. Pattern Anal. Mach. Intell. **25**(6), 713–724 (2003)
3. Shwartz, S., Namer, E., Schechner, Y.Y.: Blind haze separation. In: IEEE Conference on Computer Vision and Pattern Recognition (CVPR 2006), pp. 1984–1991, June 2006
4. Tan, R.: Visibility in bad weather from a single image. In: IEEE Conference on Computer Vision and Pattern Recognition (CVPR 2008), pp. 1–8, June 2008
5. Fattal, R.: Single image dehazing. In: International Conference on Computer Graphics and Interactive Technique, vol. 72, pp. 1–9. ACM SIGGRAPH Press, USA (2008)
6. He, K.M., Sun, J., Tang, X.O.: Single image haze removal using dark channel prior. IEEE Trans. Pattern Anal. Mach. Intell. **33**(12), 2341–2353 (2011)
7. He, K.M., Sun, J., Tang, X.O.: Guided image filtering. IEEE Trans. Pattern Anal. Mach. Intell. **35**(6), 1397–1409 (2013)
8. Kopf, J., Neubert, B., Chen, B., Cohen, M., Cohen-Or, D., Deussen, O., Uyttendaele, M., Lischinski, D.: Deep photo: model-based photograph enhancement and viewing. In: ACM SIGGRAPH Asia 2008 Papers (SIGGRAPH Asia 2008), pp. 116:1–116:10. ACM, New York (2008)
9. Tarel, J.P., Hautiere, N.: Fast visibility restoration from a single color or gray level image. In: 2009 IEEE 12th International Conference on Computer Vision, pp. 2201–2208, September 2009
10. Cai, B.L., Xu, X.M., Jia, K., Qing, C.M., Tao, D.: DehazeNet: an end-to-end system for single image haze removal. IEEE Trans. Image Process. **25**(11), 5187–5198 (2016)
11. Chen, S.Z., Ren, Z.G., Lian, Q.S.: Single image dehazing algorithm based on improved dark channel prior and guided filter. Acta Automatica Sinica **42**(3), 455–465 (2016)
12. Xing, X.M., Liu, W.: Haze removal for single traffic image. J. Image Graph. **21**(11), 1440–1447 (2016)
13. Liu, X.Y., Dai, S.K.: Halo-free and color-distortion-free algorithm for image dehazing. J. Image Graph. **20**(11), 1453–1461 (2015)
14. Wu, X.T., Lu, J.F., He, B.G., Wu, C., Zhu, M.: Fast restoration of haze-degraded image. Chin. Optics **6**(6), 892–899 (2013)
15. Liu, H.B., Yang, J., Wu, Z.P., Zhang, Q.N., Deng, Y.: A fast single image dehazing method based on dark channel prior and Retinex theory. Acta Automatica Sinica **41**(7), 1264–1273 (2015)
16. Fattal, R.: Dehazing using color-lines. ACM Trans. Graph. (2014)
17. Kim, J.H., Jang, W.D., Sim, J.Y., Kim, C.S.: Optimized contrast enhancement for real-time image and video dehazing. J. Vis. Commun. Image Represent. **24**(3), 410–425 (2013)
18. Li, J.T., Zhang, Y.J.: Improvements of image haze removal algorithm and its subjective and objective performance evaluation. Optics Precis. Eng. **25**(3), 735–741 (2017)
19. Chu, H.L., Li, Y.X., Zhou, Z.M., Shen, J.: Optimized fast dehazing method based on dark channel prior. Acta Electronica Sinica **41**(4), 791–797 (2013)

The Method of Crowd Density Alarm for Video Sequence

Mengnan Hu[ID], Chong Li[ID], and Rong Wang[✉][ID]

People's Public Security University of China, Beijing, China
361868422@qq.com

Abstract. A method of crowd density alarm for video surveillance based on the compressive sensing (CS) is proposed in this paper. Firstly, the video sequence is preprocessed to obtain the gray images or foreground images. Secondly, CS measurement is calculated and principal components analysis (PCA) is implemented to extract crowd density features. Finally, according to the feature vector, crowd density is divided into medium, high, very high by support vector machine (SVM). Compared with other methods, the test is carried out at the entrance of a school. Results of experiment show that the proposed method has higher accuracy and better real-time performance and the alarm target can be accomplished when the crowd density reaches a specified level.

Keywords: Compressive sensing (CS)
Principal components analysis · SVM · Crowd density alarm

1 Introduction

In recent years, with the increasing of violent terrorist incidents, stampede incidents and mass incidents, crowd behavior analysis has become a research hotspot in the field of video surveillance. Crowd density, as the main attribute of the population, has the important significance in the field of public security and group management. However, the crowd cannot be fully and continuously supervised only relying on the traditional means of civil air defense and anti- technology. With the development and popularization of video analysis technology, crowd density estimation technology is used to monitor the crowd density in real time to discover high density crowd and alarm.

The methods of crowd density estimation based on video sequence mainly include pixel based method and texture feature based method. The pixel based method is suitable for the low crowd density estimation and has low accuracy when the density is large [1–4]. Reference [5] firstly proposed the method based on Gray Level Co-occurrence Matrix (GLCM) and neural network to estimate the crowd density. The texture feature based method, using the principle that the image texture feature is closely related to the crowd density level, is suitable for high crowd density estimation

This work is supported by National Key Research and Development Plan under Grant No. 2016YFC0801005.

Y. Wang et al. (Eds.): IGTA 2017, CCIS 757, pp. 85–95, 2018.
https://doi.org/10.1007/978-981-10-7389-2_9

but the real-time performance is poor [6–9]. Reference [10] proposed the method combined GLCM and fractal to improve the accuracy rate. Foreground feature and texture feature were combined by PCA to represent the crowd density Ref. [11]. To reduce the computation and improve the real-time performance, Ref. [12] proposed the method of extracting sparse feature.

In this paper, a method of crowd density alarm based on CS and PCA is proposed. The features of crowd density are represented by CS measured value using sparse representation to reduce the calculation of feature extraction to shorten the extraction time. The dimension of CS measurement is reduced by PCA to reduce the dimension of the density feature vector to shorten the time of crowd density classification. The simulating experiment results show that the method proposed in this paper can get better effect for crowd density alarm.

The rest of the paper is organized as follows. The method of crowd density alarm is discussed in Sect. 2. Simulation experiment and analysis are presented in Sect. 3. Conclusions are given in Sect. 4.

2   Method of Crowd Density Alarm

As shown in Fig. 1, the method of crowd density alarm is divided into four parts, video sequence reading, preprocessing, crowd density feature extraction, and the crowd density estimation, in which the crowd density feature extraction and crowd density estimation are the two key links.

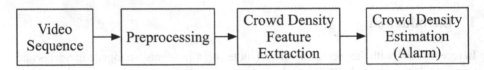

Fig. 1. Flowchart of crowd density estimation alarm system

2.1   Preprocessing

In this paper, foreground image of original video is obtained by the algorithm of gray scale, thresholding, template mask, object detection and so on, as shown in Fig. 2.

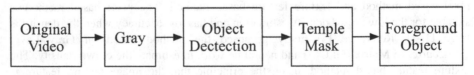

Fig. 2. Flowchart of preprocessing

As the method is not affected by the color feature, so the input video is grayed to transform the multi-channel color image to the single channel image.

Moving object detection is based on the Background Model Average algorithm. Firstly, the average value of each pixel is used as the initial background. Secondly, threshold is determined by the mean and standard deviation of gray difference between adjacent frames. And then, background model and threshold are updated in real time according to the inter frame data. Finally, foreground scene can be obtained by the subtraction between the gray value of current frame pixel and the background model.

Since the extracted foreground scene contains non-interested regions in which there are no pedestrians or only a very small number of pedestrians, so these regions are eliminated through the template mask. The template image is a binary image where the gray values are zero corresponding to non-interested regions and others are one. Non-interested regions can be blocked by 'and' operation between the original image and the template.

2.2 Crowd Density Feature Extraction

The process of crowd density feature extraction is divided into three parts, image block, CS measurement, PCA, as shown in Fig. 3. The crowd density feature vector is represented by CS measurement, which is divided into two steps, sparse representation and signal measurement.

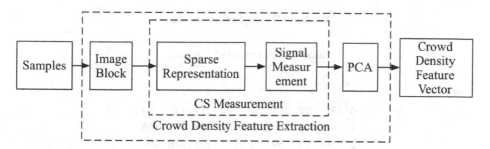

Fig. 3. Flowchart of crowd density feature extraction

For the signal $x = \{x_1, x_2, \ldots, x_N\}$, if the majority of elements are zero, the signal is sparse signal [13]. By mapping to vector s through sparse basis, if the majority of elements in the vector s are zero, the original signal can be regarded as sparse signal, as shown in formula (1) showing that s is the sparse representation for x. Then, mapping the sparse signal to a low dimensional space through the measurement matrix, the CS measured value is obtained, as shown in the formula (2).

$$x = \Psi s \tag{1}$$

$$y = \Phi x = \Phi \Psi s \tag{2}$$

where $\Phi \in R^{N \times N} (M \ll N)$ is the measurement matrix and the measured value $y \in R^N$.

Firstly, due to strong local correlation, the original image is divided into sub images which can not only maintain the spatial correlation of image but also have gentle changes and low spatial frequency, contributing to the image sparse representation.

Secondly, according to formula (1), choose DCT as sparse basis and perform DCT transform for each sub image to obtain the DCT transform coefficient matrix. The input image $f(i,j)$ of DCT transform is shown in Fig. 4, sub image f_1 is obtained by taking $i,j \in [0,7]$ and the pixel value of f_1 is shown in Table 1. DCT transform coefficient matrix $\mathbf{F} : \{F(u,v)|u,v \in [0,7]\}$ is obtained by performing DCT transform for f_1, as in Table 2, $F(0,0)$ is the DC (Direct Current) coefficient which reflects the average luminance of the image, and others are AC (Alternating Current) coefficient which reflect the spatial frequency size.

Fig. 4. DCT transform input image

Table 1. Pixel value of sub image

j \ i	0	1	2	3	4	5	6	7
0	230	228	238	241	244	211	188	204
1	195	188	185	172	150	135	157	165
2	50	54	59	67	76	133	220	208
3	64	69	62	64	86	158	232	180
4	103	107	102	104	112	143	173	119
5	164	164	163	161	137	105	105	78
6	144	144	145	146	122	93	103	80
7	112	117	116	119	117	129	163	121

DCT transform coefficients reflects different frequency components of the image, the upper left corner referring to the lower frequency, the lower right corner referring to the higher frequency. So the value of DCT transform coefficient in the upper left corner is larger and the value of the lower right corner is closer to zero. In order to increase the number of zero in the DCT transform coefficient matrix, DCT transform coefficient matrix is quantified, as shown in formula (3):

$$F_q(u,v) = (\text{rounding})\frac{F(u,v)}{Q(u,v)} \tag{3}$$

Table 2. DCT transform coefficient matrix of sub image

j \ i	0	1	2	3	4	5	6	7
0	1115.5	58.409	32.066	0.88925	31.750	40.812	31.683	12.670
1	169.07	58.456	30.838	12.424	12.484	12.061	12.615	0.72754
2	172.70	133.93	50.477	22.217	40.442	22.328	12.666	0.58977
3	144.48	182.08	78.695	0.79181	31.542	22.409	11.960	0.87558
4	48.500	76.849	1.0756	32.033	22.250	0.49053	0.63687	0.14881
5	0.86083	40.525	0.074455	1.2828	0.84450	0.64360	0.18740	0.29935
6	1.1772	48.232	0.41574	1.1270	0.29614	0.097803	0.27271	0.069211
7	31.638	41.036	0.22710	0.34020	0.24825	0.97601	0.073059	0.60901

where $F(u, v)$ is the DCT coefficient, $Q(u, v)$ is the quantization step using JPEG standard brightness quantization and $F_q(u, v)$ is the quantized DCT coefficient, as shown in Fig. 5 and Table 3.

16	11	10	16	24	40	51	61
12	12	14	19	26	58	60	55
14	13	16	24	40	57	69	56
14	17	22	29	51	87	80	62
18	22	37	56	68	109	103	77
24	35	55	64	81	104	113	92
49	64	78	87	103	121	120	101
72	92	95	98	112	100	103	99

Fig. 5. JPEG standard brightness quantization

Through Z shape scanning the quantified DCT transform coefficient matrix, as in Fig. 6, 1D sparse signal $x_1 = \{69\ 5\ 14\ 12\ 4\ 3\ 0\ 2\ 10\ 10\ 2\ 10\ 3\ 0\ 1\ 1\ 0\ 0\ 3\ 3\ 0\ 0\ 1\ 0\ 0\ 1\ 0\ 0\ 0\ 0\ 0\ 0\ 0\ 0\ 0\ 0\ 0\ 0\ 0\ 0\ 0\ 0\ 0\ 0\ 0\ 0\ 0\ 0\ 0\ 0\ 0\ 0\ 0\ 0\ 0\ 0\ 0\ 0\ 0\ 0\ 0\ 0\ 0\ 0\}$ is obtained. Then, CS measurement is obtained by choosing random Gauss matrix as the measurement matrix. All the measured value of the sub image can be got and converted into a 1D signal by repeating the above steps.

Finally, 6D crowd density feature vector through PCA to reduce the dimension.

Table 3. Quantized DCT transform coefficient matrix of sub image

j \ i	0	1	2	3	4	5	6	7
0	69	5	3	0	1	1	0	0
1	14	4	2	0	0	0	0	0
2	12	10	3	0	1	0	0	0
3	10	10	3	0	0	0	0	0
4	2	3	0	0	0	0	0	0
5	0	1	0	0	0	0	0	0
6	0	0	0	0	0	0	0	0
7	0	0	0	0	0	0	0	0

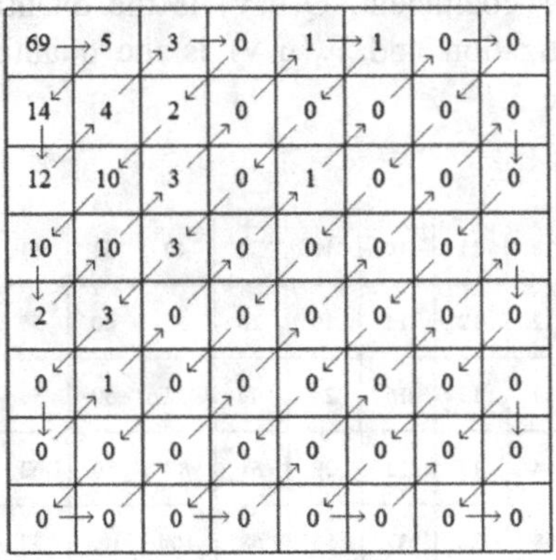

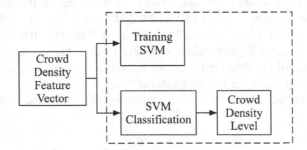

Fig. 6. Z shape scanning the quantified DCT transform coefficient matrix

2.3 Crowd Density Estimation

Crowd density estimation process is shown in Fig. 7, a number of known samples are collected and features are extracted in advance to constitute the training set to train the SVM classifier, and then the crowd density feature vector is put into the classifier.

Fig. 7. Flowchart of crowd density estimation

According to the definition of the crowd density level proposed by Polus [14] in Table 4, higher crowd density is divided into 3 categories: medium, high and very high.

Table 4. Definition of crowd density level by Polus

Crowd density (person/m²)	Font size and style
0–0.6	Extremely sparse
0.6–0.75	Sparse
0.75–1.25	Medium
1.25–2.0	Crowded
Above 2.0	Extremely crowded

'Voting method' strategy [14] is adopted, as shown in Fig. 8, and two classifiers are constructed by three SVM. SVMa is in the first level to realize a medium and high category classification. SVMb and SVMc are in the second level to realize medium, high and very high categories, respectively.

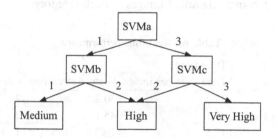

Fig. 8. SVM classification

3 Simulation Experiment and Analysis

The test video sequence is from the entrance of a middle school, in which the real scene area is about 10 m² and the image size is 320 × 240. 750 frames are extracted at 15 frames intervals for the experiment. Among them, the total number of training images is 450 frames, medium, high, very high density is 150 frames respectively; the total number of test images is 300 frames, medium, high, very high density is 100 frames.

3.1 Experiment Results

According to Table 1, the crowd density is divided into three classes, medium, high and very high, as shown in Table 5 and Fig. 9.

The method performance is evaluated in terms of real time and accuracy compared with the former methods, as shown in Tables 6 and 7. The real time performance is represented by the time of processing a single image including the crowd density

Table 5. Crowd density level in this paper

Crowd density (person/m²)	Total number of people in the scene	Density level	Alarm or not
0.8−1.5	8−15	Medium	No
1.6−2.5	16−25	High	No
Above 2.5	16−25	Very high	No

(a)Medium   (b)High   (c)Very High

Fig. 9. Crowd density level

feature extraction time and classification time. The accuracy performance is represented by the proportion of correct classified images in each category.

Table 6. Real-time performance

Method	Time (ms)		
	Total time per image	Feature extraction	Classification
GLCM	32.2	30.2	2
GLCM and Fractal	47.1	45.1	2
CS	17.5	16.5	1
CS and Fractal	31.2	30.2	1

Table 7. Accuracy performance

Method	Accuracy			
	Medium	High	Very high	Average
GLCM	73.2%	77.9%	75.9%	75.67%
GLCM and Fractal	75.4%	78.6%	79.5%	77.93%
CS	93.4%	97.2%	97.7%	96.1%
CS and Fractal	95.1%	98.8%	98.4%	97.53%

The video gray and foreground extraction are performed through preprocessing and crowd density is estimated preliminarily according to the proportion of the target pixel. If the proportion is lower than 0.15, which means that the crowd is sparse and is in a relatively safe condition, crowd density estimation based on SVM will not be carried out, otherwise, it will be carried out. The results of crowd density are divided into low, medium, high, and very high.

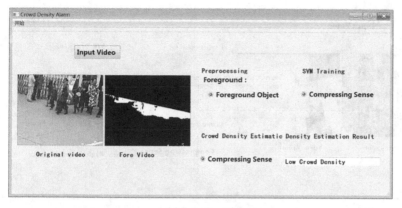

(a) Low Level

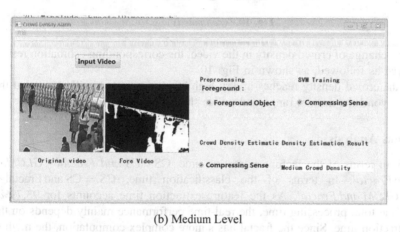

(b) Medium Level

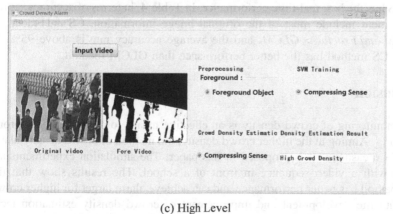

(c) High Level

Fig. 10. Results of crowd density estimation

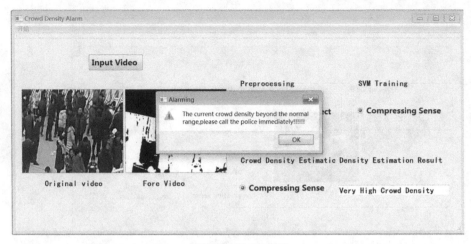

(d) Very High Level

Fig. 10. (*continued*)

With the change of crowd density in the video, the corresponding estimation results are displayed as followed, as shown in Fig. 10.

When the crowd density reaches a very high level, the system will alarm that the density is beyond the normal range and police should be called immediately.

3.2   Results Analysis

In Table 3, in terms of the feature extraction time, $CS < CS$ *and Fractal* $< GLCM <$ *GLCM and Fractal*. In terms of the classification time, $CS = CS$ and Fractal $<$ $GLCM = GLCM$ *and Fractal*. As the feature extraction time accounts for 93.79%–96.79% of the total processing time, the real-time performance mainly depends on the feature extraction time. Since the fractal has a more complex computation, the method based on CS has the best real-time performance. In Table 4, in terms of accuracy, as the CS measurement include most of the original image information, CS and Fractal > $CS > GLCM$ and Fractal $> GLCM$, and the average accuracy rate is above 95%. In conclusion, CS method has the better performance than GLCM method.

4   Conclusion

Real-time monitoring of crowd density is an effective means to alarm auxiliary group of events early. Aiming at the higher crowd density, the method of crowd density alarm based on CS measurement is proposed in this paper. The simulation experiments are carried out with a video sequence in front of a school. The results show that the proposed method has better performance and can achieve alarm target for higher crowd density. With the development and improvement of crowd density estimation technology, the technology will play a more important role in the field of intelligent video analysis.

References

1. Davies, A.C., Yin, J.H., Velastin, S.A.: Crowd monitoring using image processing. Electron. Commun. Eng. J. **7**(1), 37–47 (1995)
2. Choudri, S., Ferryman, J.M., Badii, A.: Robust background model for pixel based people counting using a single uncalibrated camera. In: 12th IEEE International Workshop on Performance Evaluation of Tracking and Surveillance, pp. 1–8. IEEE, Snowbird, UT, USA (2009)
3. Conte, D., Foggia, P., Percannella, G., et al.: A method for counting people in crowded scenes. In: IEEE International Conference on Advanced Video & Signal Based Surveillance, pp. 225–232 (2010)
4. Ding, Y., Chen, S., Liu, J., et al.: Crowd density estimation based on normalised target pixels. Comput. Appl. Softw. **33**(4), 212–214 (2016)
5. Marana, A.N., Velastin, S.A., Costa, L.F., et al.: Automatic estimation of crowd density using texture. Saf. Sci. **28**(3), 165–175 (1998)
6. Ma, W., Huang, L., Liu, C.: Crowd density analysis using co-occurrence texture features. In: 2010 5th International Conference on Computer Sciences and Convergence Information Technology (ICCIT), pp. 170–175. IEEE, Seoul, Korea (South) (2010)
7. Li, Y., Wang, G., Lin, X.: A crowd density estimation algorithm combining local and global features. J. Tsinghua Univ. **53**(4), 542–638 (2013)
8. Wang, B., Bao, H., Yang, S., et al.: Crowd density estimation based on texture feature extraction. J. Multimed. **8**(4), 331–337 (2013)
9. Xie, L., Wang, P.: Method for estimation of crowd density using neural network with PSO optimization based on gray level co-occurrence matrix. Int. J. Mach. Learn. Comput. **3**(6), 520–523 (2013)
10. Zhang, W.: Crowd density estimation based on grey co-occurrence matrix and fractal. Electron. Test **5**, 36–39 (2012)
11. Hu, L.I., Zhang, E., Duan, J.: Crowd counting method based on PCA and multivariate statistical regression. Comput. Eng. Appl. **50**(11), 206–209 (2014)
12. Foroughi, H., Ray, N., Zhang, H.: Robust people counting using sparse representation and random projection. Pattern Recogn. **48**(10), 3038–3052 (2015)
13. Candes, E.J., Tao, T.: Near optimal signal recovery from random projections and universal encoding strategies. IEEE Trans. Inf. Theor. **52**(12), 5406–5425 (2007)
14. Polus, A., Schofer, J.L., Ushpiz, A., et al.: Pedestrian flow and level of service. J. Transp. Eng. **109**(1), 46–56 (1983)
15. Liu, Z.: An analytical overview of methods for multi-category support vector machines. Comput. Eng. Appl. **40**(7), 10–15 (2004)

A Novel Three-Dimensional Asymmetric Reconstruction Method of Plasma

Junbing Wang[1(✉)], Songhua He[1], and Hui Jia[2]

[1] College of Computer Science and Electronic Engineering, Hunan University, Changsha, China
junb_wang@163.com
[2] College of Science, National University of Defense Technology, Changsha, China

Abstract. In Inertia Confinement Fusion (ICF), the symmetry and uniformity of plasma compression are of great importance for plasma diagnostics, which has great significance for in-depth analysis of the physical state in the process of implosion and the high gain ignition parameter design. Most traditional three-dimensional reconstruction methods are based on the symmetric structure, however, potential instability will make plasma to become asymmetry. This paper proposes a novel three-dimensional plasma reconstruction method based on asymmetric layered 3D distribution model. Firstly, with the analysis of the forward imaging process of plasma, we put forward a asymmetric layered model and the calculation model of emission coefficient. Then a GA-LS combined algorithm also is adopted for the reconstruction via several pictures of plasma. Numerical simulation result shows high accuracy and robustness of this method.

Keywords: 3D reconstruction · Asymmetric plasma model · Genetic algorithm
Imaging process simulation

1 Introduction

Inertial Confined Fusion (ICF) is an effective way to achieve the controlled thermonuclear fusion, it can uniformly irradiate the target via a strong drive source and use the inertia of capsule to realize the ignition [1]. As we all know, there are lots of complicated interactions between pellet and laser, analysis the physical conditions of plasma can provide a lot of important information for ignition, such as electron temperature, ion density. The picture obtained from traditional x-ray imaging equipment is the result of the line integral along the space, which can't reflect the symmetry and uniformity in three-dimensional space. The 3D reconstructions of plasma's radiation parameters utilize some x-ray pictures of plasma to get the 3D distribution of important parameters, which is a good way to diagnose the symmetry and uniformity of plasma. The research group of R.C. Mancini in LLNL did a lot of pioneering works for the diagnosis of plasma in ICF [2, 3], they proposes a layered slicing symmetric model and combined with PGA(pareto genetic algorithm) optimization algorithm for multi-objectives optimization, successfully reconstruct the gradient distribution of the temperature and density [4–6]. After that, some researcher in china also do some relevant works in recent years [7, 8]. At the base

© Springer Nature Singapore Pte Ltd. 2018
Y. Wang et al. (Eds.): IGTA 2017, CCIS 757, pp. 96–103, 2018.
https://doi.org/10.1007/978-981-10-7389-2_10

of layered symmetric model, Mr. Dong use the multi-objective genetic algorithm to deduce the spatial profile of temperature and density for plasma and prove that the model is suitable for realistic experiment [9]. As we can see, due to the limited numbers of the projection pictures, traditional 3D reconstruction of plasma is almost based on the symmetry structure. However, in the realistic process in ICF, the Rayleigh-Taylor instability will make the plasma become asymmetry, it is necessary to study the asymmetry model and the asymmetry reconstruction method.

In order to consider the situation of asymmetric plasma, this paper proposed a novel 3D reconstruction method. Firstly, we utilize the spherical harmonic functions to form an asymmetric layered 3D structure. After that, we also analyze the asymmetric emission calculation model to get the projection of plasma. Lastly, the GA-LS combinatorial optimization algorithm is adopted for the reconstruction.

2 Asymmetric Layered 3D Distribution Model

X-ray pictures are always considered as the projection of the emission intensity of plasma in different angles. Before the reconstruction, we should think about the three-dimensional distribution of the emission and the calculation model, to get the 2D projections.

The initial design of target is layered, and different layers have different physical condition in the process of fusion. In order to obtain the asymmetric distribution, as Fig. 1 shows, an asymmetric model is proposed which consists of symmetric spherical model and spherical harmonic function. Spherical harmonic function is a special basis function, and any asymmetric function on a sphere can be expanded to a linear combination of the spherical harmonic functions. If we change the spherical harmonic coefficients to be random, the spherical function will change to be asymmetry. So, the asymmetric layered three-dimensional distribution model can be expressed as a-mathematical formula:

$$E(r, \theta, \varphi) = G\left(\frac{r}{R(\theta, \varphi)}, \theta, \varphi\right) \tag{1}$$

$$R(\theta, \varphi) = \sum_{l=0}^{N} \sum_{m=-l}^{l} a_{lm} \gamma_l^m(\theta, \varphi) \tag{2}$$

Where $G(r, \vartheta, \varphi)$ is the symmetric spherical model based on spherical coordinates, $R(\vartheta, \varphi)$ is the disturbance function formed by linear combination of the spherical harmonic functions, a_{lm} is the disturbance coefficients and N is the degree of spherical harmonic function.

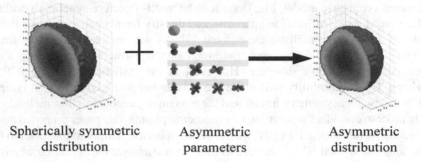

Spherically symmetric   Asymmetric   Asymmetric
distribution   parameters   distribution

Fig. 1. Asymmetric 3D model of emission

3   Asymmetric Emission Calculation Model

After obtaining the 3D distribution of emission coefficient, it is needed to think about radiation transport process, in this paper, we assume that the plasma is optically thin, ignoring the influence of the scattering and absorption.

Figure 2 shows a slice of the plasma, these rings represent different areas in the plasma. For example, as Fig. 2(a) shows, the projection of outer three emission intensity can be expressed as:

$$I(1) = e(1)L_{11} \tag{3}$$

$$I(2) = e(1)L_{12} + e(2)L_{22} + e(1)L_{21} \tag{4}$$

$$I(3) = e(1)L_{12} + e(2)L_{23} + e(3)L_{33} + e(2)L_{32} + e(1)L_{21} \tag{5}$$

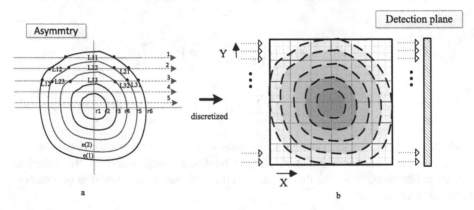

Fig. 2. Asymmetric emission calculation model

Here I is the intensity of projection, e is the layered emission coefficient and L is the length of radiation.

Then, in Fig. 2(b), the slice of the plasma is assigned to each mesh point with the discrete way, and Fig. 3 shows the projections that get from different angles. Therefore, the reconstruction problem can be considered as a progress that calculating the 3D distribution of emission coefficients in the case of that the projection of emission co-efficients are already known.

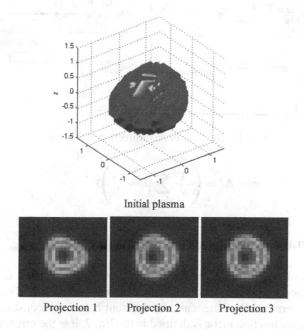

Initial plasma

Projection 1   Projection 2   Projection 3

Fig. 3. The projections of different angles

4 GA-LS Reconstruction Method

For the asymmetric reconstruction method, we adopt Genetic Algorithm (GA) and Least-Squares (LS) combinatorial optimization algorithm. GA is a kind of widely used intelligent algorithm, with good global search capability and strong expandability. Compared with the traditional numerical methods, GA has strong adaptability and doesn't depend on specific problem. However, the local search ability of GA is not very well. Thus after obtaining the result of GA, using LS optimization algorithm to enhance the local search ability making the result become more accurately. The flow of reconstruction algorithm is shown in Fig. 4.

In the reconstruction algorithm, $[e(1), e(2), \ldots, e(10), a(1), a(2), \ldots, a(15)]$ represent the reconstructed parameters, here e are emission coefficients for each spherical layer, in our paper, the numbers of the layers of the emission coefficients is 10, a are disturbance coefficients. For instances, the degree of spherical harmonic function is 3, but we ignored the 0 degree harmonic coefficient, so the numbers of disturbance coefficients is $3 + 5 + 7 = 15$. The objective function of GA and LS optimization algorithm are the same, which can be defined as Eq. 6, it is aimed to minimize the difference between reconstructed projection and initial projection.

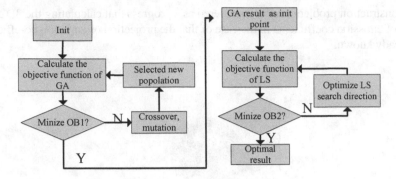

Fig. 4. The flow of reconstruction algorithm

$$\min(\Delta I) = \left(\frac{1}{N_c} \sum_{i=1}^{N_c} |I_i^o - I_i| \right) \tag{6}$$

5   Result Analysis of the Numerical Simulation

In order to examine the model and algorithm, we did a numerical simulation in MATLAB. The accuracy and robustness of the reconstruction method can be measured by three different errors, all of them are the different between reconstructed result and initial result. Reconstruction error is defined in the Eq. 7, it is the error of very volume in 3D mesh model, similarly, emission coefficient error is defined in the Eq. 8 and disturbance coefficient error is the Eq. 9.

$$\Delta I = \left(\frac{1}{N_c} \sum_{i=1}^{N_c} \frac{|E_i^o - E_i|}{E_i} \right) \tag{7}$$

$$\Delta E = \left(\frac{1}{10} \sum_{i=1}^{10} \frac{|e_i^o - e_i|}{e_i} \right) \tag{8}$$

$$\Delta K = \left(\frac{1}{15} \sum_{i=1}^{15} \frac{|a_i^o - a_i|}{a_i} \right) \tag{9}$$

Figure 5 is the comparison of the 3D reconstruction result and the initial data, it can be clearly see from the picture that the reconstruction result is almost consist with the original data, which means that the high accuracy of method that we adopted. What is more, the result also demonstrate that the layered 3D distribution model which we proposed can successfully achieve the asymmetric structure of plasma.

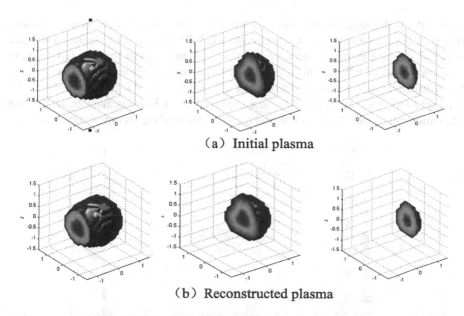

(a) Initial plasma

(b) Reconstructed plasma

Fig. 5. 3D reconstruction result of emission coefficient

Figure 6 is the result of the reconstruction error with different noise, as we can see from Fig. 6, all of the errors are very low in low noise environment, with the increase of noise, three errors also appear gradual growth tendency. Emission coefficient error is very low and no more than 2%, it means that the reconstructed emission coefficient is very good. In the same time, disturbance coefficient error also no more than 6% and reconstruction error is under 9%. The reason why the reconstruction error is higher than others is that it is a combined result of two others. When the noise is below 1%, all of these error are under 2%, it represents that our model and reconstructed algorithm has strong noise immunity and high accuracy.

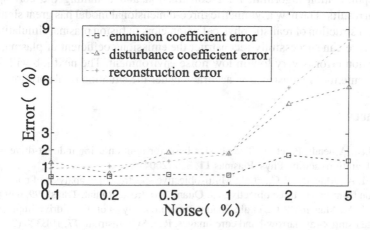

Fig. 6. Reconstruction error as a function of noise

In order to demonstrate the improvement of the reconstruction method, we make a comparison of the reconstruction error between GA-LS optimization algorithm and GA. As Fig. 7 shows, the reconstruction error of GA is much higher than the GA-LS optimization algorithm, when the noise is below 1%, the reconstruction error of GA is around 4%, in comparison, the reconstruction error of GA-LS method is less than 2%, what is more, when the noise is 2% and 5%, the accuracy of GA-LS also is much better than the GA, which reflect the improvement and the innovation of the reconstruction method.

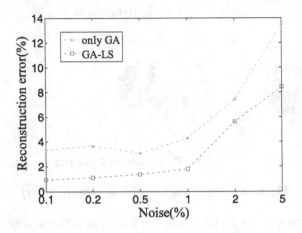

Fig. 7. Comparison of different reconstruction methods

6   Conclusion

This paper proposes a novel 3D plasma reconstruction method based on asymmetric layered 3D distribution model, and builds an asymmetric emission calculation method via the analysis of x-ray radiation transportation. Besides, the study also adopts the GA and LS optimization algorithm for reconstruction and obtaining the corresponding simulation results. The new asymmetric three-dimensional model has great significance for the reconstruction of realistic physical parameters in fusion plasma, simulation result shows that we can successfully reconstruct the emission coefficient of plasma, and the reconstruction error is very low in low noise environment. The next job will focus on the improvement of reconstruction accuracy under the situation of absorption.

References

1. Lindl, J.D., Amendt, P., et al.: The physics basis for ignition using indirect-drive targets on national ignition facility. Phys. Plasmas **11**, 339 (2004)
2. Welser, L.A., Mancini, R.C., et al.: Multi-objective spectroscopic analysis of core gradients: extension from two to three objectives. J. Quant. Spectrosc. Radiat. Transf. **99**, 649 (2006)
3. Welser, L.A., Mancini, R.C., et al.: Spatial structure analysis of direct drive implosion cores at omega using x-ray narrow-band core images. Rec. SCI. Instrum. **77**, 10E320 (2006)

4. Nagayama, T., Mancini, R.C., et al.: Four-object analysis including an optically thick line to extract electron temperature and density profiles in ICF implosion cores. J. Phys: Conf. Ser. **112**, 022014 (2008)
5. Nagayama, T.: Polychromatic Tomography of High Density Plasmas, Doctor of Philosophy in Physics, University of Nevada, Reno (2011)
6. Nagayama, T., Mancini, R.C., et al.: Investigation of a polychromatic tomography method for the extraction of the three-dimensional spatial structure of implosion core plasmas. Phys. Plasmas **19**, 082705 (2012)
7. Kai, H., Wenyong, M., et al.: Effects of capsule parameters on diagnosis of convergent geometry rayleigh-taylor instability. Acta Optica. Sinca. **37**(2), 0214002 (2017)
8. Jianjun, D., Yongkun, D., et al.: Calculation of spatial temperature of implosion core zone. J. High. Pow. Las. Part. Beam. **25**(3), 646–650 (2013)
9. Jianjun, D., Bo, D., et al.: Deduction of temperature and density spatial profile for implosion core by multi-objective optimization. Acta Phys. Sin. **63**(12), 125209 (2014)

Pose Measurement of Drogue via Monocular Vision for Autonomous Aerial Refueling

Yun Ye[1(✉)], Yingjie Yin[1], Wenqi Wu[1], Xingang Wang[1], Zhaohui Zhang[2], and Chaochao Qian[2]

[1] Institute of Automation, Chinese Academy of Sciences, Beijing 100190, China
{yeyun2014,yingjie.yin,wenqi.wu,xingang.wang}@ia.ac.cn
[2] Beijing Information Science & Technology University, Beijing 100192, China
{Zhaohui.Zhang,Chaochao.Qian}@mail.bistu.edu.cn

Abstract. In the probe-and-drogue refueling system, pilots need to operate carefully to dock probe with drogue, autonomous aerial refueling technology can assistant pilots to accomplish this operation. In this paper, we proposed a novel framework to measure pose of drogue via monocular vision, pose information of drogue can further lead control system accomplish aerial refueling automatically. This framework is consisted of three parts: detecting landmarks of drogue, locating contour of drogue in image, figuring out pose of drogue. Experiment results indicate that this pose measurement system is both accurate and efficient.

Keywords: Autonomous aerial refueling · Monocular vision
Landmark detection · Local feature · Pose measurement

1 Introduction

Aerial refueling is the most effective approach to enhance duration of flight for aircraft. Nowadays, mature aerial refueling system including boom-and-receptacle refueling system and probe-and-drogue refueling system [1]. In the probe-and-drogue refueling system, flying tanker will release drogue, pilots need to dock probe with drogue, autonomous aerial refueling technology will greatly reduce difficulty for pilots to accomplish this operation, a typical probe-and-drogue refueling system is shown in Fig. 1.

Martinez [8] and Yin [9] proposed autonomous aerial refueling framework exactly based on monocular vision, they set up a simplified pose measurement model, which supposes the optic axis of camera is perpendicular to drogue. In this paper, we come up with an accurate framework to figure out pose of drogue, this framework consists of three parts, including detection landmarks of drogue, locating circular contour of drogue in image, figuring out pose of drogue. Experiment results indicate that, our algorithm could obtain higher accuracy in various pose.

Y. Wang et al. (Eds.): IGTA 2017, CCIS 757, pp. 104–112, 2018.
https://doi.org/10.1007/978-981-10-7389-2_11

Fig. 1. Probe-and-drogue refueling system

2   Related Work

Landmark Detection. Landmark detection is now widely used in face recognition, face pose estimate and human pose estimate. For the past few decades, active shape model [10] and active appearance model [11] are widely used in industrial. At present, CNN based method [12] can usually boost landmarks detection accuracy, but requires more computing resource. To get a better balance between accuracy and efficiency, we proposed to combine local feature with global constraint of landmarks by random forest.

Pose Measurement. Pose measurement is an important link in automatic assembly system. In some occasion with particular targets, we can design suitable algorithm based on monocular vision to measure pose of target. At present, several algorithms based on monocular vision have been proposed to figure out pose of targets that have circular contour [8, 9, 13]. Accurate pose measurement algorithm can be used, once we can locate circular contour of drogue. Monocular vision based algorithms have lower computation complexity, and can be applied in real-time.

3   Pose Measurement Framework

3.1   Landmark Detection Based on Random Forest

Random forest has been used to detect landmarks, this algorithm needs to train a random forest for each landmark.

The conventional random forest regression only considers local feature of each landmark, which loses the global constraint of all landmarks, such as the shape information. For solving this problem, Ren [14] proposed to use random forest as an encoder to encode local feature of each landmark, then combined local features of all landmarks to train a regression weights to get final result. In this paper, we proposed to use random forest to calculate initial regression result for each landmark, and also made it as feature encoder to encode local feature of each landmark, then combined local feature as global feature for drogue. We used this global feature and the initial regression result to get final result. The process of training random forests for each landmark is just the same to conventional algorithm based on random forest. With trained random forests, we first calculate pre-designed feature for each landmark, input these features to corresponding random forest, for a tree in this forest, the sample will finally reach a leaf-node. We use results of all trees in this forest to get encode feature vector of this landmark. Specifically, we mark the position of reached leaf-node as 1, and mark the position of un-reached leaf-node as 0, combining all marks to form the feature vector, this process can be demonstrated as Fig. 2.

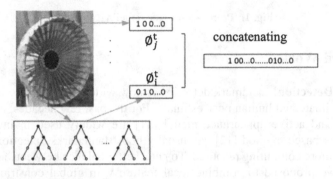

Fig. 2. Local feature encoding operation

For each landmark, we use its corresponding random forest to encode local feature: $\emptyset_i, i = 1, 2, 3, \ldots, l$, l is number of total landmarks in target, $\emptyset_i$ is a feature vector with length of n, and we can also get initial regression result $\Delta\tilde{D}_i, i = 1, 2, 3, \ldots, l$ for each landmark, we use the following loss function to fit a global regression weight W:

$$\min_{W^t} \sum_{i=1}^{N} \left\| \Delta D_i^t - \Delta\tilde{D}_i^t - W^t\Phi^t\left(I_i, D_i^{t-1}\right) \right\|_2^2 + \lambda\|W^t\|^2 \tag{1}$$

To get higher locating accuracy, we apply this process t times iteratively. In formula (1), W^t is global regression weight in the t step, ΔD_i^t is the regression target of ith landmark in t step, which is calculated by minus the normed ground-truth coordinate of this landmark with initial position in this step t. $\Delta\tilde{D}_i^t$ is the regression result of random forest corresponding to ith landmark in step t. Φ^t is the combined global feature of this target in step t.

In the process of reference, for the regression step of t, $\Delta\tilde{D}_i^t$ and Φ^t can be obtained by random forest, predict coordinate of this step can be figured out by formula 2:

$$D_i^t = W^t\Phi^t\left(I_i, D_i^{t-1}\right) + D_i^{t-1} + \Delta\tilde{D}_i^t \tag{2}$$

Predicted coordinates of step $t-1$ are used as initial positions for the regression step of t.

3.2 Pose Measurement

Chen [13] proposed a pose measurement algorithm based on monocular vision, presuppose of this algorithm is that contour of target is circular. Once the diameter of drogue is known, and contour of drogue can be located on image, we can also apply this algorithm to figure out pose of drogue under the coordinate system of camera. To improve the robustness of our pose measurement framework on various illumination, we first applied histogram equalization algorithm. Next, we use the landmark detection algorithm described above to locate landmarks in this image. Then, we use RANSAC algorithm to select suitable detected landmarks to fit contour. Finally, we use monocular vision-based pose measurement algorithm [13] to figure out exact post of drogue.

4 Experimental Results

4.1 Datasets

There is no public dataset of drogue so far. To validate the practicability of our framework, we built a dataset with 455 images of drogue via a two-robots system on the ground, this simulation system is shown as Fig. 3.

Fig. 3. Data acquisition system. It is consisted of two robots, one plays the role of flying tanker, we installed a drogue on its flange, the other one plays the role of receiver aircraft, we installed a camera on its flange. Pose information of drogue can be read from controller, we use this as ground-truth to validate our pose measurement framework.

4.2 Landmark Detection

We also choose pixel-difference feature to build each random forest, each forest has 12 trees, each tree has a deepest depth of 5, and the t is set as 6. We use detected landmarks to fit circular or elliptical contour of drogue, and use artificial annotation coordinates to fit circular or elliptical contour of drogue as ground-truth. For each fitted ellipse, marking the center point as (x, y), length of major axis as a, length of minor axis as b, axial angle of major axis as θ.

We compared our results on validation images with conventional random forest based method, results are shown as Fig. 4.

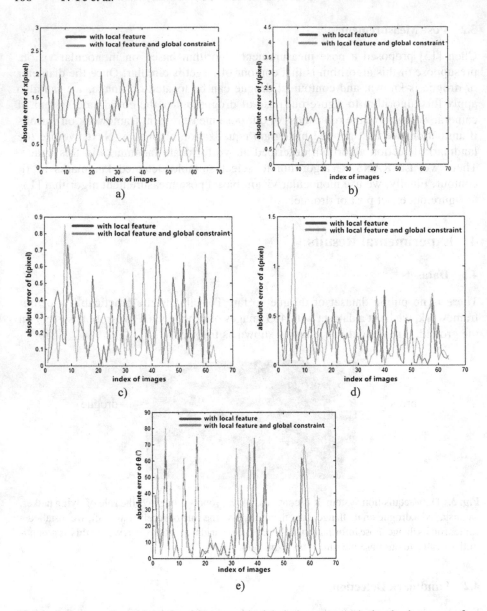

Fig. 4. Influence of combining local feature with global constraint, (a) is the absolute error of x, (b) is the absolute error of y, (c) is the absolute error of b, (d) is the absolute error of a, (e) is the absolute error of θ. It can be seen that results with combining local feature and global constraint gets lower detection error with most samples.

We also quantify the effect of image pre-processing and RANSAC algorithm, results are shown as Fig. 5 and Table 1.

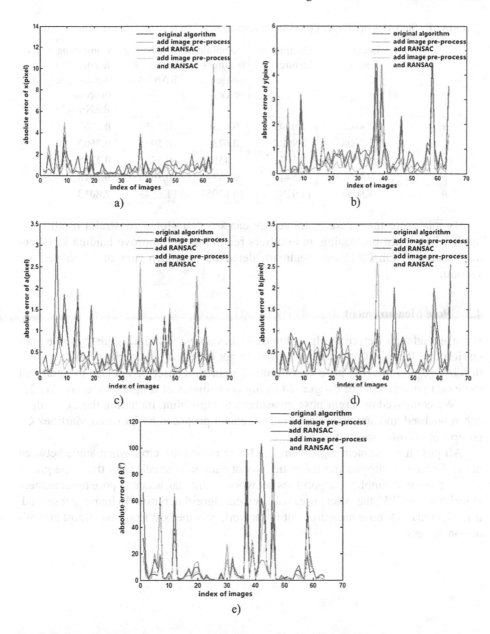

Fig. 5. Influence of image pre-process and outliers removing. (a) is the absolute error of x, (b) is the absolute error of y, (c) is the absolute error of b, (d) is the absolute error of a, (e) is the absolute error of θ. It is obvious that image pre-processing and outliers removing can improve landmarks detection accuracy. Getting both methods involved obtains highest detection accuracy.

Table 1. Statistics of different processing approaches. Value in each blank is mean error.

	Local feature	Combining feature	Combining feature + image pre-process	Combining feature + RANSAC	Combining feature +image pre-process + RANSAC
x	1.4861	1.0299	0.8639	0.7055	**0.3957**
y	1.3908	0.9007	0.6731	0.5936	**0.3503**
a	0.6568	0.5672	0.4352	0.3939	**0.2338**
b	0.7591	0.5441	0.3577	0.3924	**0.2010**
θ	24.8054	11.9183	10.1395	11.6543	**7.8013**

By analyzing these results above, we can see that global constraint of all landmarks, image pre-processing and outliers removing can improve landmarks detection accuracy. On CPU, our landmark detection approach runs at 58 frames per second.

4.3 Pose Measurement

We use landmark detection algorithm describes above with image histogram equalization and RANSAC outliers removing to get detected landmarks of each validation image, and then use pose measurement algorithm described in [13] to figure out the exact posture data of drogue. Marking coordinates of drogue center as (Xc, Yc, Zc), We compared different pose measurement algorithm, including the exact algorithm we used and simplified pose measurement proposed by Yin. and Martinez C., comparing results are shown in Fig. 6.

All pose measurement algorithms get lower measuring error when angle between normal vector of drogue and the optic axis of camera is smaller. As the angle grows larger, those two simplified algorithms get worse result than accurate pose measurement algorithm. On CPU, the exact pose measurement algorithm runs at 46 frames per second. It is clear that our pose measurement framework gets the best result on almost all validation images.

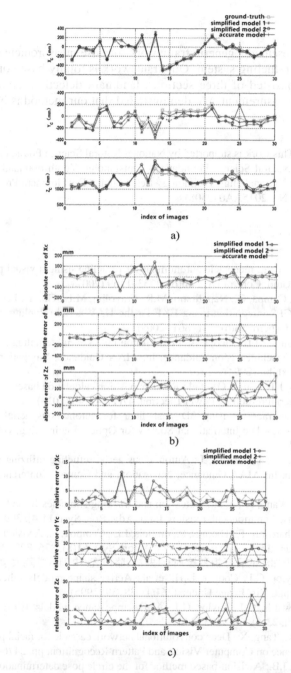

Fig. 6. (a) is coordinate values of drogue center under camera coordinate system, (b) is absolute pose measurement error of three different methods, (c) is relative pose measurement error of three different methods. Simplified model 1 represent pose measurement method proposed by Yin [9], simplified model 2 represents pose measurement method proposed by C. Martinez [8].

5 Conclusion

In this paper, we presented a generic framework for pose measurement of drogue in autonomous aerial refueling system. Our framework is totally based on monocular vision, and it is consisted of three sections: landmark detection, circular contour locating and pose measurement. We demonstrated that our method is both accurate and real time.

Acknowledgment. This work is supported by National Natural Science Foundation (Grant No. 61573349), National Natural Science Foundation—Outstanding Youth Foundation (Grant No. 5140051852) and The National High Technology Research and Development Program of China (863 Program) (Grant No. 2015AA042308).

References

1. Doebbler, J.: Boom and receptacle autonomous air refueling using a visual pressure snake optical sensor. J. Guid. Control Dyn. **30**(6), 1753–1769 (2007)
2. Mammarella, M., Campa, G., Napolitano, M.R., Fravolini, M.L., Gu, Y., Perhinschi, M.G.: Machine Vision/GPS integration using EKF for the UAV aerial refueling problem. IEEE Trans. Syst. Man Cybern. **38**(6), 791–801 (2008)
3. Campa, G., Fravolini, M.L., Ficola, A., et al.: Autonomous aerial refueling for UAVs using a combined GPS-machine vision guidance. In: AIAA Guidance, Navigation, and Control Conference and Exhibit (2004)
4. Song, C.H., Zhao, J.T., Liu, H.C., et al.: Relative position calculation based on near-infrared for autonomous aerial refueling. Power Electron. **47**(1), 41–43 (2013)
5. Chen, C.: Drogue tracking using 3D flash lidar for autonomous aerial refueling. In: Proceedings of SPIE - The International Society for Optical Engineering, vol. 8037(1), pp. 2362–2375 (2011)
6. Kimmett, J., Valasek, J., Junkins, J.: Autonomous aerial refueling utilizing a vision based navigation system. In: AIAA Guidance, Navigation, and Control Conference and Exhibit. (2013)
7. Yin, Y., Xu, D., Wang, X., et al.: Detection and tracking strategies for autonomous aerial refueling tasks based on monocular vision. Int. J. Adv. Rob. Syst. **11**(4), 399–412 (2014)
8. Martinez, C., Richardson, T., Thomas, P., du Bois, J.L., Campoy, P.: A vision-based strategy for autonomous aerial refueling tasks. Robot. Auton. Syst. **61**(8), 876–895 (2013)
9. 尹英杰. 自主空中加油的目标视觉检测与跟踪策略研究. 中国科学院大学 (2016)
10. Cootes, T.F., Taylor, C.J., Cooper, D.H., et al.: Active shape models—their training and application. Comput. Vis. Image Underst. **61**(1), 38–59 (1995)
11. Cootes, T.F., Edwards, G.J., Taylor, C.J.: Active appearance models. IEEE Trans. Pattern Anal. Mach. Intell. **23**(6), 681–685 (2001)
12. Sun, Y., Wang, X., Tang, X.: Deep convolutional network cascade for facial point detection. In: IEEE Conference on Computer Vision and Pattern Recognition, pp. 3476–3483 (2013)
13. Chen, Z., Huang, J.B.: A vision-based method for the circle pose determination with a direct geometric interpretation. IEEE Trans. Robot. Autom. **15**(6), 1135–1140 (2000)
14. Ren, S., Cao, X., Wei, Y., et al.: Face Alignment at 3000 FPS via regressing local binary features. In: IEEE Conference on Computer Vision and Pattern Recognition, pp. 1685–1692 (2014)

Recognition of Group Activities Based on M-DTCWT and Elliptic Mahalanobis Metrics

Gensheng Hu[1,2(✉)], Min Li[1], Dong Liang[1], and Wenxia Bao[1,2]

[1] School of Electronics and Information Engineering, Anhui University, Hefei 230601, China
hugs2906@sina.com, 2451108054@qq.com, dliang@ahu.edu.cn
[2] Anhui Key Laboratory of Polarization Imaging Detection Technology, Hefei 230031, China
bwxia@ahu.edu.cn

Abstract. A group activities recognition algorithm is proposed by combining M-DTCWT (multi directional dual tree complex wavelet transform) with elliptic Mahalanobis metric. M-DTCWT is composed of directional filter bank in cascade with dual tree complex wavelet transform. By using the M-DTCWT to decompose the human images in videos for multi-scale and multi-direction, the high and low frequency coefficients can be obtained. The texture features of the high and low frequency coefficients are extracted by using improved local binary pattern and gray level co-occurrence matrix and classified by using elliptic Mahalanobis metric. According to the results of classification, group activities are recognized. Experimental results on Group activity video set and self built video set show that the proposed algorithm has higher recognition accuracy than the existing algorithms and Euclidean metric algorithm.

Keywords: Video surveillance · Group activities recognition · M-DTCWT
Elliptic Mahalanobis metric

1 Introduction

Group activity refers to the relative motion of two or more individuals that interact with and depend on each other. Group activity widely exists in a variety of large-scale commercial exhibitions, sports competitions, traffic junctions, stations and activity centers. On the one hand, the group activity promotes the economic development and cultural exchange. On the other hand, the group fighting and illegal gathering also make social security be under threat. If the group illegal activity can be real-time monitored and automatically recognized, we can prevent danger and reduce the losses. Therefore, recognition of group activities in videos has become a project with research value in the field of video surveillance, and has a prospective application.

At present, scholars have made great progress in the recognition of group activity. Zhang et al. [1] introduced a causal relationship to reflect the interaction between groups, and achieved the recognition of group activity through a linear support vector machine model learning. Yin et al. [2] proposed a social network structure based on feature set to represent the group activity and a probabilistic framework to learn and recognize the group activity. Andrade et al. [3] extracted the optical flow features, and constructed a hidden

© Springer Nature Singapore Pte Ltd. 2018
Y. Wang et al. (Eds.): IGTA 2017, CCIS 757, pp. 113–122, 2018.
https://doi.org/10.1007/978-981-10-7389-2_12

Markov model to implement the abnormal group activity detection. Ryoo et al. [4] proposed a hierarchical interaction probability algorithm to identify the specific activity, but the activity recognition method is only limited to one or two people. Choi et al. [5] used crowd context and random forest model to identify group activity. Antic et al. [6] achieved the recognition of different groups activity through automatic learning between the potential components of different people. Nabi et al. [7] proposed a semantic based spatio-temporal descriptor, which can cope with the interaction between different scales and multiple activities in the video. Owning to difficulties for feature extraction and activity description caused by the scene diversity, the difference of population density, and groups of mutual occlusion, the group activity recognition algorithm for videos has disadvantages of high computational complexity and low recognition accuracy.

In this paper, we propose a group activity recognition algorithm for videos based on multiple direction dual tree complex wavelet transform (M-DTCWT) and elliptic Mahalanobis metric. Compared with the wavelet transform and dual tree complex wavelet transform (DTCWT), M-DTCWT can more effectively represent the geometrical features such as edges and textures in the image. Elliptic Mahalanobis metric is more suitable for modeling and measuring data with complex geometric structures. The human body image in the video is decomposed by M-DTCWT. The high frequency and low frequency coefficients features are extracted, which are used to implement the group activity recognition for video by employing the elliptic Mahalanobis metric.

2   M-DTCWT

Discrete wavelet transform (DWT) is shifting variant, that is to say, small input signal translation will cause drastic change of the transform coefficient. DWT can only capture the signal at the horizontal, vertical and diagonal directions in detail [8]. DTCWT consists of two parallel wavelet trees. After transformation, we can get the real and imaginary part coefficients of the signal. Two wavelet trees of each layer provide the necessary signal delay and double the sampling interval to eliminate the aliasing effect and achieve translation invariance [9]. For each level of DTCWT, signal is decomposed into 2 low frequency sub-bands and 6 directional high frequency sub-bands [10].

In order to further increase the directional selection of the DTCWT, an improved M-DTCWT filter banks are constructed by adding an hourglass filter banks to the DTCWT filter banks. The schematic diagram of decomposition and reconstruction of M-DTCWT is shown in Fig. 1.

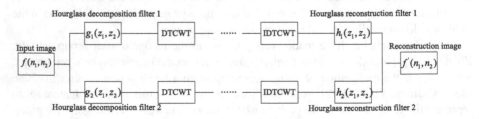

Fig. 1. Schematic diagram of decomposition and reconstruction of input image by M-DTCWT

M-DTCWT decomposition of two-dimensional image $f(n_1, n_2)$ can be expressed by a series of complex scaling function and complex wavelet function:

$$f(n_1, n_2) = \sum_{k \in Z^2} c_{j,k} \Phi_{j,k}(n_1, n_2) + \sum_{i=1}^{8} \sum_{j \geq j,} \sum_{k \in Z^2} d_{j,k}^{(i)} \Psi_{j,k}^{(i)}(n_1, n_2) \tag{1}$$

where Z is a natural number set, j, k are dilation and translation indices, $c_{j,k}$ is scale coefficient, and $d_{j,k}^{(i)}$ is complex wavelet coefficients at ith direction. The schematic diagram of the frequency tiling of M-DTCWT of two levels is shown in Fig. 2:

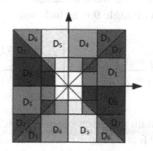

Fig. 2. Schematic diagram of frequency tiling of M-DTCWT of two levels

3 Feature Extraction

In this paper, an improved local binary pattern (ILBP) with rotation invariance and directional selectivity is used to extract the features of high frequency coefficients of the human image in video decomposed by M-DTCWT. Gray level co-occurrence matrix is used to extract the features of low frequency coefficients. High and low frequency coefficient features are concatenated to form the group activity features.

LBP can be used to describe the local texture of image [11, 12], whereas the traditional LBP is subject to the influence of the center pixel and the relative position of the pixel. On the basis of the traditional LBP operator, we get a set of binary sequence of the center pixel, and then rotate the neighborhood to get a series of initial LBP value, and eventually take the minimum value as the center pixel LBP value [13]:

$$V_{\text{LBP}^{\text{ri}}} = \min\{f_R(V_{\text{LBP}}, i) | i = 0, \cdots, 7\} \tag{2}$$

where V_{LBP} is initial LBP value and rotation function $f_R(x, i)$ represents x shifts i bit to right cyclically.

The image moments of image $G(x, y)$ is computed as:

$$m_{p,q} = \sum_{x,y} x^p y^q G(x, y) \tag{3}$$

Using the first order moment m_{10} and m_{01} and zero order moment m_{00}, we can calculate the centroid C of the center pixel neighborhood [14]:

$$C = \left(\frac{m_{10}}{m_{00}}, \frac{m_{01}}{m_{00}} \right) \tag{4}$$

According to the imaging principle of the camera, the distribution of pixels in image area is non-uniform, thus the centroid C and the geometric center O of the image $G(x, y)$ are not in the same position, then we can construct a vector $\overrightarrow{OC}$ from O to C. The angle between $\overrightarrow{OC}$ and X are defined as the main direction of the central pixel in a neighborhood. The calculation formula of angle θ is as follows:

$$\theta = \tan^{-1} \left(\frac{m_{01}}{m_{10}} \right) = \tan^{-1} \left(\frac{\sum\limits_{x,y} yG(x, y)}{\sum\limits_{x,y} xG(x, y)} \right) \tag{5}$$

So we can determine the main direction of the local texture in the neighborhood of the center pixel, and form LBP features with orientation selectivity. Then the ILBP with rotation invariance and directional selectivity is obtained. ILBP can be used to extract the high frequency coefficient features of the human images in video decomposed by M-DTCWT.

Gray level co-occurrence matrix reflects the information of the image gray level distribution [15]. In this paper, we choose four directional $(0°, 45°, 90°, 135°)$ gray level co-occurrence matrix of the low frequency coefficients of the human images in video decomposed by M-DTCWT and calculate the mean and standard deviation of three kinds of texture feature statistics: correlation, energy and homogeneity. The texture features with six rotation invariant characteristics of low frequency coefficients are obtained. The features of high frequency and low frequency coefficients are concatenated to form the group activity feature vector.

4   Elliptic Mahalanobis Metric

Assuming a multivariate vector x whose mean is μ and covariance matrix is $\sum$, its Mahalanobis metric is defined as:

$$D_M(x) = \sqrt{(x - \mu)^T \sum{}^{-1} (x - \mu)} \tag{6}$$

Given sample set $\{X_i \subset R^n, i = 1, \cdots, N\}$, the elliptic Mahalanobis metric [16] is defined as follows:

$$D_M(X_i, X_j) = \frac{k}{2i} \log \left(\frac{\rho_{ij} + \sqrt{\rho_{ij}^2 - \rho_{ii}\rho_{jj}}}{\rho_{ij} - \sqrt{\rho_{ij}^2 - \rho_{ii}\rho_{jj}}} \right) \tag{7}$$

where $\rho_{ij} = (X_i - m)^T \sigma^{-1} (X_j - m) + c$, m is sample mean vector, σ^{-1} is generalized inverse matrix of sample covariance matrix and c is a positive constant.

Since the covariance matrix is positive semidefinite, its generalized inverse is also positive semidefinite. There exists a linear transformation, so that the Mahalanobis metric and the Euclidean metric in the transformed space are the same. In addition, the elliptic Mahalanobis metric reflects the nonlinear transformation of the sample spatial structure information, which makes the corresponding recognition algorithm have better discrimination.

5   Recognition Steps

Firstly, the multi-scale and multi-direction decomposition of human body image in videos is performed by M-DTCWT, and the high and low frequency subband coefficients are obtained. Secondly, subband coefficients are divided into blocks, and the high and low frequency coefficient features of the block regions are extracted by using the ILBP and gray level co-occurrence matrix method. Thirdly, the elliptic Mahalanobis metric of the feature vectors between testing samples and training samples is calculated, and the feature similarity is evaluated by using the minimum value of the elliptic Mahalanobis metric. Finally, we obtain the feature vector of the human image in video to be recognized and calculate the elliptic Mahalanobis metric of the feature vectors between it and the testing sample to realize the group activity recognition in video. The specific steps of the algorithm are as follows:

Step 1. Human image in video is decomposed by M-DTCWT, and the high and low frequency subband coefficients are obtained. Subband coefficients are divided into blocks.

Step 2. ILBP is used to extract the features of the high frequency coefficients of each block region, and gray level co-occurrence matrix is used to extract the features of low frequency coefficient of each block region. The high and low frequency coefficients features are concatenated to form the group activity feature vector.

Step 3. The covariance matrix σ_j, $j = 1, 2, \cdots, N$ of each activity category is calculated from the group activity feature vector extracted in step2, where N is the number of activity categories.

Step 4. The elliptic Mahalanobis metric $D_{(j)}^{(i)}(\omega_1, \omega_2)$ between the training samples and the i th testing sample is calculated by using (7), where ω_1 is group activity feature vector of test sample, ω_2 is mean feature vector of group activity of all training samples and j is activity category.

Step 5. The minimum value of the above elliptic Mahalanobis metric is obtained to select the testing sample who is most similar to the training samples. Namely we get $i_0 = D_{(j)}^{(i)}(\omega_t, \omega_{i_0})$.

Step 6. For human image in video to be identified, we can get $S_j^t = D_{(j)}^{(t)}(\omega_t, \omega_{i_0})$ following the similar steps, where $t = 1, \cdots, n$ is the video frames to be identified, ω_t is the feature vector of tth frame to be identified, and ω_{i_0} is the feature vector of i_0th test sample.

Step 7. Calculating the mean and variance of each row vector in the smallest elliptic Mahalanobis metric similarity matrix by using (8). Then, the activity category with the minimal sum of the mean and variance is the category of group activity to be recognized in video.

$$\begin{cases} \sigma_j^{mean} = \dfrac{\sum_{t-1}^N \left(1 - S[j,t]\right)}{N} \\ \sigma_j^{deviation} = \sqrt{\dfrac{\sum_{t-1}^N \left(\bar{S}[j,t] - S[j,t]\right)}{N}} \\ \sigma_j = \dfrac{\left(\sigma_j^{mean} + \sigma_j^{deviation}\right)}{2} \end{cases} \tag{8}$$

6 Experimental Results and Analysis

The video set used in this paper include Group Activity video set [17] and a self built video set. Five group activities of Crossing, Waiting, Talking, Dancing and Jogging are considered in Group Activity video set and each group activity is done by 4–5 people. Three videos are selected as training and testing samples. The self built video set consists of two scenes of fighting video with a total of 6 video clips. Each clip contains 60 frame target image with 2–5 people. One video of the first scene and two videos of the second scene are selected as training and testing samples.

The recognition accuracy of different methods on Group Activity video set is shown in Table 1. As can be seen from Table 1, the recognition accuracy of the proposed algorithm for Crossing and Jogging is similar to literature [7], but higher than literature [6] and literature [8]. The recognition accuracy of the proposed algorithm for Waiting, Talking and Dancing is higher than the other methods. Compared with the above literature, the proposed algorithm has higher recognition accuracy.

Table 1. Recognition accuracy of different methods on Group Activity video set

	The proposed algorithm	Literature [6]	Literature [7]	Literature [8]
Crossing	95.8%	76.5%	95.1%	66.9%
Waiting	93.3%	78.5%	83.1%	57.4%
Talking	89.1%	84.1%	69.3%	76.8%
Dancing	94.1%	80.5%	91.3%	86.3%
Jogging	98.3%	94.1%	100%	81.1%
Average	94.1%	82.6%	87.7%	73.7%

The following is the results of the proposed algorithm compared with the algorithm of DTCWT combined with Euclidean metric. Experimental results on different video sets are shown in Figs. 3, 4, 5 and 6, where the color of red, blue, green, rose red, cyan and white represents Fighting, Dancing, Talking, Jogging, Crossing and Waiting respectively.

Fig. 3. Experimental results of DTCWT combined with Euclidean metric on Group Activity video set (Color figure online)

Fig. 4. Experimental results of the proposed algorithm on Group Activity video set (Color figure online)

Fig. 5. Experimental results of DTCWT combined with Euclidean metric on self built video set (Color figure online)

Fig. 6. Experimental results of the proposed algorithm on a self built video set (Color figure online)

Figure 7 gives a quantitative evaluation result by using the confusion matrix. Each row element of the confusion matrix represents the probability that the group activity of this type is recognized as the group activity of different types, and the diagonal element represents the probability of correct recognition. As seen in Fig. 7, on the Group Activity video set, the average recognition accuracy of the proposed algorithm is 94.172%, the average recognition accuracy of combining DTCWT with Euclidean metric algorithm is 76.688%. Table 2 shows the comparison results of the recognition accuracy of the proposed algorithm and the DTCWT combined with the Euclidean metric algorithm on the self built video set. As can be seen from Figs. 3, 4, 5, 6, 7 and Table 2, the proposed algorithm has higher recognition accuracy.

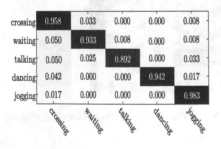 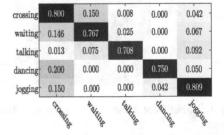

	crossing	waiting	talking	dancing	jogging
crossing	0.958	0.033	0.000	0.000	0.008
waiting	0.050	0.933	0.008	0.000	0.008
talking	0.050	0.025	0.892	0.000	0.033
dancing	0.042	0.000	0.000	0.942	0.017
jogging	0.017	0.000	0.000	0.000	0.983

	crossing	waiting	talking	dancing	jogging
crossing	0.800	0.150	0.008	0.000	0.042
waiting	0.146	0.767	0.025	0.000	0.067
talking	0.013	0.075	0.708	0.000	0.092
dancing	0.200	0.000	0.000	0.750	0.050
jogging	0.150	0.000	0.000	0.042	0.809

(a)The proposed algorithm   (b)DTCWT combined with Euclidean metric

Fig. 7. Confusion matrix of different algorithms on Group Activity video set

Table 2. Recognition accuracy of different methods on self built video set

Method	Fighting1	Fighting2	Fighting3	Average
Elliptic Mahalanobis metric	84.2%	87.4%	83.3%	84.97%
Mahalanobis metric	80.0%	83.3%	78.9%	81.1%
Euclidean metric	68.8%	70.4%	67.2%	68.8%

7 Conclusion

In order to solve the problem of low recognition accuracy of group activities recognition algorithms in video surveillance, a new group activities recognition algorithm is proposed by combining M-DTCWT with elliptic Mahalanobis metric. M-DTCWT is composed of directional filter banks and DTCWT. It further increases the directional selectivity of DTCWT and can represent the geometric characteristics such as edge and texture in two-dimensional images more effectively. The elliptic Mahalanobis metric is more suitable for modeling and measuring data with complex geometric structure. By using the M-DTCWT to decompose the human images in videos into multi-scale and multi-direction, the high and low frequency coefficients can be obtained. After extracting the features of the high and low frequency coefficients, the elliptic Mahalanobis metric is used to realize the group activity recognition in video. Experimental results show that the proposed algorithm has higher recognition accuracy than classical algorithm and DTCWT combined with Euclidean metric algorithm.

Acknowledgements. This work has been partially supported by the National Natural Science Foundation of China (61672032, 61401001), the Natural Science Foundation of Anhui Province under Grant 1408085MF121, and the Opening Foundation of polarization imaging detection technology of Anhui Key Laboratory (2016-KFKT-003).

References

1. Zhang, C., Yang, X., Lin, W., Zhu, J.: Recognizing human group behaviors with multi-group causalities. In: 2012 IEEE/WIC/ACM International Conferences on Web Intelligence and Intelligent Agent Technology (WI-IAT), Macau, pp. 44–48 (2012)
2. Yin, Y., Yang, G., Xu, J., Man, H.: Small group human activity recognition. In: 2012 19th IEEE International Conference on Image Processing, Orlando, FL, pp. 2709–2712 (2012)
3. Andrade, E.L., Blunsden, S.R.B.: Hidden Markon models for optical flow analysis in crowds. In: Proceedings of the 18th International Conference on Pattern Recognition, pp. 460–463 (2006)
4. Ryoo, M.S., Aggarwal, J.K.: Semantic representation and recognition of continued and recursive human activities. Int. J. Comput. Vision **82**, 1–24 (2009)

5. Choi, W., Shahid, K., Savarese, S.: Learning context for collective recognition. In: Proceedings of the IEEE Internation Conference on Computer Vision and Pattern Recognition (2011)
6. Antic, B., Ommer, B.: Learning Latent constituents for recognition of group activities in video. In: Fleet, D., Pajdla, T., Schiele, B., Tuytelaars, T. (eds.) ECCV 2014. LNCS, vol. 8689, pp. 33–47. Springer, Cham (2014). https://doi.org/10.1007/978-3-319-10590-1_3
7. Nabi, M., Bue, A.D., Murino, V.: Temporal poselets for collective activity detection and recognition. In: International Conference on Computer Vision Workshops (ICCVW), Sydney, NSW, pp. 500–507 (2013)
8. Kingsbury, N.: Image processing with complex wavelets. Philos. Trans. Royal Soc. Lond. Ser. A Math. Phys. Eng. Sci. 357(1760), 2543–2560 (1999)
9. Selesnick, I.W., Baraniuk, R.G., Kingsbury, N.C.: The dual-tree complex wavelet transform. Sig. Process. Mag. 22(6), 123–151 (2005)
10. Ioannidou, S., Karathanassi, V.: Investigation of the dual-tree complex and shift-invariant discrete wavelet transforms on Quickbird image fusion. IEEE Geosci. Remote Sens. Lett. 4(1), 166–170 (2007)
11. Zhang, Y.X., Zhao, Y.Q., Liu, Y., Jiang, L.Q., Chen, Z.W.: Identification of wood defects based on LBP features. In: 2016 35th Chinese Control Conference (CCC), Chengdu, China, pp. 4202–4205 (2016)
12. Song, H., Xiao, B., Hu, Q., Ren, P.: Integrating local binary patterns into normalized moment of inertia for updating tracking templates. Chin. J. Electron. 25(4), 706–710 (2016)
13. Lu, F., Huang, J.: An improved local binary pattern operator for texture classification. In: 2016 IEEE International Conference on Acoustics, Speech and Signal Processing (ICASSP), Shanghai, pp. 1308–1311 (2016)
14. Flusser, J., Suk, T., Boldyš, J., Zitová, B.: Projection operators and moment invariants to image blurring. IEEE Trans. Pattern Anal. Mach. Intell. 37(4), 786–802 (2015)
15. Imamverdiyev, Y., Teoh, A.B.J., Kim, J.: Biometric crypto-system based on discretized fingerprint texture descriptors. Expert Syst. Appl. 40(5), 1888–1901 (2013)
16. Bi, Y., Fan, B., Wu, F.: Beyond Mahalanobis metric: Cayley-Klein metric learning. In: 2015 IEEE Conference on Computer Vision and Pattern Recognition (CVPR), Boston, MA, pp. 2339–2347 (2015)
17. Choi, W., Shahid, K., Savarese, S.: What are they doing? Collective activity classification using spatio-temporal relationship among people. In: Proceedings of 9th International Workshop on Visual Surveillance (VSWS 2009) in Conjuction with ICCV (2009)

HKS-Based Feature Extraction for 3D Shape Partial Registration

Congli Yin[1,2], Mingquan Zhou[1,2(✉)], Guoguang Du[1,2], and Yachun Fan[1,2]

[1] College of Information Science and Technology, Beijing Normal University, Beijing, China
mqzhou@bnu.edu.cn
[2] Key Laboratory of Digital Protection and Virtual Reality for Cultural Heritage, Beijing, China

Abstract. Heat Kernel Signature (HKS) is an informative and multi-scale descriptor that has been widely used in shape analysis. However, current feature extraction methods based on HKS are highly affected by the time scale, which limits its performance. For the task of 3D shape partial registration, this paper proposes a feature extraction algorithm based on the overlapping diffusion time of the partial shape and the complete shape, which not only eliminates the impact of time scale but also obtains consistent and stable feature points. A registration pipeline is also put forward that guarantees the accuracy. Experiments have been conducted on various partial shapes, and the validity of the algorithm was verified. Compared with other partial registration methods based on HKS, the proposed algorithm achieved more accurate results.

Keywords: Heat kernel signature · Feature extraction · Partial registration

1 Introduction

With the rapid development of 3D model-acquisition technologies, the repositories of 3D models have grown greatly. There exist many shape analysis methods to utilize these data effectively. Among all shape analysis tasks, the topic of 3D shape partial matching has attracted much attention recently. In rigid cases, the goal of partial matching refers to partial registration, which means finding the transformation between partial shape and complete shape. A common idea for partial registration is to use methods for minimizing geometric distances, such as interactive closest points (ICP) algorithm [1]. However, these methods are strongly affected by initial positions and are time-consuming. Other methods are those using local shape descriptors [8–11], which are effective and efficient. However, these traditional descriptors are susceptible to local noise.

Shape descriptors based on diffusion geometry such as the Heat Kernel Signature (HKS) [12] and the Wave Kernel Signature (WKS) [13] have been proposed in the past few years. These descriptors are more discriminative than traditional shape descriptors and are multi-scale. However, the feature extraction algorithm based on HKS was influenced by the time scale, which is unstable at different time scales.

© Springer Nature Singapore Pte Ltd. 2018
Y. Wang et al. (Eds.): IGTA 2017, CCIS 757, pp. 123–135, 2018.
https://doi.org/10.1007/978-981-10-7389-2_13

In this paper, a novel HKS-based feature extraction algorithm is proposed to address 3D shape partial registration task. The proposed algorithm is based on the overlapping diffusion time of the partial and complete shape, which is particularly suitable to the partial matching tasks. Points on sharp regions are extracted as feature points, which are stable and consistent with the target shapes. By comparing the HKS, initial matching results are obtained. Partial registration is then achieved after refinement procedures. Experiments have been conducted on various partial shapes, which achieved accurate registration results. The proposed algorithm has achieved higher accuracy than other partial registration methods based on HKS.

The main contributions of this paper are as follows:

(1) A new HKS based feature extraction algorithm based on the overlapping diffusion time is proposed, and an optimization strategy is proposed to eliminate the influence of boundaries.
(2) A matching strategy for 3D shape partial registration is proposed, which achieves accurate results and is more effective than other methods.

2   Related Work

2.1   Methods for Minimizing Geometric Distances

Representative methods for minimizing geometric distances include the iterative closest points (ICP) algorithm [1] and its variants [2–7]. The ICP algorithm was first proposed by Besl et al. Given the source dataset, the nearest points on the target dataset were computed iteratively to update the transformation until the average geometric distance was lower than a given threshold. However, there exist some disadvantages. First, the algorithm is highly affected by initial positions, especially when the two datasets vary substantially in scale; the partial shape may be trapped in local minima. Second, it has a high time complexity. Third, the outliers in the dataset are not excluded during each iterative process, which results in large errors.

A series of algorithms were proposed that optimized the problem in different views, such as how to obtain the initial matching positions and how to remove wrong matches. The random sample consensus algorithm (RANSAC) [14] was proposed to find an optimal solution. This algorithm was first applied to the registration of 3D datasets by Chen et al. [15]; it selected a number of corresponding points randomly to compute the transformation, and then evaluated the error. These procedures were repeated many times, and the lowest transformation error was selected. Aiger and Mitra [16] proposed a 4PCS registration algorithm based on RANSAC, which was fast and robust. To improve speed and robustness further, the Super4PCS algorithm is proposed [17]. However, methods for minimizing geometric distances still cannot achieve stable and accurate results when the source dataset is relatively small compared to the target dataset.

2.2 Methods Using Local Shape Descriptors

The complexity of the problem decreases substantially by using local shape descriptors, which can also improve the matching accuracy. There exist traditional local shape descriptors and diffusion geometry based local shape descriptors. The former uses differential geometric metrics such as normals and curvatures. The latter simulates the diffusion process on the shape and characterizes the shape structure in a multi-scale way.

Spin Image [18–20] is the common local shape descriptor. A 2D image is obtained for each 3D point by counting the points in a surrounding supporting volume. Other algorithm [21] utilizes information of the normal to extract bending points and segment surface. The Shape Index [22, 23] is another local shape descriptor, which is a high order descriptor based on the principal curvatures and is well suited for describing subtle changes on the surface. Pottmann et al. [24] proposed Integral Invariant descriptors that are discriminative and have been used in surface segmentation [25]. Shapira et al. [26] proposed the Shape Diameter Function descriptor for surface segmentation and skeleton extraction. A scalar function for each point was defined, and the weighted average value was calculated as the descriptor. Signatures of Histograms of Orientations (SHOT) [27] are other descriptors based on distribution, and are suitable for partial shape registration tasks. Although all the above descriptors have certain discriminative capabilities, they are sensitive to local tessellations and local noise.

In recent years, many shape descriptors based on diffusion geometry have been proposed, such as HKS [12] and WKS [13]. Coifman et al. [28] first introduced the diffusion geometry theory into 3D shape analysis. The basic solution for the heat diffusion process is called the heat kernel. HKS is multi-scale, which means that a small time scale reflects local shape structure while a large time scale reflects global shape structure. WKS [13] simulates the energy diffusion process of a particle to obtain the description of the shapes. They are more robust and discriminative than traditional descriptors. However, the feature extraction algorithm based on HKS is affected by the time scale, which results in scattered and unstable feature points.

3 Heat Kernel Signature

In this section, we briefly recap the basic theory and properties of HKS and discuss why such a descriptor is ideal for the task.

3.1 Mathematical Background

Let M be a compact Riemannian manifold and $u(x, t)$ be the amount of heat at a point $x \in M$ at time t. The heat propagation over M is governed by the heat diffusion equation:

$$\begin{cases} \frac{\partial u(x,t)}{\partial t} = -\Delta u(x, t) \\ u(x, 0) = f(x) \end{cases} \tag{1}$$

where Δ is the Laplace-Beltrami operator and $f(x)$ is the initial temperature defined on M. If M has boundaries, u needs to satisfy the Dirichlet boundary condition $u(x, t) = 0$ for all $x \in M$ for all t. Given the initial function f, the solution to this equation at time t can be computed through the heat operator H_t:

$$u(x, t) = H_t f \qquad (2)$$

For any M, there exists a function $h_t(x, y)$ such that:

$$u(x, t) = \int_M ht(x, y) f(y) dy. \qquad (3)$$

The $ht(x, y)$ satisfying (3) is called the heat kernel, and its value can be thought as the amount of heat that is transferred from point x to point y during time t. For a compact Riemannian surface M, the heat kernel has the following eigen-decomposition:

$$ht(x, y) = \sum_{i=0}^{\infty} e^{-\lambda_i t} \Phi_i(x) \Phi_i(y), \qquad (4)$$

where $\lambda_0, \lambda_1, \cdots \lambda_i$ are eigenvalues, t is the time value and $\Phi_0, \Phi_1, \cdots, \Phi_i$ are the corresponding eigenfunctions of the Laplace-Beltrami operator, which satisfy $\Delta_M \Phi_i = \lambda_i \Phi_i$. HKS is a powerful descriptor that characterizes local and global geometry of the surface centered at each point:

$$ht(x) = \sum_{i=0}^{\infty} e^{-\lambda_i t} \Phi_i(x)^2. \qquad (5)$$

The HKS inherits many good properties from heat kernel and is quite effective in describing shapes at different scales and identifying geometric features. For a piecewise linear surface mesh, HKS can be computed from the eigenvalues and eigenvectors of the Laplace-Beltrami operator. Details are given in [12].

3.2   Properties of HKS

The HKS descriptor is adopted as a reliable descriptor for partial registration because it is multi-scale and informative.

For a small time t, the function $h_t(x, y)$ is determined by a small neighborhood of x; the neighborhood expands as t increases. The multi-scale property of the heat kernel implies that for a small t, $h_t(x, y)$ reflects only local characteristics of the shape around point x, while for large values of t, $h_t(x, y)$ captures the global structure of M from the view of point x. The explicit relationship between time and the size of the diffusion region is also discussed in [29]. It is different from local descriptors such as spin images [18–20] or global descriptors such as GPS [30]; HKS allows us to perform multi-scale comparisons between different neighboring regions of points on the same shape. Figure 1 shows an example of the HKS of the corresponding points on the complete and partial shape.

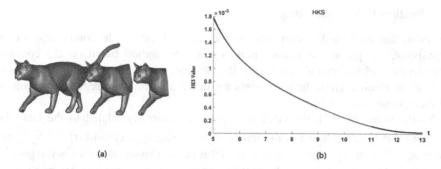

Fig. 1. Multi-scale Property. (a) Corresponding points in the complete shape and partial shapes. (b) Overlapping HKS curves of the corresponding points.

Another important property of HKS is that it is informative. Varadhan's Lemma [31] indicates that for every pair of points $x, y \in M$, the geodesic distance has the following relationship with $h_t(x, y)$: $\lim_{t \to 0} t \log h_t(x, y) = -\frac{1}{4}d^2(x, y)$. Therefore, the heat equation contains all of the information of the intrinsic geometry and hence fully characterizes the shape. The geometric information about the neighborhoods of a point x at different scales is encoded compactly in HKS $\{h_t(x, x)\}_{t > 0}$. HKS curves of three different points are shown in Fig. 2. The properties make HKS a suitable discriminative descriptor for shape registration tasks.

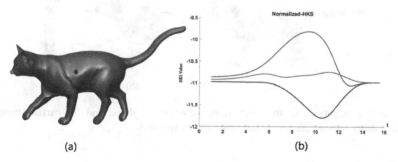

Fig. 2. Informative property. (a) Different points in a shape. (b) The corresponding HKS curves are quite different.

4   Pipeline of the Proposed Algorithm

In this section, the novel HKS-based feature point extraction algorithm is introduced firstly. Then, the registration strategy is developed depending on the features.

4.1   Feature Point Extracting

Observing that the heat diffusion between the partial shape and the complete shape are inconsistent, we propose a feature point extraction method based on the common diffusion time, which not only eliminates the influence of the time scale but also obtains more stable results. These feature points are distributed in sharp regions and contain sufficient shape information.

As illustrated in [12], the HKS of a point x is directly related to the Gaussian curvature $s(x)$ at x, as shown in the following equation: $k_t(x, x) = (4\pi t)^{-d/2} \sum_{i=0}^{\infty} a_i t^i$, where $a_0 = 1$ and $a_1 = \frac{1}{6}s(x)$. The heat diffusion is slower at points with positive curvature and faster at points with negative curvature; $k_t(x, x)$ can be interpreted as the intrinsic curvature of x under scale t. The time scale t depends on the maximum and minimum eigenvalues of the Laplace-Beltrami operator, given by:

$$t_{min} = log(\frac{4ln10}{\lambda_{max}}), \ t_{max} = log(\frac{4ln10}{\lambda_2}), \tag{6}$$

where λ_2 is the smallest non-zero eigenvalue and λ_{max} is the largest eigenvalue. Therefore, the variation of the HKS value between t_{min} and t_{max} describes the characteristics of the point. Let v_p be the variation of HKS values of p, Fig. 3 shows that v_p in sharp regions are larger than that in smooth regions during the diffusion time. That is, HKS changes greatly of the points that are more obvious.

(a)   (b)

Fig. 3. (a) The variations of the HKS value of complete shape and (b) partial shape. The changes in sharp regions are larger than the smooth region.

However, v_p for all points are not so distinct, since the partial shape and the complete shape have different diffusion times. Considering that the overlapping heat diffusion time is used in the matching task because the HKS values in the range are almost the same, the points whose HKS values change greatly during the overlapping diffusion time are extracted as the feature points, which are shown in Fig. 4. It can be observed that v_p in sharp regions are clearly much larger than in the smooth region, and the variations are consistent between the complete shape and the partial shape, except for the boundaries.

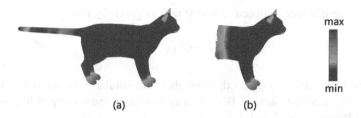

(a)   (b)

Fig. 4. (a) The variations of the HKS value of complete shape and (b) partial shape. The changes in sharp regions are consistent and apparent.

The specific process of the proposed feature extraction algorithm is the following. Let M and N be the complete and partial shapes, respectively. First, the heat diffusion time is computed by formula (6). Second, let the common diffusion time be $[t_x, t_y]$ and the HKS value of $[t_x, t_y]$ be $[k_{t_x}, k_{t_y}]$. Third, sort $d_k = |k_{t_x} - k_{t_y}|$, where $k = 1, 2, \ldots n$, and select the top K points as the feature points. The points lying in the boundary regions are also extracted as feature points since the boundary of the partial shape is sharp. A feature point optimization strategy is presented to eliminate the influence of boundaries, which finds the feature points that lie in the two-ring neighbor of the boundary and removes them.

For the calculating of HKS, the top 300 eigenvalues and eigenvectors of the Laplace-Beltrami operator are selected. The parameter K is determined by the total number of shapes, usually 15% of the complete shape and 10% of the partial shape. It can be observed in Fig. 5 that the feature points on the complete shape and the partial shape are almost identical.

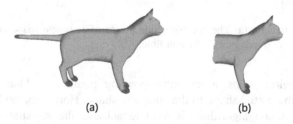

(a)   (b)

Fig. 5. (a) Complete shape and (b) partial shape, the feature points are almost identical.

4.2 Registration Strategy

Given a complete shape M and a set of partial shapes $P = \{P_i\}$, all of the feature points extracted are first put into candidate sets, denoted as $R \subseteq P_i$ and $S \subseteq M$, respectively. Then, for each point $r_i \in R (i = 1, 2, \ldots, r)$, its corresponding points $s_j \in S(j = 1, 2 \ldots, s)$ are searched. Let $\Phi^P_{r_i}(k)$ denote the HKS value at $t_k \in (t_x, t_y)$ of point r_i of partial shape P, and $\Phi^M_{s_j}(k)$ denote the HKS value at $t_k \in (t_x, t_y)$ of point s_j of complete shape M. The initial matching is as follows:

Step 1: The common heat diffusion time $[t_x, t_y]$ is evenly divided into n intervals, $n = 100$ usually and the corresponding HKS values are calculate;

Step 2: The distance between r_i and s_j at t_k is given by (7):

$$E_{(r_i,s_j)}(k) = \left\| \Phi^P_{r_i}(k) - \Phi^M_{s_j}(k) \right\| \tag{7}$$

And the variance $D(E)$ of k - th intervals is the similarity between r_i and s_j;

Step 3: The smallest value of $D(E)$ in S is selected as the corresponding point to r_i;

Step 4: Repeat steps 2 and 3 from $i = 1$ to $i = r$.

Figure 6 illustrates that HKS of the corresponding points are equal in the overlapping diffusion time, which guarantees the matching feasibility. To remove errors in the initial matching, a basis point driven refinement strategy is presented. Specifically, $r_i, r_j \in R$ and $s_i, s_j \in S$ are considered as potential corresponding pair if $|D(r_i, r_j) - D(s_i, s_j)| < \delta$, where $D(\cdot, \cdot)$ is the Euclidean distances between any two points and $\delta = 10^{-4}$. The basis points were selected first if there exists another two pairs of points whose Euclidean distances are the same. Other initial matching results will be refined if the distances to the basis points are lower than threshold.

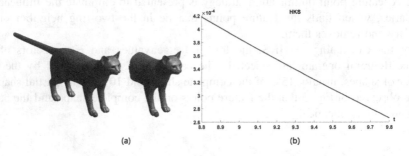

(a)   (b)

Fig. 6. Matching strategy. (a) The corresponding points of complete shape and partial shape. (b) HKS curves of the overlapping diffusion time.

After the previous steps, a few corresponding points are obtained that can be utilized to align the partial shape to the complete shape. Horn's method [32], which is an absolute orientation algorithm, is used to achieve the registration; it uses the quaternion to represent the transformation matrix and obtains accurate registration results, as shown in Fig. 7.

(a)   (b)

Fig. 7. (a) The registration results. (b) The reference error; it is extremely accurate.

5 Experimental Results and Comparisons

5.1 Experimental Results

Experiments were conducted on Intel Xeon 2.13 GHz 64-bit machines with 6 GB of memory. The experimental data come from the TOSCA dataset [34] and SHREC'16 dataset [33], which is extended from the TOSCA dataset. 6 classes 72 shapes totally are used in our experiment. 300 eigenvalues are used to evaluate the HKS, which can afford a precise approximation.

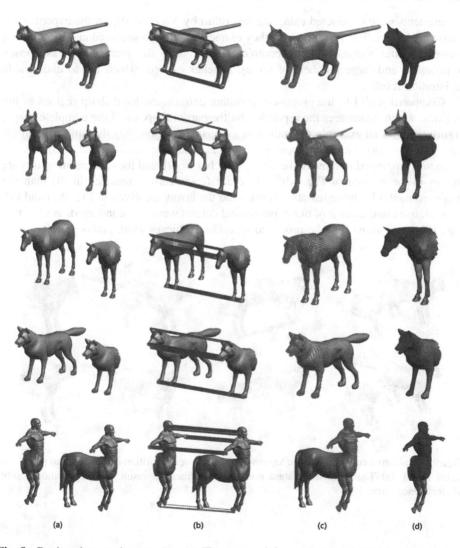

    (a)   (b)   (c)   (d)

Fig. 8. Registration result examples. (a) The extracted feature points; (b) Refinement results; (c)Registration results; (d) The reference error.

For the evaluation of the registration quality, the reference error ε_R and reference error ratio δ_R are used in this paper. ε_R is the average Euclidean distance of all the points on the partial shape to its nearest point on the complete shape. δ_R is the ratio of ε_R to the diameter of the bounding box. Qualitative examples of the registration results obtained by the proposed algorithm are given in Fig. 8. The reference error ratio δ_R of each class are reported in Fig. 10 compared with other methods, where the maximum error ratio is no more than 0.2%. The stable and consistent feature points generate a large number of correct matching, which guarantees the accurate registration results.

5.2   Comparison with Existing Methods

Experiments were conducted using the algorithm by Yu et al. [9] on the experimental datasets we used. The feature points they extracted are often scattered and inconsistent between partial shapes and the complete shape since the time scale was chosen empirically, and large numbers of wrong matches existed, which led to undesirable registration results.

Compared with [9], the proposed algorithm extracts the local sharp regions as the features, which guarantees the repetition on the partial shapes and the complete shape. Figure 9 shows an example of qualitative comparisons. Note that the time scale in [9] was set to $k = 60$, which produces more precise results generally. A RANSAC algorithm was employed to remove the wrong matches in [9], and the refinement results are shown in the bottom of Fig. 9(b). There are fewer correct matches in [9] than the proposed method. The registration results and the errors are given in Fig. 9(c) and (d). Quantitative comparisons of our experimental dataset were also conducted, as shown in Fig. 10, which show that the proposed algorithm achieves more precise result.

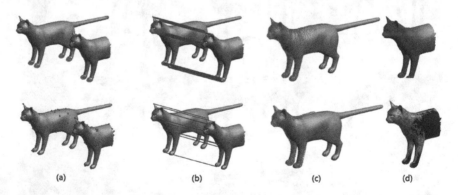

Fig. 9. Qualitative comparison. The top row is the proposed algorithm and the bottom row is the result in [9]. (a) The extracted feature points. (b) Refinement result. (c) Registration result. (d) Reference error.

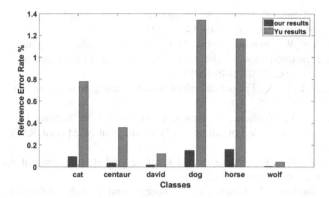

Fig. 10. Quantitative comparisons of average reference error ratio.

6 Conclusion

In this paper, a novel HKS-based feature extraction algorithm is proposed for 3D shape partial registration. The multi scale descriptor is introduced firstly and its several desirable properties are then analyzed. The feature extraction algorithm is presented that can extract the sharp features of the shape efficiently. By comparing the HKS values of the feature points, initial matching results are obtained. Partial registration results are achieved after a refinement procedure. Experiments have been conducted on various partial shapes and accurate results were achieved. The proposed approach presents improvements to a general feature extracted algorithm based on HKS. In the future, we will test the proposed approach on a large number of partial shapes that may be different sizes or have large deformations.

References

1. Besl, P.J., Mckay, N.D.: A method for registration of 3-D shapes. IEEE Trans. Pattern Anal. Mach. Intell. **14**(3), 239–256 (1992)
2. Rusinkiewicz, S., Levoy, M.: Efficient variants of the ICP algorithm. In: Proceedings of International Conference on 3-D Digital Imaging and Modeling, pp. 145–152 (2001)
3. Rusinkiewicz, S., Hall-Holt, O., Levoy, M.: Real-time 3D model acquisition. ACM Trans. Graph. (TOG) **21**(3), 438–446 (2002)
4. Haehnel, D., Thrun, S., Burgard, W.: An extension of the ICP algorithm for modeling nonrigid objects with mobile robots. In: Proceedings of IJCAI-03, Proceedings of the Eighteenth International Joint Conference on Artificial Intelligence, Acapulco, Mexico, August, pp. 915–920 (2003)
5. Wand, M., Jenke, P., Huang, Q.: Reconstruction of deforming geometry from time-varying point clouds. In: Proceedings of Eurographics Symposium on Geometry Processing, pp. 49–58 (2007)
6. Brown, B.J., Rusinkiewicz, S.: Global non-rigid alignment of 3-D scans. ACM Trans. Graph. **26**(3), 21 (2007)

7. Huang, Q.X., Adams, B., Wicke, M.: Non-rigid registration under isometric deformations. Comput. Graph. Forum **27**(5), 1449–1457 (2008)
8. Zhang, K., Yu, W., Manhein, M.: 3D fragment reassembly using integrated template guidance and fracture-region matching. In: Proceedings of IEEE International Conference on Computer Vision, pp. 2138–2146 (2015)
9. Wei, Yu., Li, M., Li, X.: Fragmented skull modeling using heat kernels. Graph. Models **74** (4), 140–151 (2012)
10. Zhang, K., Yu, W., Manhein, M.: Reassembling 3D thin shells using integrated template guidance and fracture region matching. In: Proceedings of ACM SIGGRAPH 2015 Posters, p. 88:1 (2015)
11. Li, X., Yin, Z., Wei, L.: Symmetry and template guided completion of damaged skulls. Comput. Graph. **35**(4), 885–893 (2011)
12. Sun, J., Ovsjanikov, M., Guibas, L.: A concise and provably informative multi scale signature based on heat diffusion. In: Proceedings of Computer Graphics Forum, pp. 1383–1392 (2009)
13. Aubry, M., Schlickewei, U., Cremers, D.: The wave kernel signature: a quantum mechanical approach to shape analysis. In: Proceedings of IEEE International Conference on Computer Vision Workshops, pp. 1626–1633 (2011)
14. Fischler, M.A., Bolles, R.C.: Random sample consensus: a paradigm for model fitting with applications to image analysis and automated cartography. Commun. ACM **24**(6), 381–395 (1981)
15. Chen, C.S., Hung, Y.P., Cheng, J.B.: A fast automatic method for registration of partially-overlapping range images. In: Proceedings of International Conference on Computer Vision, pp. 242–248 (1998)
16. Aiger, D., Mitra, N.J., Cohen-Or, D.: 4-points congruent sets for robust pairwise surface registration **27**(3), 85 (2008)
17. Mellado, N., Aiger, D., Mitra, N.J.: Super 4PCS fast global pointcloud registration via smart indexing. Comput. Graph. Forum **33**(5), 205–215 (2015)
18. Johnson, A.E., Hebert, M.: Using spin images for efficient object recognition in cluttered 3D scenes. IEEE Trans. Pattern Anal. Mach. Intell. **21**(5), 433–449 (1999)
19. Brusco, N., Andreetto, M., Giorgi, A.: 3D registration by textured spin images. In: Proceedings of International Conference on 3-D Digital Imaging and Modeling, pp. 262–269 (2005)
20. Dinh, H.Q., Kropac, S.: Multi-resolution spin-images. In: 2006 IEEE Computer Society Conference on Proceedings of Computer Vision and Pattern Recognition, pp. 863–870 (2006)
21. Itskovich, A., Tal, A.: Semantic 3D media and content: surface partial matching and application to archaeology. Comput. Graph. **35**(2), 334–341 (2011)
22. Koenderink, J.J., Van Doorn, A.J.: Surface shape and curvature scales. Image Vision Comput. **10**(8), 557–564 (1992)
23. Dorai, C., Jain, A.K.: COSMOS – a representation scheme for 3D free-form objects. In: Proceedings of International Conference on Computer Vision, Proceedings, pp. 1024–1029.38 (1997)
24. Pottmann, H., Wallner, J., Huang, Q.X.: Integral invariants for robust geometry processing. Comput. Aided Geom. Design **26**(1), 37–60 (2009)
25. Huang, Q.X., Flory, S., Gelfand, N.: Reassembling fractured objects by geometric matching. In: Proceedings of ACM SIGGRAPH 2006 Papers, pp. 569–578. ACM, New York (2006)
26. Shapira, L., Shamir, A., Cohen-Or, D.: Consistent mesh partitioning and skeletonisation using the shape diameter function. Visual Comput. **24**(4), 249–259 (2008)

27. Tombari, F., Salti, S., Di Stefano, L.: Unique signatures of histograms for local surface description. In: Daniilidis, K., Maragos, P., Paragios, N. (eds.) ECCV 2010. LNCS, vol. 6313, pp. 356–369. Springer, Heidelberg (2010). https://doi.org/10.1007/978-3-642-15558-1_26
28. Coifman, R.R., Lafon, S.: Diffusion maps. Appl. Comput. Harmonic Anal. **21**(1), 5–30 (2006)
29. Grigor'Yan, A.: Escape rate of Brownian motion on Riemanian manifolds. Appl. Anal. **71**, 63–89 (1998)
30. Rustamov, R.M.: Laplace-Beltrami eigenfunctions for deformation invariant shape representation. In: Proceedings of Eurographics Symposium on Geometry Processing, pp. 225–233 (2007)
31. GrigorYan, A.: Heat kernels on weighted manifolds and applications. Heat Kernels Weighted Manifolds Appl. Researchgate **398**, 93–191 (2005)
32. Horn, B.K.P.: Closed-form solution of absolute orientation using unit quaternions. J. Optical Soc. Am. A **4**(4), 629–642 (1987)
33. Cosmo, L., Rodola, E., Bronstein, M.: SHREC 2016: partial matching of deformable shapes. In: Proceedings of Conference: Eurographics Workshop on 3D Object Retrieval (2016)
34. Bronstein, A.M., Bronstein, M.M., Kimmel, R.: Numerical Geometry of Non-Rigid Shapes. Springer Publishing Company, Incorporated (2008)

U3D File Format Analyzing and 3DPDF Generating Method

Nan Zhang[1], Qingyuan Li[1,2(✉)], Huiling Jia[3], Minghui Zhang[3], and Jie Liu[1]

[1] College of Geosciences and Surveying Engineering,
China University of Mining and Technology (Beijing), Beijing 100083, China
[2] Key Laboratory of Geo-Informatics of State Bureau of Surveying
and Mapping, Chinese Academy of Surveying and Mapping,
Beijing 100830, China
liqy@casm.ac.cn
[3] Zhengzhou Xinda Institute of Advanced Technology,
Zhengzhou 450001, China

Abstract. It introduces U3D (Universal 3D) file format and the method to embed U3D data into PDF to produce a 3DPDF file which can be browsed by PDF reader. It analyzes the architecture, mechanism and data structure of U3D. C++ language is used to translate 3D model to U3D file and then embed U3D into 3DPDF file. A 3D geology model which is expressed by Geo3DML (Three Dimension Geological Model Data Transfer Format), which has been published by CGS (Chinese Geological Survey) has been translated into 3DPDF file. The results file is small in file capacity, good in visualization, convenient in operation. U3D file format is appropriate to express a variety of complicated 3D models, and expand the application of 3D computer models when embed into 3DPDF.

Keywords: U3D · 3DPDF · File structure · Execution architecture
Geo3DML

1 Introduction

3D modeling and visualization technology have been widely applying in many fields such as product design, processing and manufacturing, construction, medicine, aviation, advertising, entertainment and 3D printing. 3D modeling software adopts different 3D file formats that are dependent on the original software, making it inconvenient to browse and employ 3D model data. In order to provide a common simple and reliable 3D data format, the 3D Industry Forum defines a U3D format, which was recognized by ECMA (European Computer Manufactures Association) as the standard of 3D model data in August, 2005 [1].

Many international 3D modeling and graphics software have achieved U3D format conversion or the realization of embedded U3D PDF format storage. For instance, MeVisLab, a visualization platform for Medical image processing is used in clinical, medical education, scientific research; the extension module above Adobe PS CS3 can also convert its 3D layer into U3D format. Data of U3D format can be inserted into

© Springer Nature Singapore Pte Ltd. 2018
Y. Wang et al. (Eds.): IGTA 2017, CCIS 757, pp. 136–146, 2018.
https://doi.org/10.1007/978-981-10-7389-2_14

PDF file, realize interactive visualization in Acrobat 7.0 or later, and generate the more target file 3DPDF to be further compressed. The wide use of PDF files around the world makes it possible to browse and use 3D model data on a larger scale. Many international three-dimensional modeling software companies are seeking to support 3DPDF. 3DPDF has been used in many industries, such as medical imaging, aerospace simulations, educational demonstrations, etc. [9–12]. Miao and Su [7, 8] have explored U3D file format, but many detail of the structure and generating process of U3D file have are not been discussed deeply.

3D geological modeling has been playing more and more important role in geological work. 3D geological model is the most complex of all 3D models. CGS (China Geological Survey) has published Geo3DML (Three Dimensional Geological Model Market Language) as a exchange format standard of Chinese geological 3D model. China Geological Survey hope Geo3DML can be transformed into 3DPDF to improve Geo3DML accepted by user and market. The author undertook the work to realize convert Geo3DML to 3DPDF. During the process of converting Geo3DML into 3DPDF, the U3D file format and the generating process of 3DPDF file are carefully studied. This paper expounds the results of this research, including the data structure, operation mechanism, the details of the U3D level settings, attribute output method and embedded PDF method.

2 U3D File Format-Overall Structure [2]

A file is structured as a sequence of blocks. U3D file contains file structure blocks, node blocks, geometry generator blocks, modifier blocks and resource blocks. U3D each block stores data according to a certain structure, and each block has the same basic structure. As shown in the following Fig. 1.

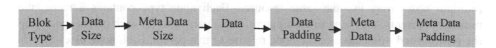

Fig. 1. The structure of blocks of U3D

Block Type identifies the type of object associated with this block. The interpretation of the data section of this block depends on the block type. Data Size is the size of the data section in bytes. Data Padding is a variable size field. Zero to three bytes are inserted to maintain 32-bit alignment for the start of the meta data section. The Meta section contains a sequence of Key/Value pairs, including the number of records to be recorded, the number of attributes, the record content, and the field value. Meta Data Padding is also a variable size field. Zero to three bytes are inserted to maintain 32-bit alignment for the start of the next block.

2.1 File Structure Block

The following six blocks is called file structure blocks.

1. File Header (block type: 0x00443355). The file header is the only required block in a file. It contains version, profile identifier, declaration size, file size, character encoding.

2. File Reference (block type: 0xffffff12). Afile reference block contains information for finding a single file that ID associated with this file and is loaded with it. A U3D file can reference other U3D file by File Reference block.

3. Modifier Chain (block type: 0xffffff14). The modifier chain contains modifier chain name, modifier chain type, modifier count, modifier declaration block and so on.

4. Priority Update (block type: 0xffffff15). Priority update blocks are in the continuation section of the file. Priority update blocks indicate the priority number of the following continuation blocks.

5. New Object Type (block type: 0xffffff16). The new object type block provides the mechanism for extending the file format. Like other object, these new object are serialized as a sequence of one or more blocks. The block contains a name, a new type of object ID, object statement block, additional blocks and other relevant information. The U3D file that contains the block needs to be specified in the configuration file identifier of header file using the extended configuration.

6. New Object Block (block type: 0x00000100 to 0x00ffffff). This section defines the syntax required for new object blocks. A New Object Type block with a declaration of the block types used shall precede the New Object Block.

2.2 Node Blocks

Nodes are the entities that populate the scene graph. Nodes (expect for the group node) also have an associated resource that is specified by name. To allow data sharing, multiple nodes may use the same resource. Each node type contains a name, the number of parents, the name of each parent, and a transform for each parent specifying the position and orientation of the node relative to that parent. Each node block type is not the same, the data part of the block is also different.

2.3 Geometry Generator Blocks

There are three kinds of geometric generator blocks: the continuous detail mesh generator, the line set generator and the point set generator. Taking the continuous detail generator as an example, the generator mainly includes the following contents:

The CLOD Mesh Generator contains the data needed to create a continuous level of detail mesh. The data includes vertices, normal vectors, faces, shade lists, and level of detail information for the base mesh and updates. The CLOD mesh declaration contains the declaration information for a continuous level of detail mesh generation. The mesh data is mesh name, mesh generator name, the name of model resource modifier chain, chain index, the position of the CLOD mesh generator in the model resource modifier chain.

Model description: CLOD description describes the range of resolution available for the continuous level of detail mesh. Resource description can set quality factors, inverse quantization and resource parameters (mesh quality factor, point quality and normal quality factor). Resource parameters control the operation of the CLOD mesh generator. Resource parameters contains normal crease parameter, normal update parameter and normal tolerance parameter. There are mesh attributes, face count, position count, normal count, diffuse color count, specular color count, texture coordinate count, shading count and so on in max mesh description.

2.4 Modifier Blocks

Modifier blocks contain the information necessary to create modifiers that can be added to a modifier chain.

1. 2D Glyph Modifier (block type: 0xffffff41). The 2D Glyph Modifier contains information used to create a 2D shape. The shape is defined by a number of control points and parameters that define how to connect the points. The shape consists of a sequence of individual glyphs called a glyph string. Each glyph in the glyph string is defined by a sequence of drawing commands.

2. Subdivision Modifier (block type: 0xffffff42). The Subdivision Modifier increases the resolution of a shape by dividing polygons into smaller polygons. The Subdivision Modifier contains modifier name, chain index, subdivision attributes, subdivision depth, subdivision tension and so on.

3. Animation Modifier (block type: 0xffffff43). The Animation Modifier block describes parameters for animating a node or a renderable group. These parameters indicate which motion resources should be used and how they should be applied. The animation modifier changes geometry data basing on skeleton and modifies bone information basing on animation resource.

4. Bone Weight Modifier (block type: 0xffffff44). The Bone Weight Modifier describes a set of bones weights that can be added to a modifier chain. The animation modifier uses the bone weights in combination with the skeleton to animate the positions in a renderable group (mesh, line set or point set).

5. Shading Modifier (block type: 0xffffff45). The Shading Modifier describes the shading group that is used in the drawing of a renderable group. The Shading Modifier contains shading modifier name, chain index, shade list count, shade count and so on.

6. CLOD Modifier (block type: 0xffffff45). The CLOD modifier adjusts the level of detail in the renderable meshes in the data packet. The CLOD modifier contains clod modifier name, chain index, and CLOD modifier level and so on.

2.5 Resource Blocks

Resource blocks contains the declarative information for resources. The resources can then be referenced by nodes to create specific instances during rendering.

1. Light Resource (block type: 0xffffff51). The Light Resource contains information regarding the type of light, color, attenuation and intensity.

2. View Resource (block type: 0xffffff52). The View Resource contains information regarding the rendered view that is not specific to a particular view instance. Fields include: fog and frame buffer properties. More field, such as view port, backdrops and overlays are stored at the node level and are specific to each instance.

3. Lit Texture Shader (block type: 0xffffff53). The Lit Texture Shader contains information needed to determine the appearance of a surface during rendering. The Lit Texture Shader includes references to material resources and texture resource and how to combine those resources when rendering.

4. Material Resource (block type: 0xffffff54). The Material Resource contain information defining how a material interacts with light in a scene, material resource names, material attributes, ambient color, diffuse color, emissive color, reflectivity and opacity.

5. Texture Resource (block type: 0xffffff55; 0xffffff5C). The Texture resource contains information for creating a texture image to be applied to geometry. The usage of the texture resource is controlled by a shade. The Texture resource is divided into two parts: the declaration and the continuation.

6. Motion Resource (block type: 0xffffff56). The Motion resource contains animation data that is stored in a number of tracks. A motion track can be used to animate a bone in a bone hierarchy and can also animate a node in the scene graph.

2.6   Serialization

Object serialization: Each object is serialized as a sequence of one or more blocks. The first block is called the declaration block. Any subsequent blocks are called continuation blocks. The declaration block contains enough information to create the object and place it in the correct palette location. Most types of objects have only the declaration blocks. Objects which require a large amount of information use continuation blocks to carry most of the data.

Block serialization: Each block is assigned a priority number used for sequencing the blocks and interleaving the blocks from multiple objects. A file is structured as a sequence of blocks which is divided into three type–the file header block, declaration blocks and continuation blocks. The file header block is followed by declaration blocks. Continuation blocks may follow the declaration blocks.

3   U3D File Format Execution Architecture [2]

The execution architecture is based on the interaction of several key elements: palettes, nodes, the scene graph, resources, and modifier chains.

3.1   Element and How They Interact

Scene: The scene is a palette container.

Palette: A palette is organized as an ordered list of entries composed of an identifying name and a reference to an object or a reference to null. Entries can be accessed through the palette by specifying a name or by iterating through the list of entries contained in a palette. The palette are: model resource palette, light resource palette, view resource palette, texture resource palette, shade resource palette, material resource palette, motion resource palette and node palette.

Node: Each node contains hierarchical information and spatial information. Nodes is stored in the node palette, and associated with the entity resource by correlating with the resource palette. The node types are: group, model, light, and view.

Resources: Each resource type has a corresponding node type. The resources contains the majority of the information needed to create a 3D object for storing light settings, view settings, geometric entities, texture settings and other source data. The model resource, motive resource, texture resource and material resource associating with the model resource are 3D model meta-data and displaying attribute meta-data. Resource is the original spatial data model and 3D display attribute data source.

Modifier and Modifier Chains: The Modifier creates outputs based on input data. The modifier chain object collects and orders the modifiers, ensures that the required inputs for each modifier are available. The modifier chain passes a data packet to a modifier and constructs a new data packet based on that modifier's outputs and then present the data packet to next modifier. Modifiers include animation modifiers, shader modifiers, etc., and some types of resources and nodes can also be used as modifiers in managing multiple data modifier chains (such as model resources, model nodes).

The relationships among the components are shown in the following Fig. 2:

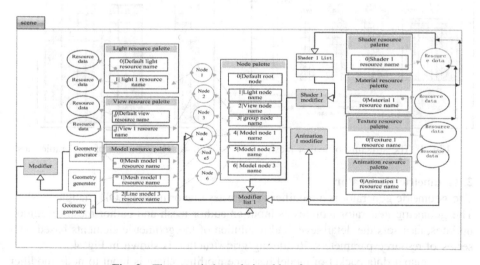

Fig. 2. The association relationship of components

3.2 Model Resource Creation Mechanism

Creating model resources includes the methods and information to create geometric models, and shading information of how to render the model. We mainly introduce the mesh resource model. U3D mesh includes two kinds of structure: the author mesh and renderable mesh. Developers can choose the model output form. The rendering grid is a reorganization of the author mesh and can choose quality parameters of reorganization (including geometric compression parameters, model rendering effects, and related parameters). Restructuring work completed by the geometric generator. The original grid is characterized by maintaining a full input geometry, without shadows and other rendering effects, and the outputting of the U3D file relatively large. Renderable meshes regroup the data in an author mesh and discard certain geometric data according to compression parameters. It has the shadow of 3D rendering, and the output U3D file is small. But if the compression quality parameter setting is too small, it will affect the accuracy of geometric model, users of high geometric accuracy requirements of the model need to set high quality of parameter.

1. Author Mesh and Author Mesh Resolution Updates

The author mesh structure is easy to modify and compress, including the list of faces, the list of vertices associated with the surface, the list of point colors, the list of colored ID, etc. Each surface in the face list has its associated colored ID, each of which contains a number of texture ID settings. The settings in the shader settings determine the properties of a surface with the property values associated with the vertices of the triangle mesh. The author mesh update describes the mesh updating method to change the resolution of the author mesh. The author mesh structure is shown in Fig. 3.

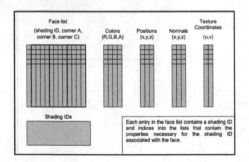

Fig. 3. The structure of author mesh

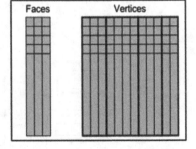

Fig. 4. The structure of renderable mesh

2. Geometric Generator

The geometric generator is a modifier that creates one or more CLOD triangle meshes. The geometric generator requires as input an author mesh and author mesh resolution updates, then sets the detail level and resolution of the geometric elements based on a series of resource parameters. Rendering grid structure is shown in Fig. 4.

The output data packet of model resource modifier chain is input to node modifier and will be proceed to the data processing. The schematic diagram of model resource creation is shown below (Figs. 5 and 6):

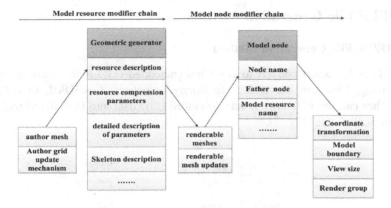

Fig. 5. The creation of model resource

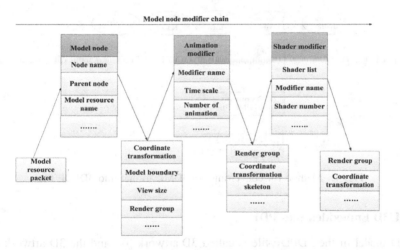

Fig. 6. Rendering and shading of model

3.3 Model Rendering Mechanism

The shader and renderer is created in the model resources, which is used to shade and render the vertices, while the shader settings can be used to shade and render the points, lines and surfaces. The renderer and shader describes some of the data elements in the last packet of the node modifier chain, and how these data elements are used to render the elements.

Steps: first create a shader resource. Then the shader resource is entered into the shader modifier. Shader resources are processed in the modifier to output the new render group.

4   3DPDF File Generation Method

4.1   3DPDF File Generation Method

G3DXML [3–5] format convert to U3D and embedded U3D PDF format using C++ programming. First call the U3D core library to convert Geo3DML to U3D data format. Then call the PDF core library to embed U3D data into PDF file to realize the output of 3DPDF file (Fig. 7).

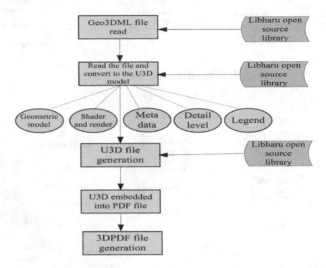

Fig. 7. Method for converting Geo3DML format into 3DPDF file

4.2   U3D Embedded into PDF

The 3D model in the 3DPDF file is called 3D artwork [6], and the 3D artwork is not displayed as a separate window or user interface element, but is rendered on the page. A page or a document can have one or more 3D artwork.

Fonts, pictures, etc. are stored and expressed in the form of object in PDF. 3D artwork presentation and storage in the file is also in the form of the object.

The U3D file embedded in PDF and output 3DPDF file can be achieved in two ways: (1) page embedding; (2) programming.

4.3   U3D Graphic Quality Control

U3D graphics can be set to whether or not to compression and the level of compression. Graphics compression is to reduce the size of the file but increase the file generation time, so the user can set compression quality based on the demand for U3D graphics.

U3D data about geometric model can be set parameters in the compilation including the compression parameters, continuous details of the hierarchy parameters.

It is important to select the compression quality, and the compression parameters include the point quality parameters, the point color quality parameters, the normal vector parameters and so on. The point quality parameter is mainly used in this paper, the value of them is between 0 and 1000, and the default quality parameter is 250. The higher the point mass parameter is, the better the output model is, the higher the coordinate precision is, and the bigger the output file is. If the selected-point quality is too low, it will impact the model visualization. If the quality of the selected- point is too high, it will be a waste of high quality and increases the size of the file.

In this paper, the result of the data through changing the point quality is compared. It was found that the output of U3D data in the PDF in the case of the default value of the data quality displayed a larger position error and the effect of the model was poorer. As is shown in Fig. 8, it is recommended that the reader should pay attention to the quality of U3D data output settings. Figure 9 point mass is 600, the effect is better.

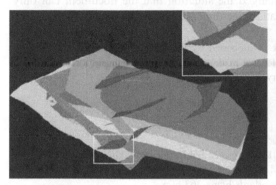 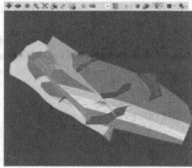

Fig. 8. Display of model using default quality parameters value

Fig. 9. U3D model of highly quality in PDF

4.4 Output of Element Attributes

The query and display of graphics elements is extremely important for the application of graphics, and equally important for 3DPDF. The element attribute is the name or value of the point, line, surface and body element of the 3D geological model. They are important contents of 3D geological model. The U3D format can store the node property values by setting, the node metadata, and a node can set multiple attribute values, that is, an element can link multiple attribute values. The "object data" of PDF reader supports the display of U3D metadata. The author's experiments show that U3D supports Chinese characters with multiple attribute values or Unicode codes. However, when U3D is embedded in PDF, attributes recorded with a Chinese character string is filtered out, and recorded in English or digital can be retained and displayed normally.

5 Conclusion

Through the analysis, it can be seen that the U3D format has the advantages of simple structure, clear structure, strong expression ability, data compression, level of detail precision control and support for 3D data stream type progressive transmission, and skeletal animation. A variety of software of Adobe support to embed the U3D format and open the 3DPDF format. With the development of 3D model data and the application of U3D data format, it is believes that more software will support U3D data format.

The Geo3DML format of the three-dimensional model file is converted to U3D and 3DPDF files using C++ programming language. The 3D geological model in the PDF has good 3D visualization effect, and also has the function of rotate, zoom, layer control, set up a variety of three-dimensional display mode, element attributes view, three-dimensional measurement and so on. This improves the scope of the use of three-dimensional model, but also changed the situation that the document can only show three-dimensional picture or static three-dimensional graphics.

Acknowledgements. The research work is supported by the National Natural Science Foundation of China (41272367) and 3D geological model data exchange support tool develop and maintain project of China Geological Survey (CGS 2016-99).

References

1. Wikipedia: Universal 3D.EB/OL (2016). https://en.wikipedia.org/wiki/Universal_3D
2. ECMA International: Standard ECMA-363 universal 3D file format (2007). http://www.ecma-international.org/publications/standards/Ecma-363.htm
3. Technical Standard of China Geological Survey DD2015-6: Three dimension geology model data transfer format. China Geological Survey (2016). (in Chinese)
4. Development Research Center of China Geological Survey: Description for drawing up three dimension geology model data transfer format Geo3DML.R (2014). (in Chinese). http://www.geo3dml.cn/
5. Li, Q., Ma, Z., Cui, Y., et al.: The research and suggestion of the application of Geo3DML in three dimensional geological model. J. Geol. **39**(9), 358–366 (2015)
6. Adobe Systems Incorporated.pdf_reference .EB/OL (2006). http://www.adobe.com
7. Miao, Y., Su, H.: Analysing U3D file format and its execution mechanism. Comput. Appl. Softw. **27**(2), 249–251, 282 (2010). (in Chinese)
8. Miao, Y., Su, H.: Applying U3D file in PDF files and its implementation with C++ programming. Comput. Appl. Softw. **27**(3), 224–227 (2010). (in Chinese)
9. Newe, A., Ganslandt, T.: Simplified generation of biomedical 3D surface model data for embedding into 3D Portable Document Format (PDF) files for publication and education. PLoS ONE **8**, e79004 (2013)
10. Dominguez, M.G., Martin-Gutierrez, J., Gonzalez, C.R., et al.: Methodologies and tools to improve spatial ability. Procedia Soc. Behav. Sci. **51**(6), 736–744 (2012)
11. Hodis, E., Sussman, J.L.: An encyclopedic effort to make 3D structures easier to understand. Trends Biochem. Sci. **34**(3), 100–101 (2009)
12. Newe, A.: Towards an easier creation of three-dimensional data for embedding into scholarly 3D PDF (Portable Document Format) files. PeerJ **3**, e794 (2015)

Estimating Cumulus Cloud Shape
from a Single Image

Yiming Zhang[1], Zili Zhang[1,2], Jiayue Hou[1], and Xiaohui Liang[1(✉)]

[1] State Key Laboratory of Virtual Reality System and Technology,
Beihang University, Beijing, China
{zyiming,zhangzili,houjiayue,liang_xiaohui}@buaa.edu.cn
[2] Shijiazhuang University, Shijiazhuang, China

Abstract. Cumulus cloud is a typical kind of low-altitude cloud and
bears detailed appearance. However, construct a cumulus cloud shape
from image remains a challenging task. In previous works, cloud thickness is first calculated from intensities of the pixels and then cloud surface shape is obtained based on symmetry assumption. Given an image,
an optimization problem is formulated based on the shape from shad-
ing(SFS) algorithm with unknown illumination. This paper addresses
this problem and presents a simple and effective method which estimates the surface shape directly by leveraging the rich details of the
cloud surface. In this paper, we propose two constraints: the boundary
constraint and relative height constraint. Meanwhile, a multi-scale optimization technique is utilized and then back surface of the cloud is constructed. The experimental results show that our method can generate
natural and realistic cumulus cloud shape with details like the image.

Keywords: Cumulus cloud shape · Boundary constraint
Shape from shading · Natural image

1 Introduction

Cloud is a critical natural element in synthesizing realistic outdoor scenes. In the
scope of image-based cloud shape modeling, the current methods estimate the
shape of cloud from a single image based on different assumptions. The method
in [1] generates cloud shape assuming that the heights of the pixels are relative
to their distance to the silhouette of the cloud. Another method recovers the
cumulus cloud shape by inverting a simplified single scattering model with other
optical parameters being fixed [2]. But these two methods cannot reproduce
natural shape or similar convex and concave regions to the cloud in the image
for lack of exploration in further on the details of the cloud surface (e.g. self-
occlusions and shading).

To address the aforementioned problems, we present a simple and effective
solution for estimating the shape of cumulus cloud with similar details to a single
input image. First, we propose two constraints on the cloud surface shape: the

© Springer Nature Singapore Pte Ltd. 2018
Y. Wang et al. (Eds.): IGTA 2017, CCIS 757, pp. 147–156, 2018.
https://doi.org/10.1007/978-981-10-7389-2_15

relative height constraint and the boundary constraint. The relative height constraint encourages that the heights of regions are proportional to their average intensities. And the boundary constraint aims to preserve the details of self-occlusions and silhouette of the cumulus cloud surface. Then, for the complex cloud model, the illumination in our method is also estimated instead of being specified in classic shape from shading algorithm. And a multi-scale optimization technique is utilized to solve the problem for the surface height field and the illumination. Finally, 3D mesh of the cloud shape is constructed using the Laplacian mesh editing technique. Experimental results show that our method with the proposed constraints imposed on the SFS algorithm can obtain a cloud surface with similar geometry structures (e.g. self-occlusion and shading details) to that of image, and the cloud surface looks more natural and realistic than previous works.

2   Related Work

A multitude of methods have been proposed to model clouds. Procedural approach is dependent on parameter adjustments, including methods based on noise functions [3], spectral synthesis [4], and interactive designs [5,6]. Physical based approach is based on a simplified atmospheric model to simulate the formation process of cloud [7,8]. The data-driven methods have proven to recover visually realistic [9], and even physically valid cloud properties [10]. There are mainly three kinds of data: satellite images [10,11], numerical simulation data [12], and natural images [1,2]. Compared with satellite images and simulation data, natural images are more suitable for modeling low-altitude cumulus clouds. Dobashi et al. [1] used a simple thickness assumption to estimate the shape of cumulus clouds, and synthesized fractal extinction values. On the contrary, Yuan [2] recovered the surface of a cumulus cloud from the image using a single scattering model, with all the other parameters being fixed. However, with the rendering parameters specified and to be uniform, the shape is not natural and like cones when viewed on the side.

In contrast to previous works, we compute the surface shape directly instead of cloud thickness. Based on shape from shading algorithm [13], we leverage the rich details to estimate the surface shape, such as self-occlusions and shading. However, a solution may not exist or not to be unique when it exists meaning that a given image can be produced from different surfaces. To make the problem well-posed, a multitude of additional priors and constraints of general or specific classes [14,15] have been proposed. Integrability constraint [16] and prior of surface isotropy [17] recover the shapes and are general enough that they work across a variety of objects. In this paper, we propose the relative height constraint and the boundary constraint suitable for cumulus cloud to rectify the ill-posed problem and obtain natural cloud shape with details similar to that of the image.

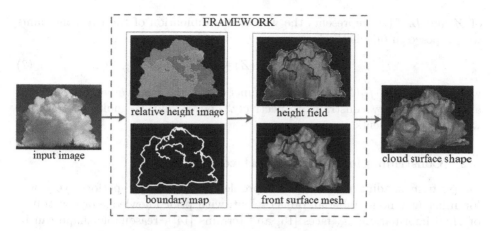

Fig. 1. The framework of our method.

3   Surface Shape Estimation

Figure 1 shows the framework of our approach. Given an image, the region of the cloud pixels is first identified by a threshold method. Next, the cloud region is clustered into several areas utilizing the K-means clustering algorithm according to the intensities and the image coordinates of the cloud pixels. In this step, two parameters are involved in: the number of the clusters k and the weight coefficient p of the image coordinates in the clustering algorithm. Next, an relative height image is calculated whose pixels hold the average brightness of the corresponding clusters they belong to. Then we construct a boundary map with the silhouette and self-occlusions of the cloud. Using the relative height image and boundary map, we estimate the front surface shape of the cloud based on the proposed optimization method. The final cloud surface shape is obtained after generating the back surface. The specific implementation details are as follows.

3.1   Problem Formulation

Given an image of cumulus cloud, we assume a Lambertian reflectance of the cloud surface. Then the desired surface shape of the cloud is defined as a height field to the image plane. Different from classic shape from shading method requiring knowledge of illumination, we estimate the illumination along with the surface shape. Thus an optimization problem is formulated as follows:

$$\min_{Z,L} \quad | I - \rho R(Z, L) | + f(Z) \tag{1}$$

where Z represents the height field viewed orthographically with the same size as I. L is a vector consisting of the coefficients needed in a spherical-harmonic model of illumination and ρ is the albedo related to the cloud specified by the user. $R(Z, L)$ denotes the synthesized image rendered with the surface normals of Z and L. $f(Z)$ represents the weighted combination of the two constraints we proposed in our method:

$$f(Z) = \lambda_I f_I(Z) + \lambda_B f_B(Z) \tag{2}$$

where $f_I(Z)$ and $f_B(Z)$ are the cost functions of the relative height constraint and the boundary constraint respectively. The λ_I and λ_B multipliers are the weighting coefficients.

3.2   Constraints for Cumulus Surface Shape

Shape from shading is an ill-posed problem and does not perform very well for inherently non-lambetian objects. But, with prior knowledge or constraints of class information(e.g. faces [15] and terrains [14]), reasonable shape can be recovered by shape from shading. In this subsection, we propose two constraints suitable for estimating the surface shape of cumulus cloud with similar details to that of the input image.

Relative Height Constraint. The outline of cumulus cloud tends to be clear cut and with horizontal bases. When the direction of the sun and the view point are on the same side of the cloud, the shading distribution of the cloud surface tends to reflect characters of the concave and convex parts. First, cumulus clouds usually have flat bases and the intensities of the bases are relatively dark. Second, as shown in Fig. 2(a), the intensities of the convex parts which are illuminated directly by the sun light tend to be brighter than that of their adjacent concave parts. Inspired by the observations, the relative height constraint on the detailed shading appearance is as follows: the average heights of large regions with brighter cloud intensities tend to be higher than adjacent regions and the average heights of large regions with darker cloud intensities tend to present lower than adjacent regions. In other words, if we segment the cloud pixels according to the brightness into several regions, the average heights of the segmentations are relatively proportional to the brightness of them. Note that, the relative height constraint does not require the height of any pixel with higher intensity to be larger than that of pixel with lower intensity. It is not imposed to single pixel but regions.

As shown in Fig. 2, we generalize the idea to cloud and use the brightness information to automatically guide height field estimation. To define the relative height constraint, the cloud pixels are first clustered using K-means clustering algorithm according to the brightness and the image coordinates of the pixels. Then the average brightness of each cluster is computed. Formally, the constraint is:

$$f_I = \sum_k \left(\bar{Z}_k - \lambda \, \bar{I}_k \right)^2 \tag{3}$$

where k denotes the index of each clustered region and λ is a scale coefficient. $\bar{Z}_k$ denotes the average desired height for the kth region and $\bar{I}_k$ the average intensity of the kth region.

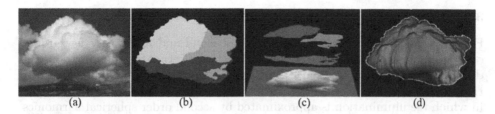

Fig. 2. The relative height constraint. (a) The input image. (b) The average brightness of each clustered region. (c) The relative height of each clustered region. (d) The estimated height field map.

Boundary Constraint. Our constraint on boundary consists of two components according to the two distinct types of boundaries: silhouette and self-occlusions. The silhouette bears rich shape information and self-occlusions play an important role in exhibiting details of cloud surface. Shape from shading algorithms can be helpfully improved incorporating these boundary cues. Although these two boundary cues have different locations, for cloud, they share the same character. That is, at the silhouette and self-occlusion boundaries, the cloud surface tends to be tangent to all rays from the vantage points. Then the z-component of the normal is 0, and the x and y components tend to be perpendicular to the boundary's tangent in the image plane. As a result, we treat these two cases in the same way.

We first obtain the silhouette and self-occlusion boundaries in our method. To separate the cumulus cloud in the image from the background, we use a chroma-based threshing method to classify each pixel belonging to the cloud or sky [9]. Then the silhouette of the cloud is detected. Due to the complexity of the self-occlusions, pixels on them are collected semi-automatically. The gradients of the intensities on the self-occlusion boundary tend to be larger than their adjacent pixels. Based on this observation, we detect the self-occlusions using the canny edge detection method. After obtaining the information at the cloud boundaries, we compute their normals in the image plane. Then the constraint is formulated as follows:

$$f_B = \sum_{i \in B} (1 - (N_i^x * n_i^x + N_i^y * n_i^y))^2 \qquad (4)$$

where B is the union boundary of the silhouette and self-occlusions. n^x and n^y are separately the x and y components of the local normal to the boundary in the image plane. N^x and N^y are the corresponding components of the surface normal of Z, defined as:

$$N^x = \frac{p}{\sqrt{p^2 + q^2 + 1}}, \quad N^y = \frac{q}{\sqrt{p^2 + q^2 + 1}} \qquad (5)$$

where $p = \partial Z / \partial x$, $q = \partial Z / \partial y$.

3.3 Illumination and Optimization

For the sophisticated illumination model of cloud and no or very few ground objects in most of cloud images, general methods estimating illumination conditions often fail for cloud image. Thus, we estimate the illumination along with the cloud shape. We employ the method used in [18] to model the illumination, in which the illumination is approximated by second order spherical harmonics. The second order harmonic approximation needs to compute only 27 coefficients (9 coefficients per color channel) for a RGB image. Thus, the shading image $R(Z, L)$ render with illumination L and the surface normals N is calculated. Then, we utilize the constraint in [17],which encourages the coefficients to match a Gaussian fit to real world spherical harmonics. See [17,18] for more details.

After modelling the illumination, we need to solve the optimization problem to estimate the height field Z and the vector L consisting of the 27 spherical harmonics coefficients. In this paper, we employ a simple and effective method similar to that of [17], in which a Gaussian pyramid constructed from the original unknowns is to be solved for using the L-BFGS. In optimization, the gradient with respect to the pyramid in each iterative step is computed in the following way: First, the original unknowns are reconstructed from the pyramid. Next, the loss and the gradient with respect to the original unknowns are computed and then the gradient is back propagated onto the pyramid. Note that, our boundary constraint is imposed on the surface normals instead of the height field Z. To calculate the gradient of the cost with respect to Z, we use the chain rule to back propagate the gradient with respect to the normal components to the height field.

3.4 Back Surface Shape Computation

After above computation of the height field , the mesh of the front surface of the cumulus is obtained by interpolating the height field. The back cloud surface needs to be generated. Cumulus clouds exhibit various shapes and appearances and it is impossible to infer the back features simply from the single image. So methods in [1,2] compute the back surface with the assumption that it is symmetric with the front surface. In this paper, we first construct the back surface B_1 based on the same assumption by inverting the front surface regarding the image plane. Next, to circumvent the unnatural appearance caused by the symmetry assumption, we create a new height field of the back surface B_2: assuming that the thickness of the clouds is proportional to the brightness of the pixels. Then the new height field is computed with the thickness and front surface. Finally, the back surface is the surface B_1 added with a small weighted B_2. If gaps exist on the boundary side of the surface after the above process, we also use the Laplacian mesh editing technique on the back surface, such as the method of [2].

4   Experimental Result

Our experiments were performed on a desktop PC equipped with an Intel Corei5-3470 3.20 GHz cpu and a NVIDIA GTX750 graphics card. The resolution of input images is approximately 400 × 300. Some parameter settings are used in our experiments. The parameters k and p denote the numbers of clusters and the weighting coefficient of image coordinates are set to be 3 and 2.5, which perform best in the experimental results.

Figure 3 shows the height field results of the clouds in natural images compared with the methods in [1,2]. With the natural image used as the input image, the shape estimating results of Dobashi et al. [1], Yuan et al. [2] and our method are shown in next three row. The method from [1] correlates the thickness of cloud with the distance of pixels to the silhouette and calculates the surface shape by translating the thickness based on the symmetry assumption, which overlooked the details on the cloud surface. And method in [2] estimates the height field by inverting the image formation model using a simplified single scattering model. With other optical parameters being specified, the errors of these parameters are propagated to the desired height field to fit the intensities of the pixels. Thus, the created shape viewed on the side is not natural and like cones in the local regions. From the results, our method can capture the details of the cloud surface such as self-occlusions and generate relatively natural shape of the cloud.

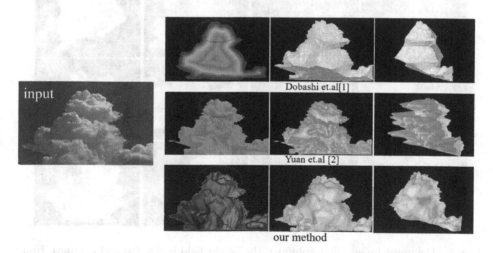

Fig. 3. Shape estimation from input natural images. First column show the height fields results of [1,2] and our method. Second column are the corresponding front view of the shapes and third column show the results of side view.

To verify the two constraints incorporated in our method, we conduct additional experiments shown in Fig. 4. From the result, height field obtained with two constraints is more similar to the ground truth. The relative height constraint (labelled as shading constraint in figure) makes the relative heights of the image more reasonable and the boundary constraint makes the self-occlusions details be more approximate to the ground truth. From experimental results, the boundary constraint can preserve the self-occlusions of the cloud better and the relative height constraint makes the relative height of different areas to be more reasonable.

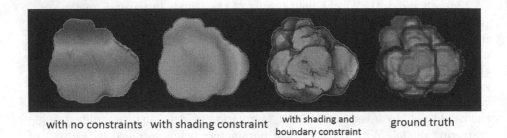

with no constraints   with shading constraint   with shading and boundary constraint   ground truth

Fig. 4. Evaluation of the proposed constraints using a constructed cloud shape.

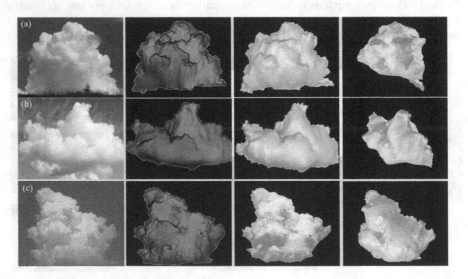

Fig. 5. The input image (first column), the height field image (second column), front view (third column) and side view of the cloud surface shape (fourth column). (Color figure online)

Experimental results of three clouds are shown in Fig. 5. The subfigures (a), (b) and (c) are the input images of the cloud in each row separately. And the second column shows the height field images computed by our optimization method.

The red color means large height values and the blue ones denote small height values instead. And the third column and the fourth column show the front view and the side view of the estimated cloud surface shapes. These results demonstrate that out method can recover the surface shape with details (e.g. shading and self-occlusions) similar to that of the image.

Additionally, Fig. 6 shows a rendering result of cumulus cloud scene. We construct particles from the 3D mesh of clouds and render the cloud scene with several clouds.

Fig. 6. Rendering results of cumulus cloud scene.

5   Conclusion

In this paper, we present an optimization problem based on shape from shading to estimate the cumulus cloud shape from a single image. And to solve the problem, we propose two constraints on cumulus cloud surface: relative height constraint and boundary constraint. In contrast to previous works, we extract the cloud surface shape using the geometry and shading cues, which can substantially reflect geometry structure of cumulus cloud. Experimental results show that our method can generate realistic cumulus cloud shape with similar details to that of the image.

Acknowledgement. This work is supported by the funds of National Natural Science Foundation of China (No. 61572058) and National High Technology Research and Development Program of China (No. 2015AA016402). The authors gratefully thank their help on this work.

References

1. Dobashi, Y., Shinzo, Y., Yamamoto, T.: Modeling of clouds from a single photograph. Comput. Graph. Forum **29**(7), 2083–2090 (2010)
2. Yuan, C., Liang, X., Hao, S., Qi, Y., Zhao, Q.: Modelling cumulus cloud shape from a single image. Comput. Graph. Forum **33**(6), 288–297 (2014). https://doi.org/10.1111/cgf.12350
3. Ebert, D.S.: Volumetric modeling with implicit functions: A cloud is born. In: Visual Proceedings of SIGGRAPH, p. 147 (1997)
4. Sakas, G.: Modeling and animating turbulent gaseous phenomena using spectral synthesis. Vis. Comput. **9**(4), 200–212 (1993)
5. Schpok, J., Simons, J., Ebert, D.S., Hansen, C.: A real-time cloud modeling, rendering, and animation system. In: Proceedings of the 2003 ACM SIGGRAPH/Eurographics Symposium on Computer Animation, pp. 160–166. Eurographics Association (2003)
6. Rana, M.A., Sunar, M.S., Hayat, M.N.N., Kari, S., Bade, A.: Framework for real time cloud rendering. In: 2004 Proceedings of the International Conference on Computer Graphics, Imaging and Visualization, CGIV 2004, pp. 56–61. IEEE (2004)
7. Harris, M.J.: Real-time cloud simulation and rendering (doctoral dissertation)
8. Dobashi, Y., Kusumoto, K., Nishita, T., Yamamoto, T.: Feedback control of cumuliform cloud formation based on computational fluid dynamics. ACM Trans. Graph. **27**(3), 94:1–94:8 (2008)
9. Dobashi, Y., Iwasaki, W., Ono, A., Yamamoto, T., Yue, Y., Nishita, T.: An inverse problem approach for automatically adjusting the parameters for rendering clouds using photographs. ACM Trans. Graph. **31**(6), 1451–14510 (2012)
10. Yuan, C., Liang, X., Hao, S., Yang, G.: Modeling large scale clouds from satellite images. In: Proceedings of Pacific Graphics (short paper), pp. 47–52 (2013)
11. Dobashi, Y., Yamamoto, T., Nishita, T.: Interactive and realistic visualization system for earth-scale clouds. In: Proceedings of Pacific Graphics 2009 (poster paper) (2009)
12. Hufnagel, R., Held, M., Schroder, F.: Large-scale, realistic cloud visualization based on weather forecast data. In: Proceedings of the 9th International Conference on Computer Graphics and Imaging, pp. 54–59 (2007)
13. Horn, B.K.P.: Obtaining shape from shading information. In: The Psychology of Computer Vision, Chapter 4 (1975)
14. Liao, I.Y., Petrou, M., Zhao, R.: A fractal-based relaxation algorithm for shape from terrain image. Comput. Vis. Image Underst. **109**(3), 227–243 (2008)
15. Kemelmacher-Shlizerman, I., Basri, R.: 3D face reconstruction from a single image using a single reference face shape. IEEE Trans. Softw. Eng. **33**(2), 394–405 (2010)
16. Durou, J.D., Falcone, M., Sagona, M.: Numerical methods for shape-from-shading: A new survey with benchmarks. Comput. Vis. Image Underst. **109**(1), 22–43 (2008)
17. Mehta, J., Sugden, R.: Shape, illumination, and reflectance from shading. IEEE Trans. Pattern Anal. Mach. Intell. **37**(8), 1670–1687 (2015)
18. Ramamoorthi, R., Hanrahan, P.: An efficient representation for irradiance environment maps. In: Conference on Computer Graphics and Interactive Techniques, pp. 497–500 (2002)

Design of a Computer-Aided-Design System for Museum Exhibition Based on Virtual Reality

Xue Gao[2], Xinyue Wang[2], Benzhi Yang[3], and Yue Liu[1,2(✉)]

[1] Beijing Engineering Research Center of Mixed Reality and Advanced Display,
Beijing Institute of Technology, Beijing 100081, China
liuyue@bit.edu.cn
[2] School of Optoelectronics, Beijing Institute of Technology, Beijing 100081, China
gao30703@126.com, 1464677442@qq.com
[3] China Mobile Communications Corporation Research Institute, Beijing, China
yangbenzhi@chinamobile.com

Abstract. Exhibition design is the process of developing an exhibit from a concept through to a physical exhibition. The realization of an attractive and friendly exhibition requires its designers to combine various disciplines and multiple techniques. However, the present design process faces such challenges as the need for designers to cooperate with each other as well as the inefficient work for the non-real-time design effects in the process of exhibition design. In this paper, we propose a computer-aided-design system based on virtual reality for museum exhibition that helps designers to design a new exhibition more efficiently. The goal of our system is to improve designers' awareness of the 3D space structure and the design effects in the process of exhibition design. We integrate and visualize the multiple exhibition information in 3D environment with the purpose of supporting the collaborative process. The experimental results show that the proposed design system can provide real-time design effects and high immersion.

Keywords: Museum design · Virtual reality · Immersion · Interaction
Visualization

1 Introduction

A museum is an institution that collects, preserves, interprets, and displays items of artistic, cultural, or scientific significance for the education of the public [1]. Museum hosts exhibition to disseminate certain messages to visitors [2]. These messages are about the collections (objects or archives) and the knowledge (facts or stories) [3].

Museum exhibitions have been regarded as the core function of the museums because they offer a transformative experience and expand the visitors' awareness, interest and valuation of many aspects of themselves and their world [4]. So, it puts forward high demands for the museum designers.

The conventional way of exhibition design for its designers should follow the steps of theme determination, content design, exhibits selection and form design. Exhibition

Y. Wang et al. (Eds.): IGTA 2017, CCIS 757, pp. 157–167, 2018.
https://doi.org/10.1007/978-981-10-7389-2_16

design is a collaborative process, integrating the disciplines of architecture, landscape architecture, graphic design, audiovisual engineering, digital media, lighting, interior design, and content development to develop an audience experience [5]. If there appears a mistake in this process, it may be modified from the ground up because one designer doesn't know the whole information or can't deal with whole complex information. At the same time, the exhibition designer could not know the real-time effects of his design so that he is not sure whether his design is suitable.

Therefore, we develop a computer-aided-design system for museum exhibition based on virtual reality [6] that helps exhibition designers to design a new exhibition more efficiently. The goal of our system is to improve designers' awareness of the 3D space structure and the design effects in the process of exhibition design. We integrate and visualize the multiple exhibition information in 3D environment with the purpose of supporting the collaborative process. We also evaluated the practical value and visual design of the proposed system based on an informal user study. And the experimental results show that the proposed design system can provide real-time design effects and high immersion.

2   Related Work

2.1   Exhibition Design

In recent years, various researchers and exhibition designers have put forward certain innovative design concepts and methodologies.

Faxing Chen et al. [7] proposed a novel virtual exhibition design concept composed of user-generated 3D exhibition contents and non-professional design that designers can build 3D models for exhibition products with their platform. Arief Syaichu Rohman et al. [8] proposed an interactive cyber exhibition on virtual museum by providing three key features: theme based exhibition, visualization [9] of the collections, and information of the collections. Their study indicated that users can get different and more interactive experiences compared to the actual exhibition in the physical museum. Angelo Chianese et al. [4] focused specifically to design an IoT (Internet of Things) architecture that could support the designing of a smart museum. Chien-Hsin Hsueh et al. [10] proposed an exhibition design framework of interactive visualization and data exploration, which combined Multiple External Representations (MERs) and tangible user interfaces (TUIs) to provide a complementary representation of the marine animal behaviors' data. Chairi Kiourt et al. [11] presented an innovative fully dynamic Web-based virtual museum framework named DynaMus that relied entirely on users' creativity. This system could connect to popular repositories, such as Europeana and Google, and retrieve content that could be used in creating virtual exhibitions. Dimitrios Charitos et al. [2] presented an approach towards designing and developing a virtual reality museum comprising ten different museums.

These design concepts and methodologies can help to guide the collaborative design process for utilizing multidisciplinary information. However, the visualization of objects and the 3D real-time design effects for exhibition designers [12] during the design process are ignored.

2.2 Virtual Museum Design

The digital age has drastically changed the traditional definition of the museum [13]. Immersive technologies such as virtual reality and augmented reality [14] have a clear potential to support the experiencing of museum by the large public. Some museums have started to digitalize many types of information concerning their own collections and to construct a virtual museum by using sensing and information technologies [15]. Michela Mortara et al. [14] have divided the serious games which are utilized in museums or cultural heritages into three categories: cultural awareness, historical reconstruction and heritage awareness.

Cultural awareness is focused on the immaterial heritage. Wenzhi Chen et al. [16] applied animations, computer games, and VR to China's famous Jing-Hang Grand Canal and this system could vividly show the canal's history and introduce humanistic and scientific knowledge related to the canal.

Historical reconstruction means the serious games are designed for reconstructing the historical period, historical events or wars for their irreversible features. Ekaterina Razuvalova et al. [17] presented cultural and historical monuments of the Middle Volga. The users became part of virtual reality and they could try different roles and do different actions they could not do in reality. Dimitrios Christopoulos et al. [18] described a virtual reality exhibit implemented for the museum of Thermopylae located at the site of the original battle. They utilized storytelling techniques and principles of modern video games to disseminate historical knowledge about the battle and the associated legends. Gaitatzes et al. [19] presented the virtual reality applications about the Olympic Games in ancient Greece. These applications were made to recreate the feeling of the games and helped the user/spectator be an interacting part of the edutainment activity.

Heritage awareness is widely used in museum because the virtual museum can be used as a reference version and allows the access of fragile, closed, destroyed, stolen or remote sites [20]. Vaz et al. [21] presented the design of a tangible user interface to enhance accessibility in geological exhibitions, specifically for the case of visitors with visual impairments. And the results showed that the interaction with the interface pleased the visitors and that it had application space within geological exhibitions. Fernández-Palacios et al. [22] employed Oculus Rift (VR visualization headset) and Kinect (depth sensor for user interaction) to create a complex 3D archaeological scene. Archaeological sites or fragile environments with forbidden access due the preservation policies could also be virtually visited and inspected.

According to these applications of virtual museum we can find that they are focused on education and exhibition for the museum visitors. But improving museum designers' awareness of the 3D space structure and the design effects in the process of exhibition design also should be paid attention to. Therefore, we propose a computer-aided-design system for museum exhibition based on virtual reality. The aim of the proposed system is to provide exhibition designers new experiences in an interactive and immersive way.

3   Design and Implementation

3.1   Requirements Analysis

To implement the computer-aided-design system for museum exhibition, requirements analysis should be implemented first.

- The core of an exhibition is the exhibits. We reconstruct the reality-based digital models through laser scanning [23] and photogrammetry [23] (Fig. 1). But the created models are composed by millions of polygons and high-resolution images, which are not benefited to interact or upload in the virtual world. To deal with these problems, the models are optimized by reducing their faces but kept their high-resolution images. In our system, we digitalize 200 collections based on Changsha Museum and generate their 3D virtual models' data set.

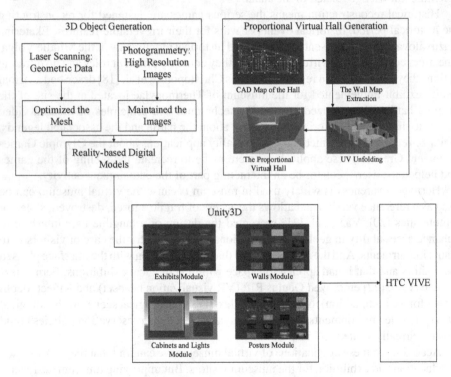

Fig. 1. Flowchart of the proposed system

- The proposed system is used to help the exhibition designers to realize the form design. The virtual scenes are arranged according to the exhibition halls in the physical world. We generate the 3D virtual exhibition halls by using the tool in 3ds Max with the halls' CAD maps (Fig. 1). Thus, the halls' models are in accordance with the real proportion. To match the virtual models of the exhibits, we build the exhibition halls' models of Changsha Museum, China.

- Form design for an exhibition is a collaborative process, integrating the disciplines of architecture, landscape architecture, graphic design, audiovisual engineering, digital media, lighting, interior design, and content development to develop an audience experience. The proposed system combines part of these to improve designers' efficiency, such as graphic design, lighting design, interior design and exhibits arrangement.

3.2 VR Implementation and Devices

The proposed system is built using the Unity3D game engine. Unity3D [22] is a commercial game engine application that allows fast implementation time and the management of externa devices for the integration of the user's movements and cooperation. And a HTC VIVE is used as the hardware. HTC VIVE is a VR head-mounted display (HMD) to provide 360° virtual and immersive environment, and it also has two controllers to make the users interact with virtual objects much naturally and conveniently. Compared to other HMDs, the HTC VIVE has 2160×1200 resolution across two screens, 90 Hz refresh rate, 110° field of view and two Lighthouses to track position [13], which make the HTC VIVE be suitable for our system. On the other hand, the HTC VIVE allows the user to move and walk in the physical world to enhance immersion and interaction with a 3 m × 4 m activity space instead of standing or sitting in one place.

3.3 Virtual Contents Design

In the proposed virtual system, a virtual exhibition hall is reconstructed and decorated with exhibits, posters, lights and cabinets. The user can visit the virtual exhibition in the similar way as a real exhibition. And the user can modify and decorate everything in the hall. Figure 2 shows the virtual exhibition hall.

- Arrangement of the exhibits is most important because the exhibits will determine which poster and text-introduction should be arranged, and what type of the cabinet and light should be used. The proposed system designs the arrangement of the exhibits as the main operation. The user can press the Application Menu key to trigger the Exhibits User Interface (UI), and this UI is bounded with the user's controller, when user's hand moves or rotates, the UI will follow the hand to move and rotate. On the Exhibits UI, there are many buttons to provide user to select which exhibit he wants to arrange. The user can place an exhibit everywhere after he selects it, following a cabinet and lights will occur with the placed exhibit.
- Decoration of the walls with different textures is also needed. The user can select a wall in the exhibition hall using the controller, and the Wall User Interface (UI) will occur bounded with the user's controller. The user selects a texture and the wall will be decorated with this selection. In the same way, the posters also can be arranged and decorated.

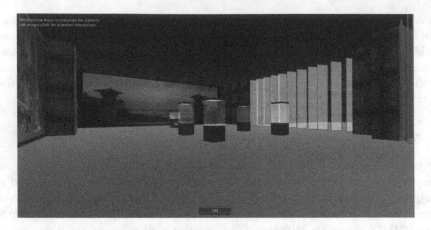

Fig. 2. Virtual exhibition hall

During the design process, the user could get the real-time effects. If the user doesn't satisfy with the design, he can destroy the unpleasant objects and arrange them again. The proposed system provides an initial scene which is a simple exhibition hall without any decorations and exhibits. It is popular with the users who want to design an exhibition completely according to their will.

4   Experimental Results

In this section, we evaluated the practical value and visual design of the proposed system based on an informal user study.

This study was based on a task-based [9] comparison between a conventional PC-based VR interactive system and our proposed HMD-based VR interactive system. Both interactive systems had the same virtual environments and tasks except their peripherals. In the PC-based VR interactive system, a monitor displayed the virtual scenes and the mouse and keyboard helped to finish the whole interaction. Differently, in the HMD-based system, the HTC VIVE was used to provide 360-degree virtual environment with its controllers providing the interaction.

As shown in Fig. 3, the tasks were to modify the posters, to decorate the walls and to arrange some exhibits in the virtual museum. The study was conducted by 16 users aged 22–34 (9 females and 7 males), and all users were asked to finish these 8 tasks. These 16 users were divided into two sample groups, one was asked to finish the PC-based version first and the other was done the HMD-based version first.

These results were examined based on the time spent for finishing each task. Figure 4 shows the average time users spent for each task. It indicated that the users were faster with conventional PC devices (the blue bars) than the HMD (the red bars), but there was not a significant difference for the average time. According to the users' interviews, we found the reasons were:

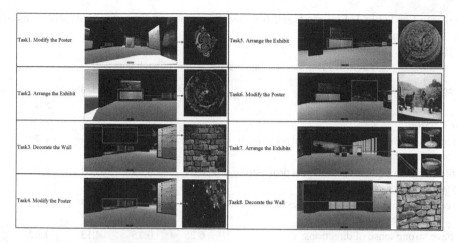

Fig. 3. The 8 tasks which the user was asked to finish.

- The users didn't very familiar with the interactive ways using HMD compare to the mouse or keyboard.
- The users needed to cooperate the virtual objects which had the same proportion with the real objects in physical world, it increased the difficulty of interaction.
- In HMD-based virtual environment, the users had the first-person perspective and it's easy to lose the sense of directions.

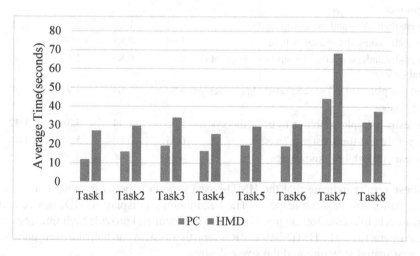

Fig. 4. Average time users spent for each task. The blue bars show the PC-based VR system and the red bars show the HMD-based VR system. (Color figure online)

After finishing the tasks, the users were given the questionnaires regarding their impression on the compared systems. The questionnaire has 16 questions that are to be evaluated using 7-point Likert scale (ranging from 1 which means "strongly disagree" to 7 which means "strongly agree") [24]. The questionnaire items and the results are presented in Table 1. Figures 5 and 6 shows the means and the standard deviations of each question.

Table 1. The means, standard deviations of each question.

Items	HMD-based		PC-based	
	M	SD	M	SD
Immersion				
I feel the 3D simulated environment provided by this system is realistic	6.25	0.89	4.25	1.79
I feel the 3D simulated environment provided by this system is immersive	6.69	0.85	3.63	1.29
I feel that the 3D environment makes me concentrate more while designing	6.56	0.61	5.13	1.22
I have strong sense of directions	6.25	0.75	4.13	1.62
Interaction				
I can easily observe 3D objects from various perspectives	6.31	0.68	4.13	1.73
I can easily move in the virtual scene	5.63	1.22	5.75	1.09
I can easily arrange the virtual objects	5.56	1.12	5.56	1.22
I can easily change the materials of the virtual objects	5.56	1.06	5.38	1.41
I can easily use the UI (User Interface)	5.63	0.93	5.50	1.46
Imagination				
I can easily understand the design tasks	5.75	1.20	5.94	1.20
I can easily know the spatial structure	5.94	0.83	4.06	1.71
I can easily understand the size and the shape of the virtual objects	5.81	0.88	4.13	1.69
I must use plenty of 3D space knowledge to design	3.94	1.64	3.94	1.60
Aided Design				
I can design a simple exhibition by using this system	5.25	1.44	5.38	1.32
I can get the real-time design effects	6.31	0.68	5.25	1.48
I can learn the exhibits' knowledge	4.44	1.46	3.75	1.35

These results indicate that the HMD-based version is better than the conventional PC-based version in some respects. The head-mounted display (HMD) device and its controllers help create 360-degree virtual environment and provide high immersive and natural interaction. The HMD-based VR interactive system can help the users gain better senses of spatial structure and the space design.

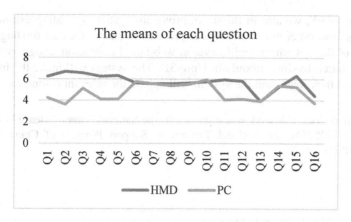

Fig. 5. The means of each question.

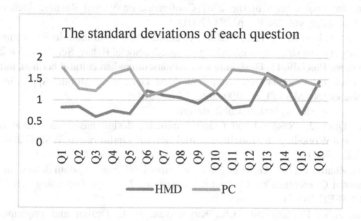

Fig. 6. The standard deviations of each question.

5 Conclusions

We propose a computer-aided-design system based on virtual reality for museum exhibition that helps designers to design a new exhibition more efficiently. The proposed system integrates multiple information and the users can get more interactive and visual experiences compared to the conventional way of exhibition design. We selected to work with a data set of 200 collections based on Changsha Museum, China. The proposed system helps to improve designers' awareness of the 3D space structure and the design effects in the process of exhibition design. We integrate and visualize the multiple exhibition information in 3D environment with the purpose of supporting the collaborative process. We evaluate the practical value and visual design of the proposed system based on an informal user study. And the experimental results show that the proposed design system can provide real-time design effects and high immersion.

As future work, we aim to further improve our system by adding exhibition halls and exhibits from other museums. And to prevent the size of the data too huge to affect the quality of the system, we will develop web-based exhibition design system using dynamic resource loading module in Unity3D. The system will make the user decide which models they need, and the system will upload the relevant resources.

Acknowledgements. This work was supported by the National Natural Science Foundation of China (No. U1605254), the National Technology Support Program of China (Grant No. 2015BAK01B05).

References

1. https://en.wikipedia.org/wiki/Museum
2. Charitos, D., Lepouras, G., Vassilakis, C., et al.: Designing a virtual museum within a museum. In: Proceedings of the 2001 Conference on Virtual Reality, Archeology, and Cultural Heritage, vol. 28(30), p. 284 (2001)
3. Ahmad, S., Abbas, M.Y., Taib, M.Z.M., et al.: Museum exhibition design: communication of meaning and the shaping of knowledge. Procedia-Social Behav. Sci. **153**, 254–265 (2014)
4. Chianese, A., Piccialli, F.: Designing a smart museum: when cultural heritage joins IoT. In: 2014 Eighth International Conference on Next Generation Mobile Apps, Services and Technologies (NGMAST), pp. 300–306. IEEE (2014)
5. https://en.wikipedia.org/wiki/Exhibit_design
6. Liu, X., Qiao, J.: Research on Chinese museum design based on virtual reality. In: International Workshop on Modelling, Simulation and Optimization, WMSO 2008, pp. 372–374. IEEE (2008)
7. Chen, F., Zhang, L., Lin, G.: Web 2.0 based virtual exhibition system design. In: 2012 2nd International Conference on Computer Science and Network Technology (ICCSNT), pp. 297–301. IEEE (2012)
8. Rohman, A.S., Prihatmanto, A.S., Kayungyun, R.D.: Design and implementation of interactive cyber exhibition on virtual museum of Indonesia. In: 2012 International Conference on System Engineering and Technology (ICSET), pp. 1–6. IEEE (2012)
9. Tanahashi, Y., Ma, K.L.: OnMyWay: a task-oriented visualization and interface design for planning road trip itinerary. In: International Conference on Cyberworlds, pp. 199–205 (2013)
10. Hsueh, C.H., Chu, J., Ma, K.L., et al.: Fostering comparisons: designing an interactive exhibit that visualizes marine animal behaviors. In: Pacific Visualization Symposium (PacificVis) 2016, pp. 259–263. IEEE (2016)
11. Kiourt, C., Koutsoudis, A., Pavlidis, G.: DynaMus: a fully dynamic 3D virtual Museum framework. J. Cult. Heritage **22**, 984–991 (2016)
12. Back, M., Gold, R., Balsamo, A., et al.: Designing innovative reading experiences for a museum exhibition. Computer **34**(1), 80–87 (2001)
13. Choi, H.S., Kim, S.H.: A content service deployment plan for metaverse museum exhibitions —centering on the combination of beacons and HMDs. Int. J. Inform. Manage. **37**(1), 1519–1527 (2016)
14. Mortara, M., Catalano, C.E., Bellotti, F., et al.: Learning cultural heritage by serious games. J. Cult. Heritage **15**(3), 318–325 (2014)
15. Tanikawa, T., Ando, M., Wang, Y., et al.: A case study of museum exhibition - historical learning in Copan ruins of Mayan civilization. In: Virtual Reality, Proceedings, pp. 257–258. IEEE, 2004

16. Chen, W., Zhang, M., Pan, Z., et al.: Animations, games, and virtual reality for the Jing-Hang Grand Canal. IEEE Comput. Graphics Appl. **30**(3), 84 (2010)
17. Mendívil, E.G., Flores, P.G.R., Gutiérrez, J.M., et al.: Virtual reconstruction of cultural and historical monuments of the Middle Volga. Procedia Comput. Sci. **75**, 129–136 (2015)
18. Christopoulos, D., Mavridis, P., Andreadis, A., et al.: Using virtual environments to tell the story: "The Battle of Thermopylae". In: Third International Conference on Games and Virtual Worlds for Serious Applications, pp. 84–91. IEEE Xplore (2011)
19. Gaitatzes, A., Christopoulos, D., Papaioannou, G.: The ancient olympic games: being part of the experience. In: International Conference on Virtual Reality, Archaeology and Intelligent Cultural Heritage, pp. 19–28. Eurographics Association (2004)
20. Awang, N., Yaakub, A.R., Othman, Z.: Assessing user acceptance towards virtual museum: the case in Kedah State Museum, Malaysia. In: International Conference on Computer Graphics, Imaging and Visualization, pp. 158–163. IEEE (2009)
21. Vaz, R.I.F., Fernandes, P.O., Veiga, A.C.R.: Proposal of a tangible user interface to enhance accessibility in geological exhibitions and the experience of museum visitors. Procedia Comput. Sci. **100**, 832–839 (2016)
22. Fernández-Palacios, B.J., Morabito, D., Remondino, F.: Access to complex reality-based 3D models using virtual reality solutions. J. Cult. Heritage **23**, 40–48 (2016)
23. Guidi, G., Russo, M., Angheleddu, D.: 3D survey and virtual reconstruction of archeological sites. Digital Appl. Archaeol. Cult. Heritage **1**(2), 55–69 (2014)
24. Huang, H.M., Rauch, U., Liaw, S.S.: Investigating learners' attitudes toward virtual reality learning environments: based on a constructivist approach. Comput. Educ. **55**(3), 1171–1182 (2010)

Research on Waves Simulation of the Virtual Sea Battled-Field

Shanlai Jin, Yaowu Wu, and Peng Jia$^{(\boxtimes)}$

Logistics Academy, Beijing, China
jiapeng1018@163.com

Abstract. Describing the dynamically waving characteristic is one of the key points in simulation of sea battled-field environment. The waving phenomenon generated by underwater explosion in sea battled-field is simulated in this paper. The state of art of waves modeling technology is introduced. The method based on wave spectrum is employed to model ocean waves in natural situation. The wave caused by the falling of water column generated by underwater explosion is modeled from the viewpoint of energy transforming. The Gerstner wave and Sine wave are used to describe the shape of the wave. The simulation results of waving phenomena generated by single explosion source and multi-explosion sources are presented. The proposed method and results enrich the means of wave simulation in sea battled-field environment.

Keywords: Energy transforming
Water waves generated by underwater explosion · Wave spectrum
Wave superposition · Sea battled-field simulation

1 Introduction

The simulation of ocean wave, which played an important assistant role in various activities of the sea battlefield, is the main component of virtual sea battlefield environment. At present, the simulation of ocean wave in sea battlefield is mainly concentrated in two aspects.

On the one hand, the simulation of ocean wave is about the ocean's surface in natural situations. There are four kinds of methods about ocean wave modeling [1]. Modeling method based on the geometric shape, including bump mapping, Stocks mode, Peachy model and Gerstner model. Such as, Tong and Wang simulated water waves which caused by raindrops and ripples which caused by gentle breeze through using Peachy model [2]. Modeling method based on dynamic model, including particle system and cellular automaton. Such as, Based on the theory of small amplitude wave and cellular automaton model, Yang et al. applied the idea of a neighborhood's spread to do dynamic modeling of ocean waves [3]. Modeling method based on the physics, which is essentially based on Navier-Stockes equations in fluid mechanics. Such as, Chen et al. used a numerical iterative method to work out simplified two-dimensional navier-stokes equations [4]. Stam presented a kind of stable fluid's method to solve the three-dimensional Navier-Stockes equations, and the method make solution of equations to be unconditionally stabilized. Modeling method based on ocean wave spectrum, which is based on the results of the Marine observation ocean wave spectrum, apply the inversion method of appropriate ocean waves spectrum to simulate the wave. There are 2 kinds of common inversion methods including linear filtering method and linear superposition addition [5]. Such as, From this respect of the frequency domain Tessendorf [6] used the FFT method to complete a rapid inversion of ocean wave spectrum, which can simulate discretionarily large sea area by using Fourier transform's periodicity [6].

Among four methods, modeling method based on the geometric shape is simpler than others, but the scene which is generated by this method is lack of authenticity and full of artificial mark. Modeling method based on dynamic model simulates ocean waves from the angle of the motion. It does not simply pursue similarity in shape but it is not fully compliant with physics laws. Modeling method based on the physics can realistically simulate all kinds of natural phenomenon. But the complexity of the method is high. It needs a large amount of calculation. So it is not convenient for real-time display and interaction. Modeling method based on ocean wave spectrum [14] is easy to widely used due to its clearly physical concept and more achievable algorithm. Meanwhile, the parameters which are obtained by a long time ocean observation possess certain truth.

On the other hand, the simulation of ocean wave is about the track of warship and the exploding of water column. At present there are two common methods including dynamic texture mapping technology and particle system modeling [7]. Dynamic texture mapping technology, according to required expressive special effects which begin texture mapping by using a series of two-dimensional image. Meanwhile according to the exchange of time and space, it dynamically adjusts on the texture image and texture coordinates, in order to achieve the required dynamic effect. Particle system modeling adopts a lot of randomness of particle elements to describe irregular fuzzy scene in nature. At different times any particle in the system has different size, color, transparency, direction and speed of movement etc. in attributes. Particle system can present a complicated natural or man-made phenomenon by a small amount of particle's combination. Such as Li et al. used particle system to generate the head waves and wakes of warship [8]. Lu Zhihui accomplished the track of warship and the special effects of water column's exploding through particle system [7]. Lasse Staff Jensen [9] adopted dynamic texture mapping technology to achieve the effect of the surface's foam, which labeled foam's texture across all the sea surface. Based on Lasse Staff Jensen method, Liu Zhendong [10] advanced the new method based on Gauss curvature texture simulation method, and use particle system to simulate the generation mechanism of spray.

However, in the sea battlefield environment the research about wave superposition between waves caused by the falling of water column of ammunition explosion under gravity and ocean waves in natural situations is less. Based on the own properties of the sea battlefield environment, this paper first studied on the property of waves in natural situations and waves caused by the falling of water column of ammunition explosion under gravity. Second, this paper experimented on wave's superposition between waves caused by the falling of water column of multi-ammunition explosion and waves in natural situations. In the end, it obtains the relevant analytical data and simulation results.

2 Waves Modeling Algorithm

The wave simulation based on sea battle-field environment not only has the common properties with wave in nature situation, but also has its own properties. When ammunition explodes under the water, the explosion energy releases quickly. It makes the surrounded pressure to increase immediately. Under the huge impact surrounded water molecules quickly spread, form the shock wave [7]. The wave in the water which speeds faster than the sound speed spreads to the free surface. It forms small amplitude fluctuations whose radius is a certain length and whose center is explosive source. The ocean surface is exploded, then the water column roll over. Finally, the water column by gravity will fall back into the water and the surface creates the transmission of ocean waves.

Because there have been a large number of papers and data, which studied shock wave caused by ammunition explosion under water. Therefore, other two main problems are studied in this section. First, the mathematical model of ocean waves in natural situations is studied. Second, the transmission properties and mathematical model of waves caused by the falling of water column of ammunition explosion is studied.

2.1   The Mathematical Model of Ocean Waves in Natural Situations

Through the last section of analysis for ocean wave modeling technology, it is concluded that the modeling method based on ocean wave spectrum is easy to realize ocean waves in natural situations. In this situation, FFT method based on Phillips spectrum is adopted, which is proposed by Tessendorf [6]. Some improvements are done in the experiments of spectrum formula.

Statistical Models and Phillips Spectrum. Oceanographers got some statistical model of water body from empirical observation. These models can describe the water wave spectrum in different environment. In statistical models, the wave height $h(x, t)$ is a random variable. It is related to the horizontal position and time. On the height field, generally the fast Fourier transform (FFT) is used, and the spatial domain information is calculated by frequency domain from statistical model.

Wave height field based on FFT expresses height $h(x, t)$ at horizontal position $x = (x, z)$ as the sum of sine function with a series of complicated, amplitudes changed over time:

$$h(x, t) = \sum_{\vec{k}} \tilde{h}(\vec{k}, t) \cdot \exp(i\vec{k} \cdot X) \tag{1}$$

where $\vec{k}$ is a two-dimensional vector (k_x, k_z). It represents the angular velocity of each harmonic component in the Fourier decomposition. $k_x = 2\pi n/L_x, k_z = 2\pi m/L_z$, n and m are integers. Meanwhile, Constraint condition are $-N/2 \leq n < N/2$, $-M/2 \leq m < M/2$. L_x and L_z are dimensions of the two directions in a generating wave height filed area. N and M is number of discrete height values generated in the two directions.

Oceanographic observation results show that Eq. 1 can well express the ocean's surface height field driven by a wind. According to statistical methods, the sea-buoy, photos, and radar monitoring data were analyzed. So marine scientists found that the spectrum coefficient $\tilde{h}(\vec{k}, t)$ of wave height is in line with stable and independent normal distribution by:

$$P_h(\vec{k}) \approx |\tilde{h}^*(\vec{k}, t)|^2 \qquad (2)$$

where $|\tilde{h}^*(\vec{k}, t)|^2 = |\tilde{h}(\vec{k}, t)|^2$, So $P_h(\vec{k}) \approx |\tilde{h}(\vec{k}, t)|^2$, and it is also the energy spectrum of surface height. There are some semi-empirical model to $P_h(\vec{k})$. Phillips spectrum is often used in wave model driven by a wind, as follows:

$$P_h(\vec{k}) = A \frac{\exp(-1/(|\vec{k}|L)^2)}{|\vec{k}|^4} |\vec{k} \cdot \vec{\omega}|^2 \qquad (3)$$

where $L = V^2/g$ is the largest waves under continuous wind of speed v, g is gravitational acceleration, $\vec{\omega}$ is wind's direction, Λ is a constant which can adjust the value of energy spectrum. The $|\vec{k} \cdot \vec{\omega}|^2$ is used to eliminate waves which are orthogonal to the direction of wind. Phillips spectrum is simpler. But when $|\vec{k}|$ is larger, the model has poor convergence properties. A simple correction method is to inhibit the wave height and make the wave height $1 \ll L$. So Phillips spectrum is multiplied by $\exp(-1/(|\vec{k}|L)^2)$.

The Coefficient of Spectrum. The spectrum coefficient $\tilde{h}(\vec{k}, t)$ of wave height is in line with normal distribution. $P_h(\vec{k}) \approx |\tilde{h}^*(\vec{k}, t)|^2 = |\tilde{h}(\vec{k}, t)|^2$. So to t = 0, $\tilde{h}(\vec{k}, t)$ by:

$$\tilde{h}(\vec{k}, 0) = 1/\sqrt{2}(\xi_1^2 + i\xi_2^2)\sqrt{P_h(\vec{k})} \qquad (4)$$

where ξ_1 and ξ_2 are random number, which meet the standard normal distribution, with mean 0 and deviation 1. So

$$\left|\tilde{h}(\vec{k}, 0)\right|^2 = (\frac{\xi_1^2 + \xi_2^2}{2})P_h(\vec{k}) \approx P_h(\vec{k}) \qquad (5)$$

In order to simulate the wave propagation effect, the spectrum coefficient of moment t is changed according to a certain acceleration. According to the Tessendorf [6] method, suppose the angular velocity $\omega(\vec{k})$, so

$$\tilde{h}(\vec{k}, t) = \tilde{h}(\vec{k}, 0) \exp\{i\omega(\vec{k})\} + \tilde{h}^*(-\vec{k}, 0) \exp\{-i\omega(\vec{k})\} \qquad (6)$$

Finally, in order to get spectrum coefficient, the equation of angular velocity $\omega(\vec{k})$ is needed to know. To deep sea area, the classic formula is

$$\omega^2(\vec{k}) = gk \tag{7}$$

where g is the gravitational acceleration. So, the spectrum coefficient can be gotten. Finally, the wave height information can be restored by IFFT (inverse fast Fourier transformation).

Choppy Waves. Waves generated by Phillips spectrum are tend to be rounded, but sometimes even in good weather the wave crest can be sharp. In order to show more real effect, choppy waves can be realized by making vertexes of the surface mesh to do certain horizontal displacement.

To the value of horizontal displacement, Tessendorf [6] gave a good quantitative formula:

$$D(\mathrm{x},t) = \sum_{\vec{k}} -i\frac{\vec{k}}{|\vec{k}|}\tilde{h}(\vec{k},t) \cdot \exp(i\vec{k} \cdot \mathrm{x}) \tag{8}$$

where $D(\mathrm{x},t)$ is horizontal displacement of one point, which is changed over time. The other parameters are in accordance with Eq. 1. So now x is $\mathrm{x} + \lambda D(\mathrm{x,t})$, but height is still $h(\mathrm{x},t)$. λ is an identified constant, which is used to adjust the horizontal shaking degree of one point. By adjusting the value of λ, all different kinds of choppy waves are simulated.

2.2 The Mathematical Model of Waves Caused by the Falling of Water Column of Ammunition Explosion

The wave caused by the falling of water column after underwater explosion has the characteristics of gravity waves. This section provides calculation of wavelength and wave height, together with the wave equation.

Calculation of Wavelength and Wave Height. As shown in Fig. 1(a), assume that the water column caused by an underwater explosion is a cylinder without air bubbles. Denote the radius of the cylinder as r and the height of the cylinder as h_0. Then the gravitational potential energy of the cylinder can be calculated as:

$$E_0 = \rho\pi r^2 h_0 gh_0/2 \tag{9}$$

where ρ is the density of water, g is the acceleration of gravity.

The water column falls down and generates a wave propagating outwards, as shown in Fig. 1(b). The wavelength is denoted as λ, the wave height is h_1 and wave velocity is c. As can be seen in Fig. 2, the potential energy of the wave can be calculated as:

$$E_p = 2\pi(r+0.5\lambda) \times \frac{1}{2}\int_0^\lambda \rho gz^2 dx = \frac{\pi(r+0.5\lambda)}{8}\rho gh_1^2\lambda \tag{10}$$

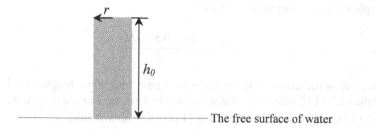

(a) The water column caused by underwater explosion

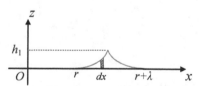

(b) The wave propagating outwards

Fig. 1. The sketch map of the water column and wave caused by underwater explosion

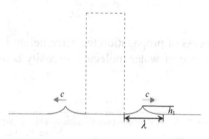

Fig. 2. The sketch map of calculating the potential energy of the wave. The coordinate origin is the circle center of the water column bottom surface. The vertical upwards direction is the positive direction of z axis.

The kinetic energy of the wave is equal to its potential energy [11], namely $E_k = E_p$. The gravitational potential energy of the cylinder is converted into the kinetic energy and potential energy of the wave, and then we have:

$$E_0 = \rho \pi r^2 h_0 g h_0 / 2$$
$$= E_k + E_p$$
$$= 2 \times \frac{\pi (r + 0.5\lambda)}{8} \rho g h_1^2 \lambda \qquad (11)$$

Simplify Eq. 11, and then we have:

$$r^2 h_0^2 = \frac{(r + 0.5\lambda)\lambda h_1^2}{2} \tag{12}$$

There are some constraints on the wavelength and wave height: h_1/λ cannot be greater than 1/7 [11], otherwise, the wave will be tattered. For the deep water wave, the following inequality should be satisfied [11]: $\frac{\lambda}{2} \leq$ water depth.

Besides, the velocity of deep water wave is related to its wavelength [11]:

$$c = \sqrt{\frac{g\lambda}{2\pi}} \tag{13}$$

And during the process of propagation the wave height is decreasing along with the energy attenuation because of water molecule viscosity consuming, air resistance and so on.

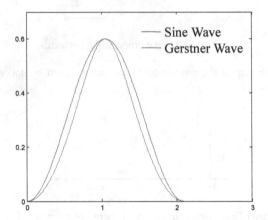

Fig. 3. Gerstner wave and Sine wave

Wave Equation. We select two types of wave equations to describe the shape of wave generated by the falling of water column after underwater explosion: Sine wave and Gerstner wave (Fig. 3). Gerstner waves describe the real shape of ocean wave. If a point on the free surface is labeled $X_0 = [x_0, z_0]$ and its undisturbed height is $y_0 = 0$. When a single wave with amplitude A passed by, the height of point on the surface at time t can be calculated as [6]:

$$\begin{aligned} x &= x_0 - (K/k)A\sin(kx_0 - \omega t) \\ y &= A\cos(kx_0 - \omega t) \end{aligned} \tag{14}$$

where K is the wave vector. K has magnitude k: $k = 2\pi/\lambda$ (λ is the wavelength). Comparing to Sine wave, the wave crest of Gerstner wave is sharper and the trough of wave is smoother.

Analysis of Wave Superposition. When there are more than one explosion sources, the phenomenon of wave superposition will appear after the waves generated by the falling of water columns after underwater explosions approaching each other. In the area of wave superposition, the wave height is summation of height of free water surface and wave heights generated by each explosion source.

3 Simulation Results

This section first presents the computing result of wavelength and wave height of the wave generated by the falling of water column after underwater explosion. Then the 2D and 3D simulation results of wave superposition when there exit multi-explosion sources are provided.

3.1 Calculation of Wavelength and Wave Height

The values of r and h_0 are set through empirical estimation. The wavelength and wave height satisfy the constraints discussed in Sect. 2.2. Assume $\lambda = 10h_1$ and some computing results are listed in Table 1.

Table 1. Computing results of wavelength and wave height

Name	Value (meter)												
r	0.5	0.6	0.7	0.8	0.9	1.0	1.1	1.2	1.3	1.4	1.5	1.6	1.7
h_0	1.0	1.2	1.4	1.6	1.8	2.0	2.2	2.4	2.6	2.8	3.0	3.2	3.4
λ	2.9	3.5	4.1	4.7	5.3	5.9	6.5	7.1	7.6	8.2	8.8	9.4	10.0
h_1	0.29	0.35	0.41	0.47	0.53	0.59	0.65	0.71	0.76	0.82	0.88	0.94	1.00

3.2 Wave Superposition When There Exit Multi-explosion Sources

In the real sea battled-field, there are more than one explosion source, and the waves caused by different explosion sources will mutually superimpose during propagation. The wave generated by the falling of water column after underwater explosion can be described by Sine wave or Gerstner wave. In the 3D simulation, the WAFO Matlab toolbox [12, 13] is employed to generate the free sea surface based on Phillips spectrum method.

The 2D and 3D simulation results of waves generated by one single explosion source and two explosion sources are shown in Table 2. The location of explosion source is randomly set. As can be seen, during the process of propagation the wave height is decreasing along with the energy attenuation because of water molecule viscosity consuming, air resistance, etc.

Table 2. The 2D and 3D simulation results of waves generated by one single explosion source and two explosion sources

Description	2D result	3D result
Single explosion source	$\lambda = 6$, $h_1 = 0.6$	
Two explosion sources	$\lambda_1 = 6$, $\lambda_2 = 3$	

The 3D simulation result of wave superposition when there exist three explosion sources are shown in Fig. 4. The bright part in the figure is the superposition of three wave crests, which means superimposing of multi-wave crests will generate large wave fluctuation.

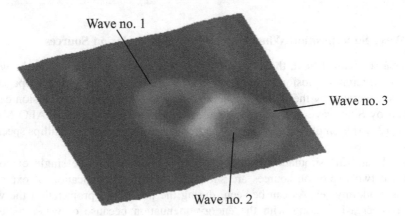

Wave no. 1

Wave no. 3

Wave no. 2

Fig. 4. The 3D simulation result of wave superposition when there exist three explosion sources.

4 Conclusions

The modeling method of the wave caused by the falling of water column generated by underwater explosion is proposed in this paper. The Gerstner wave and Sine wave are employed to describe the shape of the wave. The simulation results of waving phenomena generated by single explosion source and multi-explosion sources are presented. The proposed results have certain reference significance in furthering the research on simulation of the dynamically waving properties of sea battled-field. The future work includes: performing experiments of underwater explosion to collect and analyze the data of generated water column and wave, investigating the simulation of waving phenomena caused by underwater explosion under high-wave-level environment, etc.

References

1. Whitted, T.: An improved illumination model for shaded display. Commun. ACM **23**(6), 343–349 (1980)
2. Tong, R., Wang, G.: Waves modeling for computer animation. Chin. J. Comput. **19**(8), 594–599 (1996). (in Chinese)
3. Yang, H., Hu, S., Sun, J.: A new algorithm for water wave animation. Chin. J. Comput. **25** (6), 612–617 (2002). (in Chinese)
4. Chen, J., Lobo, N.: Toward interactive rate simulation of fluids with moving obstacles using Navier Stokes equations. Garph. Models Image Process. **57**(2), 107–116 (1995)
5. Liu, J.: Reaearch on Algorithm for Simulating Ocean Waves Based on Spectrum of Ocean Waves. Hunan University, Hunan (2005). (in Chinese)
6. Tessendorf, J.: Simulating ocean water. In: Proceeding of ACM SIGGRAPH 1999, pp. 348–367. ACM Press, New York (1999)
7. Lu, Z.: The Technology Research of Modeling and Rendering Ocean Scene in the Large-scale Virtual Battlefield Environment. National University of Defense Technology, Hunan (2005). (in Chinese)
8. Li, F., Li, S., Wang, W.: Research and implementation of generating technology of ship wakes. Softw. Eng. Appl. **3**, 121–130 (2014). (in Chinese)
9. Jensen, L., Golias, R.: Deep-water animation and rendering. In: Proceedings of Game Developer's Conference (2001)
10. Liu, Z.: Hybrid Real-Time Rendering of Large-Scale Ocean Scene. Zhejiang University, Zhejiang (2015). (in Chinese)
11. Shi, M.: Physical Oceanography. Shandong Education Press, Jinan (2004). (in Chinese)
12. WAFO-a Matlab toolbox for analysis of random waves and loads. Tutorial for WAFO version 2.5. Lund, March 2011
13. WAFO Version 2.5. http://code.google.com/p/wafo/
14. Ding, S.: Research on Generating Technique of Virtual Ocean Environment and Special Effects. Harbin Engineering University, Heilongjiang (2008). (in Chinese)

Deep-Patch Orientation Network for Aircraft Detection in Aerial Images

Ali Maher, Jiaxin Gu, and Baochang Zhang[✉]

School of Automation Science and Electrical Engineer, Beihang University, Beijing, China
ali_mtc@hotmail.com, jxgu1016@gmail.com, bczhang@buaa.edu.cn

Abstract. The aerial target detection and recognition are very challenging due to large appearance, lighting and orientation variations. We propose a Deep-patch Orientation Network *(DON)* method, which is general and can learn the encoded orientation information based on any off the-shelf deep detection framework, e.g., *Faster-RCNN* and *YOLO*, and result into higher performance in airplane target detection and classification tasks. Most existing methods neglected the orientation information, which in DON is obtained based on the structure information contained in the patch training samples. In testing process, we introduce an orientation based method to exploit patches for whole target localization. Also, we analyzed how to improve agnostic-target detection framework by tailoring the reference boxes. Experimental results on two datasets show that, our proposed DON method improves the recall at high precision rates for the deep detection framework and provide orientation information for detected targets.

Keywords: Aerial target detection · Orientation information · Faster-RCNN YOLO

1 Introduction

Reliable aircrafts detection system from aerial images is required for many critical applications nowadays. Civilian applications such as aerial visual surveillance in airports and many essential military applications. The detection of aircrafts as aerial targets is difficult and challenging, mainly for two reasons; Firstly, targets with various orientations have wide appearance and color variations, also the aspect ratios of aerial targets vary with their orientations, which brings difficulty for target localization. Secondly, different weather conditions, altitudes and complex back grounds decrease aerial target detectability. Figure 1 shows typical scenarios of aerial images. Former works [1–3] achieved average accuracy by using hand-crafted shallow features to discriminate aerial targets form complex airport scenes. Then, accuracy slightly and gradually increased by combining these shallow features [4] for detection task. Recently, deep features have been used for the same task. Where, in [5], Binarized normed gradients (BING) [6] *objectness* detector was applied to feed a three layers Convolutional Neural Networks (CNN) with region proposals to extract deep features. Although this combination approach enhances the detection accuracy but the light CNN weaken the abstraction level of the extracted features.

© Springer Nature Singapore Pte Ltd. 2018
Y. Wang et al. (Eds.): IGTA 2017, CCIS 757, pp. 178–188, 2018.
https://doi.org/10.1007/978-981-10-7389-2_18

The Region based Convolution Neural Network (R-CNN) detection framework [7] was presented in [8] based on Alexnet [9] to detect the aerial targets by concatenating multiple features from different network layers. Although [8] achieved high mean Average Precession (mAP), but at the expense of heavy computational cost which obviously appeared in R-CNN training/testing time and high feature dimension. This cost made the detection time of proposed system by [8] more than 50 s/ image. Aerial target detection is a critical task requires high detection accuracy achieved in a reasonable time. Lately, Fast R-CNN [10] has been proposed to handle the limitations of the RCNN and achieved better accuracy with speedup to 25×. Nowadays, Faster R-CNN [11] and YOLO [12] outperformed Fast R-CNN and became most successful frameworks for agnostic target detection in real time. Both of them are purely CNN-based method without using low-level features. The former comprises two main components: a fully convolutional Region Proposal Network (RPN) for regions proposal coarse candidate. Where RPN detects the presence of an object or not and also propose a box location. Followed by Fast R-CNN [10] for classification task and fine localization. The later unites the detection framework by unifying the distinct components of object detection into a single deep neural network. The architectural design of this network includes two main stages: feature extraction and detection stages. The feature extraction stage comprises 24 convolutional layers followed by 2 fully connected layers as a detection stage. YOLOv1 [12] detection layer performs poorly in detecting small aerial targets captured with high altitudes. This mainly because, the detection was carried out on low-resolution feature map (usually with a size 7 * 7). YOLOv2 [13] preserved the structure of YOLOv1, but alleviated these limitations by eliminating one pooling layer to increase the feature map resolution to (13 * 13). Moreover, the detection will be carried out directly from the last convolutional layer feature maps by means of k anchors. These anchors will resolve the spatial constraints of YOLOv1 and increase the IOU (Intersection Over Union) with GT (Ground truth) bounding boxes. In this paper, we propose a DON with Faster R-CNN and YOLOv2 to improve aerial target detection accuracy and provide orientation information within the detection task. Our contributions are three folds: (1) We propose a novel approach to train and test deep detection frameworks to increase their accuracy for aerial target detection. (2) A comprehensive study was carried out for tailoring the reference boxes (Anchors) for each framework (Faster RCNN and YOLO). (3) Our proposal will provide orientation information for each detected target at testing time. To know why predicting the target orientation is important? Considering scenarios in Fig. 2, which illustrates how a tracker based [14–16] on searching window framework seeks for the target in all possible directions (blue dashed-line window). Orientation information will reduce computational power and increase the accuracy by guiding the searching window in the direction of target orientation (yellow dashed-line window).

Fig. 1. Aerial images with multiple targets with different orientations and altitudes were taken in different weather conditions, best viewed in color.

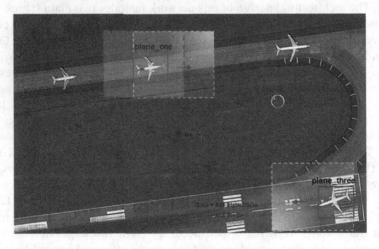

Fig. 2. The orientation information will aid the tracking system by guiding the searching window from blue dashed one to yellow one. Best viewed in color.

2   Deep-Patch Orientation Network

We investigate how to exploit the target patches in detection task for decreasing the false negative rate (FNR). In other words, the DON proposal will increase the likelihood of detecting missing targets by using features of their patches. Moreover, it will give more information about the detected targets which will be their orientations. Consequently, our *DON* proposal approach comprises three main parts:

2.1 Patch-Based with Encoded Orientation

The *DON* approach starts by representing targets by their semantic patches. Where, each airplane in training set will be separated to relevant patches e.g. plane-head and plane-tail. According to the altitude and the input image resolution, these patches will be annotated also with encoded orientation angle from 1 to 4 or from 1 to 8 to cover 90 or 45° from plan view, respectively. Where the encoded orientation describes the heading of the patch-based target in terms of numbers, simply *one* for patch-based target looking right (from −45 to +45°), *two* for patch-based looking upward (from +45 to +135°) and so on. E.g. plane-head-two is a head for a plane looking upward. Figure 3 shows how patch-based with encoded orientations was carried out.

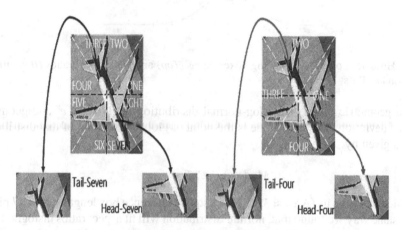

Fig. 3. Four *(right)* and eight *(left)* encoded orientations for patch-based airplane taken anti clockwise direction.

2.2 Aerial Target Anchors

In this section, we investigate how to deduce the reference boxes of Faster RCNN and YOLO for aircrafts in aerial images. Thus, the detection framework will regress the Bounding Boxes (BBs) for specific-class (aircraft) not for agnostic class. We used publicly available dataset [17] for aircraft detection in aerial images which involves (600 images with 3210 airplanes). The BBs of the training set (areas and aspect ratios) (illustrated in Fig. 4) have been used to infer appropriate reference boxes for Faster RCNN. We found that, the log-normal is the best distribution for BBs areas histogram, where it has the lowest Anderson-Darling statistic (AD) with highest P-value.

$$P(x) = \frac{1}{x\sigma\sqrt{2\pi}} \exp - \left[\frac{\ln x - \mu}{\sigma^2} \right] \tag{1}$$

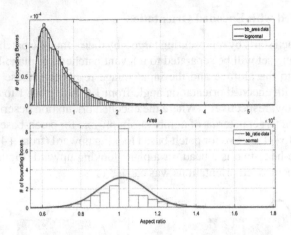

Fig. 4. Histogram of target bounding boxes Areas *(Top)* and their aspect ratios *(Bottom)* with corresponding Pdfs.

The geometric mean of the log-normal distribution is given by e^{μ} and geometric standard deviation is e^{σ}. The mode is the point of global maximum of that distribution and it is given by:

$$Mode(x) = e^{\mu - \sigma^2} \tag{2}$$

Which will give us (Area $\approx$ 3245) for a square reference box length side $\approx$ 57 pixels. By the same way we found that, normal distribution will fit aspect ratios histogram with $\mu = 1.018$ and $\sigma = 0.125$. Thus, we have three aspect ratios for width and height of the reference BBs. For YOLOv2 [13] anchors, we used k-mean clustering with Euclidean distance. We deduce anchors for the training dataset as follows: Each BBs (width and height) tuple is rescaled by multiplying by the ratio between the network input resolution and the size of the input image contains that BB.

$$\left(w_r, h_r \right) = \left(\frac{W_n}{W_i} * w_t, \frac{H_n}{H_i} * h_t \right) \tag{3}$$

Where, (w_t, h_t) and (w_r, h_r) are GT BB and rescaled BB width and height, respectively. (W_n, H_n) and (W_i, H_i) are the network input resolution and the input image width and height, respectively. All rescaled BBs will be clustered by means of k-mean clustering algorithm. We choose k which gives the highest silhouette average coefficient [18]. The resulting k centroids tuples (w_c, h_c) were divided the by feature map stride $feat_{st}$ of the network.

$$\left(w_a, h_a \right) = \left(\frac{w_c}{feat_{st}}, \frac{h_c}{feat_{st}} \right) \tag{4}$$

We have k (wa, ha) tuples, each one is the resulting anchors (width and height). $feat_{st}$ is the last feature map stride, which represents the number of pixels on the input image corresponding to one-pixel stride on the feature map. Here, $feat_{st} = 32$.

2.3 Manipulating Patch-Based Bounding Box Method

At testing time for Deep patch-based proposal, we have BBs with patch-based labels; *head − orientation* or *tail − orientation*. For target localization/scale, we applied orientation based process on patch-based BBs as follows:

- Two BBs with patch-based labels (head and tail) have the same encoded orientation (e.g. head-three, tail-three) and located near to each other (The distance between their centers within an empirical threshold). Both of them will be combined to get one BB with *plane − orientation* label. Finally, the plane BB will be reported with the average score of its patch-based scores.
- BB with patch-based label (head or tail) alone and located far away from the complementary patch. In this case, the orientation information will be used to expand the patch-based BB to get the missing complementary part. E.g. if we have only a patch-based label *head − two* (head for airplane looking upward) then we expect to find its complementary part (tail) beneath of it, then its BB will expand downward by same aspect ratio of that head. Finally, plane BB will be reported with the same score of its patch-based. Figure 5 shows the patch-based BBs manipulating policy.

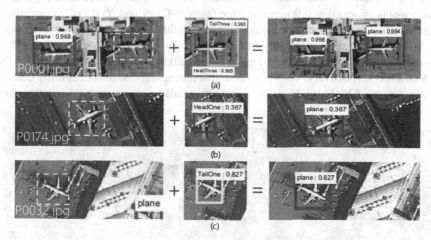

Fig. 5. Shows how the patch-based bounding boxes combined *(a)* or expanded *(b)* and *(c)* to detect the whole plane. Targets within dashed boxes on left column are missed by detection system but captured by our proposal.

3   Implementation Details and Experiments

Each framework was trained twice with orientation information and anchors adoptions, but once with patch-based and one more without it (baseline). We made overlap 40% between the patch-based patches. We experimented Faster R-CNN with the ZF network, adapted the 9 (anchors) as mentioned in Sect. 2.2. The cross-boundary anchors during fine-tuning were activated like [19].

We set the NMS to 0.3. Other parameters of RPN and Fast R-CNN are as in [11]. On the other hand, regarding YOLOv2, the input resolution is 608 * 608. We got 6 anchors (k-mean centroids) as explained in Sect. 2.2 which values are: (0.80, 1.29), (1.59, 2.32), (1.71, 3.82), (0.82, 2.03), (1.1, 2.77), (1.19, 1.70). The last convolutional layer output feature map (filter size) was set to 78. It is very important to mention that; the flipping in the training phase was disabled to achieve the correct detection for orientations in horizontal case. Other training parameters were set as in [13]. Qualitatively, Figs. 6 and 7 show the output of our proposal with both frameworks YOLOv2 and faster R-CNN, respectively. Here, we can notice that, most aircrafts were detected successfully by two overlapped patches with same encoded orientations or only one patch with encoded orientation. Quantitatively, the evaluation done according to the PASCAL VOC [20] object detection evaluation protocol, a detected bounding box and a ground truth are recognized as matched if their IOU is greater than 50%. Table 1 summarizes the Recall at high precession rates on the testing set of the first dataset [17] for Faster R-CNN and YOLOv2 with and without *DON*. Thus, we have more than **3%** and **1%** enhancements in recall at **0.9** precision for faster R-CNN and YOLOv2, respectively. We used the first dataset's trained models directly with the testing set of second dataset [21] to approve the generalization of our *DON* proposal. As mentioned in Table 2, we have more than **12%** and **14%** enhancements in recall at **0.9** precision for faster R-CNN and YOLOv2, respectively. We argue that, this increasing due to successfully detected missing targets *FN* (False Negative) at high recall value (low confidence scores).

Fig. 6. *DON* proposal results with YOLO detection framework.

Inferring that, *the DON* will improve Recall at high Precision rates, which is crucial for the aerial target detection system (Figs. 8 and 9).

Fig. 7. *DON* proposal results with Faster RCNN detection framework.

Table 1. Recall at different high precision rates of Faster R-CNN and YOLO with and without *DON* proposal on first dataset [17].

Method	Rec. at 0.8 Pr.	Rec. at 0.85 Pr.	Rec. at 0.9 Pr.
Faster R-CNN	0.9693	0.9565	0.9335
Faster R-CNN + DON	**0.9761**	**0.9702**	**0.9659**
YOLO	0.9812	0.9804	0.9787
YOLO + DON	**0.9898**	**0.9898**	**0.9872**

Table 2. Recall at different high precision rates of Faster R-CNN and YOLO with and without *DON* proposal on second dataset [21].

Method	Rec. at 0.8 Pr.	Rec. at 0.85 Pr.	Rec. at 0.9 Pr.
Faster R-CNN	0.6887	0.6512	0.6159
Faster R-CNN + DON	**0.7991**	**0.7704**	**0.7395**
YOLO	0.6392	0.6755	0.6093
YOLO + DON	**0.8124**	**0.7925**	**0.7461**

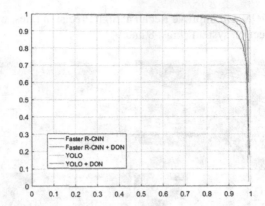

Fig. 8. Precision-Recall curve with and without *DON* proposal for first dataset [17].

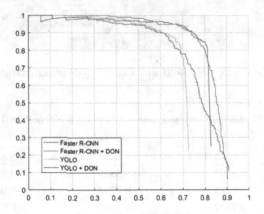

Fig. 9. Precision-Recall curve with and without *DON* proposal for the second dataset [21].

4 Conclusion and Discussion

The proposed *DON* network will enhance the detection framework performance and involve the orientation information with the detection task. Also, we investigate how to tailor the anchors of the deep detection framework. We applied our proposal with two deep detection frameworks (Faster R-CNN and YOLOv2) on two different datasets. Our proposal with that investigation improve the recall at high precision rates for both frameworks. In the future, we are looking forward to exploit the orientation information to aid the tracking systems.

Acknowledgments. The work was supported in part by the Natural Science Foundation of China under Contract 61672079, 61473086 and 61601466. The work of B. Zhang was supported in part by the Program for New Century Excellent Talents University within the Ministry of Education, China, and in part by the Beijing Municipal Science and Technology Commission under Grant Z161100001616005.

References

1. Liu, G., Sun, X., Fu, K., Wang, H.: Aircraft recognition in high-resolution satellite images using coarse-to-fine shape prior. IEEE Geosci. Remote Sens. Lett. **10**(3), 573–577 (2013)
2. Sun, H., Sun, X., Wang, H., Li, Y., Li, X.: Automatic target detection in high-resolution remote sensing images using spatial sparse coding bag-of-words model. IEEE Geosci. Remote Sens. Lett. **9**(1), 109–113 (2011)
3. Li, W., Xiang, S., Wang, H., Pan, C.: Robust airplane detection in satellite images. In: IEEE International Conference on Image Processing (ICIP 2011), Brussels, Belgium, pp. 2821–2824, September 2011
4. Razakarivony, S., Jurie, F.: Discriminative autoencoders for small targets detection. In: IAPR International Conference on Pattern Recognition, pp. 3528–3533 (2014)
5. Wu, H., Zhang, H., Zhang, J., Xu, F.: Fast aircraft detection in satellite images based on convolutional neural networks. In: IEEE International Conference on Image Processing, pp. 4210–4214 (2015)
6. Cheng, M.M., Zhang, Z., Lin, W.Y., Torr, P.: Bing: binarized normed gradients for objectness estimation at 300 fps, pp. 3286–3293 (2014)
7. Girshick, R., Donahue, J., Darrell, T., Malik, J.: Rich feature hierarchies for accurate object detection and semantic segmentation. In: Proceedings of the IEEE Conference on Computer Vision and Pattern Recognition, pp. 580–587 (2014)
8. Zhu, H., Chen, X., Dai, W., Fu, K., Ye, Q., Jiao, J.: Orientation robust object detection in aerial images using deep convolutional neural network. In: 2015 IEEE International Conference on Image Processing (ICIP), pp. 3735–3739. IEEE (2015)
9. Krizhevsky, A., Sutskever, I., Hinton, G.E.: Imagenet classification with deep convolutional neural networks. In: Advances in Neural Information Processing Systems, pp. 1097–1105 (2012)
10. Girshick, R.: Fast R-CNN. In: Proceedings of the IEEE International Conference on Computer Vision, pp. 1440–1448 (2015)
11. Ren, S., He, K., Girshick, R., Sun, J.: Faster R-CNN: towards real-time object detection with region proposal networks. In: Advances in Neural Information Processing Systems, pp. 91–99 (2016)
12. Redmon, J., Divvala, S., Girshick, R., Farhadi, A.: You only look once: unified, real-time object detection. arXiv preprint arXiv:1506.02640 (2015)
13. Redmon, J., Farhadi, A.: YOLO9000: better, faster, stronger. arXiv preprint arXiv: 1612.08242 (2016)
14. Zhang, B., Li, Z., Perina, A., Bue, A.D., Murino, V.: Adaptive local movement modelling for object tracking. In: IEEE Transactions on Circuits and Systems for Video Technology (2016)
15. Zhang, B., Perina, A., Li, Z., Murino, V., Liu, J., Ji, R.: Bounding multiple Gaussians uncertainty with application to object tracking. Int. J. Comput. Vis. **118**(3), 364–379 (2016)
16. Zhang, B., Li, Z., Cao, X., Ye, Q., Chen, C., Shen, L., Perina, A., Ji, R.: Output constraint transfer for kernelized correlation filter in tracking. IEEE Trans. Syst. Man Cybern. Syst. **PP**(99), 1–11 (2016)
17. http://www.ucassdl.cn/resource.asp
18. Bora, M., Jyoti, D., Gupta, D., Kumar, A.: Effect of different distance measures on the performance of k-means algorithm: an experimental study in matlab. arXiv preprint arXiv: 1405.7471 (2014)

19. Zhang, L., Lin, L., Liang, X., He, K.: Is faster R-CNN doing well for pedestrian detection? In: Leibe, B., Matas, J., Sebe, N., Welling, M. (eds.) ECCV 2016. LNCS, vol. 9906, pp. 443–457. Springer, Cham (2016). https://doi.org/10.1007/978-3-319-46475-6_28
20. Everingham, M., Van Gool, L., Williams, C.K., Winn, J., Zisserman, A.: The Pascal Visual Object Classes (VOC) challenge. Int. J. Comput. Vis. **88**(2), 303–338 (2010)
21. https://github.com/wuhuiIOS/AircraftsDataset

Real-Time Salient Object Detection
Based on Fully Convolutional Networks

Guangyu Nie[1], Yinan Guo[2], Yue Liu[1(✉)], and Yongtian Wang[1]

[1] Beijing Engineering Research Center of Mixed Reality and Advanced Display School of Optoelectronics, Beijing Institute of Technology, Beijing 100081, China
{gynie,liuyue,wyt}@bit.edu.cn
[2] China Mobile Communications Corporation Research Institute, Beijing 100053, China
guoyinan@chinamobile.com

Abstract. Salient object detection allows to take into account the visual content of images. In this paper, we train a real-time saliency model based on fully convolutional network (FCN), and then combine the energy maps with Gaussian filters to generate a multi-resolution image. The proposed method has been tested both qualitatively and quantitatively, by considering a representative set of ground truth images labeled with corresponding salient objects. Experimental results demonstrate that the proposed deep model significantly is superior to the-state-of-the-art approaches.

Keywords: Saliency detection · FCN · Real-time

1 Introduction

Visual saliency has been studied by researchers in computer vision for a long time, and there are many applications for visual saliency, for example, video summarization, content-aware image editing, image/video compression. Salient object detection approaches can be classified into two main groups: bottom-up and top-down methods. For the bottom-up methods, local and global information are generally used for detecting salient region. While the contrast between each element (pixel, region, or patch) and its locally surrounding neighborhood are considered as the salient cues in local methods (e.g. [1, 2]), the global contrast based method is used to separate a large-scale object from its surroundings [3]. For the top-down methods, the prior knowledge semantic information can be used to improve the performance, which is usually task-dependent, such as flash cues [4], boundary and background priors [5], and other interesting priors (e.g. [6, 7]).

In this paper, we propose a novel real-time method for salient object detection. We first train a deep network for salient object detection to predict the salient area. Then we use the Gaussian filter for non-salient area blurring. The proposed salient object detection approach has been tested and compared, both qualitatively and quantitatively, against state-of-the-art approaches, which shows the effectiveness of the proposed approach in terms of preservation of salient regions.

© Springer Nature Singapore Pte Ltd. 2018
Y. Wang et al. (Eds.): IGTA 2017, CCIS 757, pp. 189–198, 2018.
https://doi.org/10.1007/978-981-10-7389-2_19

2   Saliency

We predict the salient pixels contained in the image by the properties of the FCN.

2.1   Architecture

The FCN is originally introduced for semantic segmentation task on images [8], which can take arbitrary size of input and produce a dense map with corresponding size. As is shown in Fig. 1, we use the AlexNet [9] and cast it into fully convolutional form as suggested in [8] by replacing fully connected layers with corresponding convolutions, which we call FCN-32s. Then we define a skip architecture to extend the FCN-32s into a two-stream net (FCN-16s) with sixteen pixel stride and extend it into three-stream net (FCN-8s) with eight pixel stride. Different from the traditional semantic segmentation problem, the proposed approach segments an image only into two classes: the foreground with visual salient information and the background with ignored visual information. The network is fine-tuned from the pre-trained AlexNet model [9].

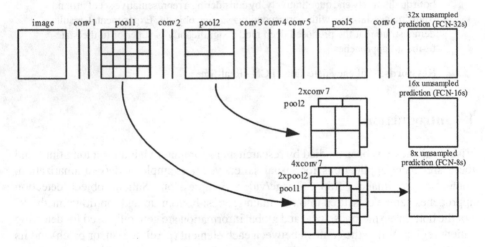

Fig. 1. Our nets learn to combine coarse features produced by shallow layers with fine features produced by high layers. Pooling and prediction layers are represented by grids that reveal relative spatial coarseness, while intermediate layers are represented by bi-vertical lines. First row (FCN-32 s): Our single-stream net with upsampling stride size of 32 back to original size in one single step. Second row (FCN-16s): finer details produced by combining predictions from both the final layer and the pool2 layer with stride 16, retaining high-level semantic information. Third row (FCN-8s): deeper predictions by combining the final layer and pool1 with stride 8, provide further precision.

2.2   Neural Network Training

The size of the input image that the model requires is [500, 500, 3], a finer dense map with the same size is output. The feature maps that pass through our model can be treated as a three dimensional volume of size [h, w, c], which h and w are the height and width of the feature map respectively, and c is the channel of the feature map. A raw image can be treated as input feature map, and it passes our architecture with basic components, including convolutional operation, pooling operation, and activation function:

$$f_{i,j}^{t+1} = h_{k,s}(f_{i,j}^t) \tag{1}$$

where $f_{i,j}^t$ is the feature vector at location (i, j) in t^{th} layer, and $f_{i,j}^{t+1}$ in $(t + 1)^{th}$ layer. Besides, k and s denotes the kernel size and stride, respectively, and $h_{k,s}$ denotes the layers type: matrix multiplication for convolutional layer, max operation for pooling layer, an element-wise nonlinear operation for activation function. Finally, we calculate the loss based on following function:

$$l(x, m; \theta) = \sum_{i,j} l'(x, m_{i,j}; \theta) \tag{2}$$

where x is the input RGB image, m is the dense map that we need to learn, and θ is model parameter. The loss value is the sum of each pixel loss $\sum_{i,j} l'(x, m_{i,j}; \theta)$ with location (i, j) over the spatial domain.

To generate the finer results, we use the bilinear interpolation to convert the pixels from coarseness to denseness which is corresponding to the deconvolution layer. We compute the output $y_{i,j}$ from the nearest four inputs by a linear map that only depends on relative positions of the input and output cells:

$$y_{i,j} = \sum_{\alpha,\beta=0}^{1} |1 - \alpha - \{i/f\}||1 - \beta - \{i/j\}|x_{\lfloor i/f \rfloor + \alpha, \lfloor i/f \rfloor + \beta} \tag{3}$$

where f is the upsampling factor, and $\{\bullet\}$ denotes the fractional part.

3   Content-Aware Image Blurring

Content-aware image blurring smooths non-salient area in order to emphasize salient regions. Differing saliency maps will emphasize different areas in the resulting image. Our trained model outputs two probability maps for each class (including background and foreground) of corresponding size. To generate the multi-resolution results, we first smooth the whole image based on Gaussian filter. The output pixel's value $g(i, j)$ is determined as a weighted sum of input pixel values $f(i + k, j + l)$:

$$g(i,j) = \sum_{k,l} f(i + k, j + l)h(k, l) \tag{4}$$

where $h(k, l)$ is the weight at the location (k, l) in Gaussian kernel. Then we blur the non-salient visual information and extract the salient visual information as:

$$P(i,j) = p_{bg}(i,j) \times g(i,j) + p_{fg}(i,j) \times f(i,j) \tag{5}$$

where $P(i,j)$ is the output value at location (i,j), $p_{bg}(i,j)$ is the probability value in non-saliency map at location (i,j), and $p_{fg}(i,j)$ is the probability value in saliency map at corresponding location.

4   Experiment

4.1   Experiment Setup

Benchmark Datasets. We evaluate the performance of our method on six public datasets: MSRA10K [3], ECSSD [10], PASCALS [11], DUT-OMRON [12], HKU-IS [13] and SED1 [14]. MSRA10K dataset contains the pixel accurate salient object labeling for 10000 images from MSRA dataset. ECSSD dataset contains 1,000 images with a variety of image from Internet. PASCALS dataset contains 850 natural images built from the validation set of PASCAL VOC 2010 segmentation challenge. DUT-OMRON dataset contains 5168 images with one or more salient objects and relatively complex background. Note that none of the existing saliency models has achieved a high accuracy on this dataset. HKU-IS dataset contains 4447 challenge images. SED1 dataset has 100 images only containing one salient object. All the datasets contain manually annotated ground masks for its corresponding images.

Evaluation Criteria. We evaluate the performance of our model using precision-recall (PR) curves and mean absolute error (MAE) score. We convert the continuous dense map into binary masks by using discrete thresholds, and then compare these binary masks against the corresponding ground truth. The PR curve is drawn by calculating the average precision and recall over saliency maps in the dataset. Besides, MAE calculates the average numerical distance of each pixels between the saliency map S and the binary ground truth G:

$$MAE = \frac{1}{w \times h} \sum_{i=1}^{w} \sum_{j=1}^{h} |S(i,j) - G(i,j)| \tag{6}$$

which is useful to estimate the performance of a saliency model in segmentation task.

Implementation. Our proposed model is implemented based on Caffe [15], an open source deep learning framework. At present, the pixel-wise ground truth annotation of the MSRA10K dataset is the largest dataset that is suitable for salient object detection, however, it still suffers from overfitting when being used for 10,000 images, so we augment the MSRA10K dataset for fine-tuning. The dataset is augmented 10 times as follows: we first resize each image into [500, 500, 3], then sample random patches from the images with size of [400, 400, 3] due to center-bias of this dataset, and finally perform random horizontal flips and resize images into [500, 500, 3]. We divide our augmented dataset into two parts: 90,000 images are selected randomly for training and the remaining 10,000 images are selected for validation. We resize all the images with the size [500, 500, 3] for training, and set the batch size to 20. Although there is a considerable oscillation, but it has no effects on the results with such batch size. The three networks are trained by stochastic gradient descent (SGD). In all cases, gradient descent is run with a momentum of 0.9, an L2 penalty on the network's parameters of 0.0005 and doubled learning rate for biases. We fine-tune the single-stream FCN-32s, the two-stream FCN-16s and the three-stream FCN-8s sequentially. In each stage the net is learned end-to-end, and initialized with the parameters of the former net. We start to train with a fixed learning rate of 1e−4, then the learning rate is dropped 100 times in each initialization. It takes around one month to train our deep learning model on the PC with NVIDIA Titan X GPU and core i7 6700 k CPU. Finally, after fine-tuning the three substructures, the loss value of the three-stream decreases to 0.04805.

4.2 Comparison with the State of the Art

We compare our saliency model against such methods, as COV [16], DSR [17], FES [18], GR [19], KSR [20], LPS [21], MC [22], PCA [23], RBD [24], RC [3] and SWD [25]. As can be seen from the visual comparison as shown in Fig. 2, our model shows more accurate saliency maps than most of challenging cases. As part of the quantitative evaluation, we first evaluate our method using precision-recall (PR) curves. As shown in the first row of Fig. 3, our method achieves the high precision in almost the entire recall range on all datasets. Moreover, we report a quantitative comparison with MAE in Table 1. Our model has the lowest score on MSRA10K, SED1, ECSSD and HKU-IS datasets, and the second lowest score on PASCALS dataset. However, our model reaches the relative low score on DUT-OMRON dataset, which shows that our model can generate the high performance on most of the public benchmarks. At the same time, we also quantitatively compare the average running time of all 12 methods, and the processing refers to inputting the arbitrary size and output the corresponding saliency map. As is shown in Table 2, our model can process 45 fps which is faster than any other methods except SWD. However, as shown in Fig. 3, the PR curves of the method SWD in each dataset are lower than that of our method obviously in each graph. Moreover, the MEA scores of our model are lower than those of the SWD model in every dataset. It can be seen from the above comparisons that our model shows its best performance among all these methods, which means that our model can achieve real-time image processing and can be applied to video saliency detection.

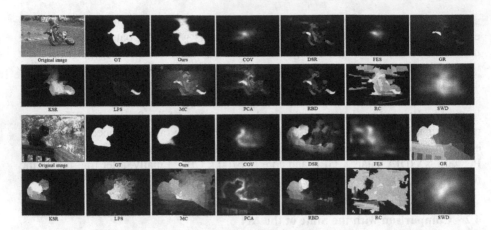

Fig. 2. Visual comparison of saliency maps generated from 12 different methods. Each two rows correspond to an example. The ground truth (GT) is shown at the location of (1, 2). We compare our method against COV, DSR, FES, GR, KSR, LPS, MC, PCA, RBD, RC, and SWD.

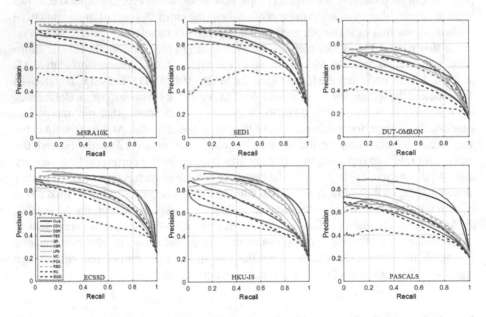

Fig. 3. Precision (vertical axis) and recall (horizontal axis) curves of saliency methods on 6 popular benchmark datasets, including MSRA10K, SED1, DUT-OMRON, ECSSD, HKU-IS, and PASCALS.

Table 1. Comparison of quantitative results based on MAE (smaller is better). **Red**: best, **blue**: second best, **green**: third best.

Dataset	Ours	COV	DSR	FES	GR	KSR
MSRA10K	0.069	0.195	0.108	0.173	0.184	0.120
SED1	0.104	0.238	0.161	0.223	0.224	0.149
DUT-OMRON	0.183	0.156	0.135	0.153	0.252	0.131
ECSSD	0.123	0.218	0.144	0.209	0.252	0.132
HKU-IS	0.118	0.172	0.119	0.162	0.246	0.120
PASCALS	0.183	0.201	0.193	0.195	0.303	0.154
Dataset	LPS	MC	PCA	RBD	RC	SWD
MSRA10K	0.127	0.130	0.178	0.095	0.266	0.262
SED1	0.163	0.170	0.235	0.145	0.246	0.282
DUT-OMRON	0.149	0.181	0.200	0.136	0.339	0.307
ECSSD	0.185	0.175	0.237	0.141	0.291	0.308
HKU-IS	0.171	0.166	0.216	0.128	0.276	0.312
PASCALS	0.217	0.229	0.227	0.201	0.306	0.314

Table 2. Quantitative comparison in terms of average running time (frames per second). Red: best, blue: second best.

Method	Speed	Code	Method	Speed	Code
Ours	45	Python + C++	DSR	1.3	Matlab + C++
LPS	0.85	Matlab	PCA	1.2	Matlab + C++
FES	43.3	Matlab + C++	RC	0.23	C++
RBD	25.8	Matlab	DSR	1.3	Matlab + C++
KSR	5	Matlab	PCA	1.2	Matlab + C++
COV	0.39	Matlab	GR	10.3	Matlab + C++
MC	46	Matlab + C++	SWD	**51.7**	Matlab

4.3 Content-Aware Image Blurring

The performance of a content-aware image blurring strongly depends on the saliency map. As described in the previous section, we propose a quick blur method based on Gaussian filter to build and select the area during the blurring. Figure 4 shows the content-aware background blurring examples from MSRA10K dataset with variable kernel size. Each row corresponds to an example. The first and the second column show the original images, ground truth images and the saliency maps. From the fourth to the ninth columns show the background blur results with 6 different kernel sizes which is positive and odd, respectively, leading to blurring the non-salient pixels but emphasize the salient area. We choose the probability maps rather than the final binary maps because it will generate the sharp boundary when using the binary mask and lead to be uncomfortable and unnatural for viewers. The blurring processing is also real-time when we run the code based on C++.

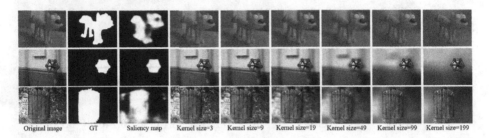

Original image   GT   Saliency map   Kernel size=3   Kernel size=9   Kernel size=19   Kernel size=49   Kernel size=99   Kernel size=199

Fig. 4. Example of content-aware background blurring with variable kernel size. Each row corresponds to an example. The columns are the original images, ground truth images, saliency maps, background blur results with 6 different kernel sizes, respectively.

5   Convolutions

In this paper we have introduced a real-time content-aware saliency detection method which exploits information extracted through training an end-to-end deep network for saliency detection, and then we apply this real-time method to content-aware image blurring. Firstly, we train a saliency model based on FCN to establish the energy maps. We compare the model against the-state-of-the-art eleven saliency models on six popular public benchmarks. Experimental results demonstrate that our deep model outperforms most of the state of the art approaches. Then we extract the important information based on saliency maps and combine probability maps with Gaussian filter to emphasize the visual salient information.

Acknowledgment. This work has been supported by the National Natural Science Foundation of China (Grant No. 61661146002) and the National Technology Support Program of China (Grant No. 2015BAK01B05).

References

1. Jonathan, H., Koch, C., Perona, P.: Graph-based visual saliency. NIPS **1**(2), 545–552 (2006)
2. Liu, T., Yuan, Z., Sun, J., Wang, J., Zheng, N., Tang, X., Shum, H.Y.: Learning to detect a salient object. IEEE Trans. Pattern Anal. Mach. Intell. **33**(2), 353–367 (2011)
3. Cheng, M., Mitra, N.J., Huang, X., Torr, P.H., Hu, S.: Global contrast based salient region detection. IEEE Trans. Pattern Anal. Mach. Intell. **37**(3), 569–582 (2015)

4. He, S., Rynson, W.L.: Saliency detection with flash and no-flash image pairs. In: European Conference on Computer Vision, pp. 110–124 (2014)
5. Wei Y., Fang, W., Zhu, W., Sun, J.: Geodesic saliency using background priors. In: European Conference on Computer Vision, pp. 29–42 (2012)
6. Ali, B.: Boosting bottom-up and top-down visual features for saliency estimation. In: Proceedings of the IEEE Conference on Computer Vision and Pattern Recognition, pp. 438–445 (2012)
7. Yang, J., Yang, M.: Top-down visual saliency via joint CRF and dictionary learning. IEEE Trans. Pattern Anal. Mach. Intell., 438–445 (2016)
8. Jonathan, L., Evan, S., Trevor, D.: Fully convolutional networks for semantic segmentation. In: Proceedings of the IEEE Conference on Computer Vision and Pattern Recognition, pp. 3431–3440 (2015)
9. Krizhevsky, A., Ilya, S., Geoffrey, E.H.: Imagenet classification with deep convolutional neural networks. In: Advances in Neural Information Processing Systems, pp. 1097–1105 (2012)
10. Wang, L., Qiao, Y., Tang, X., Van, G.L.: Actionness estimation using hybrid fully convolutional networks. In: Proceedings of the IEEE Conference on Computer Vision and Pattern Recognition, pp. 2708–2717 (2016)
11. Li, Y., Hou, X., Koch, C., Rehg, J.M., Yuille, A.L.: The secrets of salient object segmentation. In: Proceedings of the IEEE Conference on Computer Vision and Pattern Recognition, pp. 280–287 (2014)
12. Yang, C., Zhang, L., Lu, H., Ruan, X., Yang, M.: Saliency detection via graph-based manifold ranking. In: Proceedings of the IEEE Conference on Computer Vision and Pattern Recognition, pp. 3166–3173 (2013)
13. Li G., Yu, Y.: Visual saliency based on multiscale deep features. In: Proceedings of the IEEE Conference on Computer Vision and Pattern Recognition, pp. 5455–5463 (2015)
14. Alpert, S., Galun, M., Brandt, A., Basri, R.: Image segmentation by probabilistic bottom-up aggregation and cue integration. IEEE Trans. Pattern Anal. Mach. Intell. **34**(2), 315–327 (2012)
15. Jia, Y., Evan, S., Jeff, D., Sergey, K., Jonathan, L., Ross, G., Sergio, G., Trevor, D.: Caffe: convolutional architecture for fast feature embedding. In: Proceedings of the 22nd ACM International Conference on Multimedia, pp. 675–678 (2014)
16. Kavak, Y., Erkut, E., and Aykut, E.: Visual saliency estimation by integrating features using multiple kernel learning, arXiv:1307.5693 (2013)
17. Li, X., Lu, H., Zhang, L., Ruan, X., Yang, M.H.: Saliency detection via dense and sparse reconstruction. In: Proceedings of the IEEE International Conference on Computer Vision, pp. 2976–2983 (2013)
18. Tavakoli, H.R., Rahtu, E., Heikkilä, J.: Fast and efficient saliency detection using sparse sampling and kernel density estimation. In: Scandinavian Conference on Image Analysis, pp. 666–675 (2011)
19. Yang, C., Zhang, L., Lu, H.: Graph-regularized saliency detection with convex-hull-based center prior. IEEE Signal Process. Lett. **20**(7), 637–640 (2013)
20. Wang, T., Zhang, L., Lu, H., Sun, C., Qi, J.: Kernelized subspace ranking for saliency detection. In: European Conference on Computer Vision, pp. 450–466 (2016)
21. Li, H., Lu, H., Lin, Z., Shen, X., Price, B.: Inner and inter label propagation: salient object detection in the wild. IEEE Trans. Image Process. **24**(10), 3176–3186 (2015)
22. Zhao, R., Ouyang, W., Li, H., Wang, X.: Saliency detection by multi-context deep learning. In: Proceedings of the IEEE Conference on Computer Vision and Pattern Recognition, pp. 1265–1274 (2015)

23. Margolin, R., Tal, A., Zelnik-Manor, L.: What makes a patch distinct? In: Proceedings of the IEEE Conference on Computer Vision and Pattern Recognition, pp. 1139–1146 (2013)

24. Zhu, W., Liang, S., Wei, Y. and Sun, J.: Saliency optimization from robust background detection. In: Proceedings of the IEEE conference on Computer Vision and Pattern Recognition, pp. 2814–2821 (2014)

25. Duan, L., Wu, C., Miao, J., Qing, L., Fu, Y.: Visual saliency detection by spatially weighted dissimilarity. In: Proceedings of the IEEE conference on Computer Vision and Pattern Recognition, pp. 473–480 (2011)

Boosting Multi-view Convolutional Neural Networks for 3D Object Recognition via View Saliency

Yanxin Ma[1], Bin Zheng[2], Yulan Guo[1,3($\boxtimes$)], Yinjie Lei[4], and Jun Zhang[1]

[1] College of Electronic Science and Engineering,
National University of Defense Technology, Changsha, China
yulan.guo@nudt.edu.cn
[2] Henan Information and Engineering College, Zhengzhou, China
[3] Institute of Computing Technology, Chinese Academy of Sciences, Beijing, China
[4] College of Electronics and Information Engineering,
Sichuan University, Chengdu, China

Abstract. 2D views of objects play an important role in 3D object recognition. In this paper, we focus on 3D object recognition using the 2D projective views. The discriminativeness of each view of an object is first investigated with view saliency using 2D Zernike Moments. The proposed view saliency is then used to boost a multi-view convolutional neural network for 3D object recognition. The proposed method is compared with several state-of-the-art methods on the ModelNet dataset. Experimental results have shown that the performance of our method has been significantly improved over the existing multi-view based 3D object recognition methods.

Keywords: 3D object recognition · Convolutional neural networks
View saliency · 2D Zernike moments

1 Introduction

The rapid development of 3D sensors (such as LiDAR and RGB-D cameras) in recent years leads to a significant growth of 3D data. 3D scene understanding have been widely used in numerous applications, including self-driving cars and autonomous robots. As one of the most challenging tasks for scene understanding, 3D object recognition have been extensively investigated in 3D computer vision and computer graphics. Although significant progress has been achieved, there still remain several challenges.

One crucial step for 3D object recognition is to extract informative and discriminative features of 3D objects. Traditional hand-crafted 3D shape feature extraction methods are designed according to specific tasks [7,8]. These features have been widely used in the fields of 3D object recognition and retrieval [7]. However, these features highly rely on the domain knowledge of the designer

© Springer Nature Singapore Pte Ltd. 2018
Y. Wang et al. (Eds.): IGTA 2017, CCIS 757, pp. 199–209, 2018.
https://doi.org/10.1007/978-981-10-7389-2_20

or the specific task to be addressed. Consequently, it is challenging for these task-specific feature to work on large-scale 3D object repositories from different domains or tasks.

With the availability of large-scale public 3D object repositories [2,22,26], deep neural network based feature learning is growing rapidly. Existing deep neural network based 3D object recognition methods can be divided into two categories according to their data representation: 3D data based and 2D view based methods. The 3D data based methods learn features from voxels or point clouds of 3D shapes. These methods extend 2D filters to 3D filters and then implement different 3D neural networks on sparse or dense occupancy grid representations of 3D shapes [6,12,15,18,19,26]. Similarly, deep neural network can also be worked on 3D point clouds directly [11,14,16]. These methods have achieved a high category recognition accuracy for 3D object recognition. However, the computational complexity of 3D deep neural networks grows rapidly with respect to 3D data resolution. Furthermore, it is difficult to build 3D complete models (especially mesh models) for many real-world applications, which is essential for 3D data based methods.

In contrast, a 3D object can also be represented with a set of 2D projection views rendered by a specific rule. As a result, several promising 2D CNN models pretrained on image datasets (e.g., ImageNet [4]) can be used to achieve 3D object recognition using 2D multi-view representation [10,15,23,27]. 2D multi-view representation is more effective than 3D data representation since the rendered 2D views have a higher resolution than the corresponding 3D data. Consequently, 2D multi-view representation is possible to achieve a higher recognition accuracy than 3D data based methods [15,23]. However, most multi-view methods assume that a fixed number of viewpoints are provided and each viewpoint contributes equally for object recognition. In fact, a 3D object can be easily discriminated from other objects by some particular viewpoints but confused by other viewpoints. It is clear that the difference between viewpoints is overlooked in the previous 2D view based methods. Johns *et al.* [10] extracted the information of viewpoints for object recognition. Specifically, an image sequence is first divided into a set of image pairs over unconstrained camera trajectories. Then, each pair is classified and a final prediction is made by weighting the contribution of image pairs.

Motivated by [10], view saliency is introduced to analyze the different contribution of each 2D view for 3D object recognition. Since different views comprise different information of a 3D object, object recognition performance can be improved by investigating the recognition contribution of each view. In this paper, a new method is first introduced to measure the discriminativeness (i.e., saliency) of each view, and the weight of each view is computed according to its saliency. Then, a modified multi-view CNN architecture is proposed for 3D object recognition using the weighted view information. Experimental results show that our view saliency boosted method achieves a higher category recognition accuracy on benchmark datasets.

The remainder of this paper is organized as follows. The view saliency and view weights are studied in Sect. 2.1. The proposed View Saliency boosted Multi-View CNN (VS-MVCNN) is presented in Sect. 2.2. Experimental results and analyses are provided in Sect. 3. Finally, the conclusion and discussion are given in Sect. 4.

2   View Saliency Boosted Multi-view CNN

In this section, the view saliency is analyzed based on the confusion of different views using 2D Zernike moments, a view saliency boosted CNN architecture is then proposed for feature learning. Next, linear SVMs are trained for each view to classify 3D objects using their image features learned by the proposed CNN. Finally, score-level fusion of multiple SVM outputs is used to determine the category of the input 3D object. An illustration of the framework of our proposed method is shown in Fig. 1.

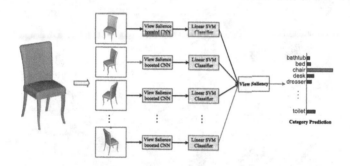

Fig. 1. The framework of our 3D object recognition method. 80 different images are firstly rendered using the Phong reflection model [13]. View saliency boosted CNN is then used to extract image features. Finally, linear SVMs with view saliency are used to predict the object category.

Different from [23], we use multi-view representation of 3D shapes without assumption on consistent upright orientation of objects. For rendering, 20 virtual cameras are placed at the 20 vertices of an icosahedron enclosing the object (as shown in Fig. 1). Each camera centroid is directed towards the object centroid and the resolution of each view is set to 224×224. Four different views are generated for each camera by rotating the camera around the virtual optical axis by 0, 90, 180, 270°. Consequently, 80 views are obtained for each object.

2.1   View Saliency

Human vision is always selectively sensitive to object parts. It implies us that only a few parts of an object (which attract human attention) are useful for object recognition while the others are not. For a particular object, only a specific set of parts can be seen from a fixed viewpoint. Therefore, images rendered from different viewpoints contribute unequally to 3D object recognition. Consequently, object recognition performance can be improved by employing the view saliency of each view.

Figure 2 illustrates some confusing views of 6 different objects. From some views (third row in Fig. 2), the objects can be easily classified. In contrast, other views may contain limited distinctive information of an object, as shown in the second row in Fig. 2. It is clear that different views have different contributions for 3D object recognition. To improve the recognition performance, the contribution of each view should be measured. Wang *et al.* [25] quantitatively evaluates the view saliency using category classification performance. It is observed that the discriminativeness of each view is quite different and some views may puzzle the object recognition method. Consequently, the discriminativeness of each view was measured using the shortest Mahalanobis distance between different categories. A significant improvement has been achieved for 3D object retrieval using the proposed measure.

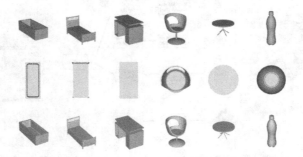

Fig. 2. View examples of six 3D objects with different discriminativeness. The first row shows the model of the six objects, the second and the third rows show the projection images acquired from different views.

For 3D object recognition, a view with a high discriminativeness should be helpful for distinguishing an object from objects of other categories and clustering objects of the same category. Different from [25], a new saliency measure is developed using both the inter-class and intra-class distances. The saliency measure is different in training and testing stages.

Given a training set $X = \{X_1, X_2, \cdots, X_N\}$ from N categories, N_i objects are presented in the training set $X_i = \{X_{i,1}, X_{i,2}, \cdots, X_{i,N_i}\}$ for category i. For each object, K views are obtained. A 56-dimensional Zernike moment x is then extracted for each training view, resulting in a set of features $X = \{x_{i,n}^k\}$, where $i = 1, 2, \cdots, N$, $n = 1, 2, \cdots, N_i$, and $k = 1, 2, \cdots, K$. The saliency for the training set is $P = \{p_{i,n}^k\}$.

During the training phase, the distance between the k-th view of object n in category i and all the views in other categories is defined as:

$$d\left(x_{i,n}^k, V\right) = \min_{v \in V} d\left(x_{i,n}^k, v\right) \tag{1}$$

where V is the set of X excluding X_i, $d\left(x, y\right)$ denotes the Mahalanobis distance between the features of two views. $d\left(x_{i,n}^k, V\right)$ represents the shortest distance from all views of other categories to $x_{i,n}^k$. A large distance value means that the view $x_{i,n}^k$ is discriminative. Therefore, the view saliency of $x_{i,n}^k$ during training can be defined as:

$$p_{i,n}^k = \frac{d\left(x_{i,n}^k, X/X_i\right)}{\sum\limits_{k=1}^{K} d\left(x_{i,n}^k, X/X_i\right)} \tag{2}$$

Since the category information is available in the training set, the inter-class distance is not used.

During the testing phase, the saliency is generated by the training set. Given an object in the testing set, K views are firstly obtained. Then, a 56-dimensional Zernike moment y^k is extracted for each view. The saliency for the testing views are donated as $Q = \{q^k\}$. The distance between the given view and all the training views belonging to category j can be defined as:

$$d_j\left(y^k, X_j\right) = \min_{v \in X_j} d\left(y^k, v\right) \tag{3}$$

where $j = 1, 2, \cdots, N$. Then, a set of distances $d^k = \{d_j\}$ is obtained. The shortest distance is:

$$d\left(y^k, X\right) = \min_{v \in X} d\left(y^k, v\right) \tag{4}$$

The second shortest distance can be defined as:

$$\tilde{d}\left(y^k, X\right) = \operatorname{smin}_j d_j\left(y^k, X_j\right) = \operatorname{smin}_j \left\{ \min_{v \in X_j} d\left(y^k, v\right) \right\} \tag{5}$$

The distance set d^k provides low-level discriminative information for object classification. That is, the shortest distance $d\left(y^k, X\right)$ provides the category information of the test view y^k. The second shortest distance $\tilde{d}\left(y^k, X\right)$ indicates the most similar category from other categories to y^k. If $\tilde{d}\left(y^k, X\right)$ is large and $d\left(y^k, X\right)$ is small, the view y^k is discriminative. We can then define the view saliency during testing as:

$$q^k = \frac{\alpha^k}{\sum\limits_{k=1}^{K} \alpha^k} \tag{6}$$

where $\alpha^k = \frac{\tilde{d}(y^k, X)}{d(y^k, X)}$.

Figure 3 shows the saliency values during training for different views of 3 objects in the ModelNet10 dataset. 12 views is showed for each object and the top 5 discriminative views are highlighted by red boxes. It can be seen from Fig. 3 that the views with high saliency contain significantly more information for the discrimination of 3D objects.

Fig. 3. The view saliency values of 3 sample objects in the ModelNet10 dataset. (Color figure online)

2.2   Recognition Based on View Saliency Boosted Multi-view CNN

Our proposed architecture consists of two parts: multi-view CNN based feature learning and linear SVMs based object recognition.

Feature learning. Our network is implemented with the VGG-M architecture [3], which consists of 8 trainable layers (5 convolutional layers and 3 fully connected layers) and a softmax classification layer. The network is pre-trained on the ImageNet Large Scale Visual Recognition Challenge 2012 (ILSVRC 2012) dataset [17], which contains 1,431,167 labeled images of 1000 categories. The network is then fine-tuned using the 2D views of 3D objects in the training set. The view saliency is used in the last softmax layer with the loss function. For each batch with a size of B given to the network, the overall loss l is obtained by the view saliency p_b and the loss l_b of each view using Eq. 7.

$$l = \sum_{b=1}^{B} l_b p_b \tag{7}$$

The output of the fully connected layer after ReLU (i.e., fc7) is used as the learned descriptor, which is a 4096 dimensional vector.

Object recognition. For object recognition, the learned image features are used to train a one-vs-rest linear SVM for each category and each view is used as a separate training sample. During testing, for each view of a given object, the SVM decision values $\boldsymbol{S}^k = \left\{ s_1^k, s_2^k, \cdots, s_N^k \right\}$ are obtained, where s_i^k denotes the prediction probability of belonging to category i for the k-th view. To improve the recognition performance, the saliency q^k of each view is used to weight the decision values over the K views as:

$$s_i = \sum_{k=1}^{K} q^k s_i^k \tag{8}$$

where s_i denotes the prediction probability of belonging to category i for an object. Finally, the object class c is determined by the one with the highest prediction probability.

$$c = \operatorname*{argmax}_{i} \left\{ s_i \right\} \tag{9}$$

3 Experiments

We tested our 3D object recognition method on the Princeton ModelNet dataset [26] and compared our method to the state-of-the-arts. The ModelNet10 and ModelNet40 are two commonly used subsets in ModelNet, which contain 4,899 shapes from 10 categories and 12,311 shapes from 40 categories, respectively. All the shapes in ModelNet10 are clean and manually aligned while the shapes in ModelNet40 are clean but not aligned. In our experiments, the training and testing datasets are split following the same setting as [26].

The GPU-accelerated multi-view CNN network was implemented with the MatConvNet library [24]. Training was conducted on a machine with an Intel Core-i7 CPU, an NVIDIA GTX1080 GPU, and a 48 GB RAM. The training time is less than 2 h on ModelNet10 and less than 6 h on ModelNet40. The linear SVM was implemented on the same machine with the liblinear library [5] using cross validation.

3.1 Recognition Experiments

To evaluate our 3D object recognition method, a Stochastic Gradient Descent (SGD) with a momentum value of 0.5 and view saliency were used to fine-tune our network. The average category recognition accuracy achieved by our method and the state-of-the-arts are shown in Tables 1 and 2.

Table 1. Recognition accuracy results achieved by our method and the state-of-the-art 2D view based methods on the ModelNet10 and ModelNet40 datasets. Best results and our results are shown in bold face. The result of MVCNN [23] on ModelNet10 (as shown in italic font) was obtained by our implementation. '-' means that the corresponding result is not provided.

Method	Data representation	ModelNet10	ModelNet40
DeepPano [20]	Panoramic image	88.66%	82.54%
Geometry image [21]	Geometry image	88.4%	83.9%
CNN [23]	Greyscale image Single-view	-	85.1%
MVD-ELM [27]	Depth image Multi-view (20 views)	88.99%	81.39%
MVCNN [23]	Greyscale image Multi-view (80 views)	*93.0%*	90.1%
MVCNN-v2 [15]	Greyscale image Multi-view, Multi-resolution	-	**91.4%**
Pairwise [10]	Greyscale+Depth image Multi-view (12 constrained views)	93.2%	91.1%
FusionNet [9]	Volumetric+Greyscale image Multi-view (60 views)	93.11%	90.8%
VS-MVCNN	Greyscale image Multi-view (80 views)	**93.5%**	**90.9%**

Table 2. Recognition accuracy results achieved by our method and the state-of-the-art 3D data based methods on the ModelNet10 and ModelNet40 datasets. Best results and our results are shown in bold face. '-' means that the corresponding result is not provided.

Method	Data representation	ModelNet10	ModelNet40
3D ShapeNets [26]	Volumetric	83.54%	77.32%
VoxNet [12]	Volumetric	92.0%	83.0%
ORION [18]	Volumetric	93.8%	-
LightNet [28]	Volumetric	93.39%	86.9%
PointNet [6]	Volumetric	77.6%	-
Voxception [1]	Volumetric	93.28%	90.56%
VRN [1]	Volumetric	93.61%	91.33%
VRN Ensemble [1]	Volumetric	**97.14%**	**95.54%**
PointNet [14]	Point clouds	-	89.2%
Deep Kd-Networks-15 [11]	Point clouds	94.0%	91.8%
Set-conv [16]	Point clouds	-	90.0%
VS-MVCNN	Greyscale image Multi-view (80 views)	**93.5%**	**90.9%**

It can be observed from Table 1 that our method outperforms the existing 2D view based methods on the ModelNet10 dataset. It achieves a high accuracy of 93.5%. Meanwhile, a significant high accuracy of 90.9% is achieved by our method on the ModelNet40 dataset. It is clear that our method outperforms the single-view networks (i.e., [20,21,23]). That is mainly because, our method is benefited from the multi-view data representation. Compared to the multi-view networks, significant improvement in recognition performance is obtained by our method due to the use of view saliency. Compared to [23], although the same basic CNN structure is used in our view saliency boosted network, a higher recognition accuracy is achieved by our method on the ModelNet40 dataset. Compared to the multi-view networks with data fusion [9,10], our method uses a simple greyscale image representation and achieves almost the same recognition performance. It is clearly demonstrated that the view saliency used in this paper enhances the ability of our method to learn discriminative features.

Table 2 shows the results achieved by our method and 3D data based methods. The VRN Ensemble method [1] achieves the best performance on both the ModelNet10 and ModelNet40 dataset. Our method achieves a comparable recognition performance among the unensemble methods (the methods in Table 2 except VRN Ensemble). This observation further demonstrates that view saliency can be used to boost the 3D recognition performance.

3.2   The Number of Views

We then tested our VS-MVCNN method and MVCNN [23] on the ModelNet10 dataset with different number of views for an object. The results are shown in Fig. 4, it is shown that our method consistently outperforms MVCNN [23]. That is because, our method is benefited from the view saliency. When the number of views is increased to 20, the performance of our model and MVCNN is increased. The recognition performance reaches its peak value when the number of views is larger than 20. That means the discriminativeness power of the learned feature does not increase further when the number of views is larger than 20. That is, the projection images acquired from 20 views of an object have provided the majority discriminative information of an object.

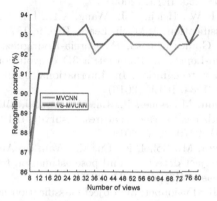

Fig. 4. Recognition accuracy achieved by our VS-MVCNN and MVCNN methods on the ModelNet10 dataset with different number of views.

4   Conclusion

In this paper, we have proposed a view saliency boosted multi-view CNN to exploit the discriminativeness of each view for 3D object recognition. The inter-class and intra-class distances of 2D Zernike Moments are used to measure the view saliency. Then, the view saliency information is used to boost a multi-view CNN. The view saliency is able to obtain discriminative information of a 3D object. Experiments have demonstrated that our proposed method outperforms all the 2D view based CNNs and several 3D data based methods (such as 3D ShapeNets and VoxNet). Our method also achieves the state-of-the-art recognition performance on the ModelNet10 dataset.

Acknowledgments. This work was supported by the National Natural Science Foundation of China (Nos. 61602499, 61601488, 61471371, 61403265), the National Postdoctoral Program for Innovative Talents (No. BX201600172), the Science and Technology Plan of Sichuan Province (No. 2015SZ0226), and China Postdoctoral Science Foundation.

References

1. Brock, A., Lim, T., Ritchie, J.M., Weston, N.: Generative and discriminative voxel modeling with convolutional neural networks. arXiv preprint arXiv:1608.04236 (2016)
2. Chang, A.X., Funkhouser, T., Guibas, L., Hanrahan, P., Huang, Q., Li, Z., Savarese, S., Savva, M., Song, S., Su, H.: Shapenet: an information-rich 3D model repository. arXiv preprint arXiv:1512.03012 (2015)
3. Chatfield, K., Simonyan, K., Vedaldi, A., Zisserman, A.: Return of the devil in the details: delving deep into convolutional nets. In: British Machine Vision Conference (2014)
4. Deng, J., Dong, W., Socher, R., Li, L.J., Li, K., Fei-Fei, L.: Imagenet: a large-scale hierarchical image database. In: IEEE Conference on Computer Vision and Pattern Recognition, pp. 248–255. IEEE (2009)
5. Fan, R.E., Chang, K.W., Hsieh, C.J., Wang, X.R., Lin, C.J.: Liblinear: a library for large linear classification. J. Mach. Learn. Res. **9**, 1871–1874 (2008)
6. Garcia-Garcia, A., Gomez-Donoso, F., Garcia-Rodriguez, J., Orts-Escolano, S., Cazorla, M., Azorin-Lopez, J.: Pointnet: a 3D convolutional neural network for real-time object class recognition. In: International Joint Conference on Neural Networks, pp. 1578–1584. IEEE (2016)
7. Guo, Y., Bennamoun, M., Sohel, F., Lu, M., Wan, J.: 3D object recognition in cluttered scenes with local surface features: a survey. IEEE Trans. Pattern Anal. Mach. Intell. **36**(11), 2270–2287 (2014)
8. Guo, Y., Bennamoun, M., Sohel, F., Lu, M., Wan, J.: An integrated framework for 3-D modeling, object detection, and pose estimation from point-clouds. IEEE Trans. Instrum. Meas. **64**(3), 683–693 (2015)
9. Hegde, V., Zadeh, R.: Fusionnet: 3D object classification using multiple data representations. arXiv preprint arXiv:1607.05695 (2016)
10. Johns, E., Leutenegger, S., Davison, A.J.: Pairwise decomposition of image sequences for active multi-view recognition. In: IEEE Conference on Computer Vision and Pattern Recognition, pp. 3813–3822 (2016)
11. Klokov, R., Lempitsky, V.: Escape from cells: deep kd-networks for the recognition of 3D point cloud models. arXiv preprint arXiv:1704.01222 (2017)
12. Maturana, D., Scherer, S.: Voxnet: a 3D convolutional neural network for real-time object recognition. In: IEEE/RSJ International Conference on Intelligent Robots and Systems, pp. 922–928. IEEE (2015)
13. Phong, B.T.: Illumination for computer generated pictures. Commun. ACM **18**(6), 311–317 (1975)
14. Qi, C.R., Su, H., Mo, K., Guibas, L.J.: Pointnet: deep learning on point sets for 3D classification and segmentation. arXiv preprint arXiv:1612.00593 (2016)
15. Qi, C.R., Su, H., Nießner, M., Dai, A., Yan, M., Guibas, L.J.: Volumetric and multi-view CNNs for object classification on 3D data. In: IEEE Conference on Computer Vision and Pattern Recognition, pp. 5648–5656 (2016)
16. Ravanbakhsh, S., Schneider, J., Poczos, B.: Deep learning with sets and point clouds. arXiv preprint arXiv:1611.04500 (2016)
17. Russakovsky, O., Deng, J., Su, H., Krause, J., Satheesh, S., Ma, S., Huang, Z., Karpathy, A., Khosla, A., Bernstein, M., Berg, A.C., Fei-Fei, L.: Imagenet large scale visual recognition challenge. Int. J. Comput. Vision **115**(3), 211–252 (2015)
18. Sedaghat, N., Zolfaghari, M., Brox, T.: Orientation-boosted voxel nets for 3D object recognition. arXiv preprint arXiv:1604.03351 (2016)

19. Sharma, A., Grau, O., Fritz, M.: VConv-DAE: deep volumetric shape learning without object labels. In: Hua, G., Jégou, H. (eds.) ECCV 2016. LNCS, vol. 9915, pp. 236–250. Springer, Cham (2016). https://doi.org/10.1007/978-3-319-49409-8_20
20. Shi, B., Bai, S., Zhou, Z., Bai, X.: Deeppano: deep panoramic representation for 3D shape recognition. IEEE Signal Process. Lett. **22**(12), 2339–2343 (2015)
21. Sinha, A., Bai, J., Ramani, K.: Deep learning 3D shape surfaces using geometry images. In: Leibe, B., Matas, J., Sebe, N., Welling, M. (eds.) ECCV 2016. LNCS, vol. 9910, pp. 223–240. Springer, Cham (2016). https://doi.org/10.1007/978-3-319-46466-4_14
22. Song, S., Lichtenberg, S.P., Xiao, J.: Sun RGB-D: a RGB-D scene understanding benchmark suite. In: IEEE Conference on Computer Vision and Pattern Recognition, pp. 567–576 (2015)
23. Su, H., Maji, S., Kalogerakis, E., Learned-Miller, E.: Multi-view convolutional neural networks for 3D shape recognition. In: IEEE International Conference on Computer Vision, pp. 945–953 (2015)
24. Vedaldi, A., Lenc, K.: MatConvNet - convolutional neural networks for MATLAB. In: Proceeding of the ACM International Conference on Multimedia (2015)
25. Wang, D., Wang, B., Zhao, S., Yao, H.: View-based 3D object retrieval with discriminative views. Neurocomputing (2017)
26. Wu, Z., Song, S., Khosla, A., Yu, F., Zhang, L., Tang, X., Xiao, J.: 3D shapenets: a deep representation for volumetric shapes. In: IEEE Conference on Computer Vision and Pattern Recognition, pp. 1912–1920 (2015)
27. Xie, Z., Xu, K., Shan, W., Liu, L., Xiong, Y., Huang, H.: Projective feature learning for 3D shapes with multi-view depth images. Comput. Graph. Forum **34**(7), 1–11 (2015)
28. Zhi, S., Liu, Y., Li, X., Guo, Y.: Lightnet: a lightweight 3D convolutional neural network for real-time 3D object recognition. In: Eurographics Workshop on 3D Object Retrieval (2017)

Spacecraft Component Detection in Point Clouds

Quanmao Wei[1,2], Zhiguo Jiang[1,2], Haopeng Zhang[1,2(✉)], and Shanlan Nie[1,2]

[1] School of Astronautics, Image Processing Center, Beihang University,
Beijing 100191, People's Republic of China
zhanghaopeng@buaa.edu.cn
[2] Beijing Key Laboratory of Digital Media, Beijing 100191,
People's Republic of China

Abstract. Component detection of spacecraft is significant for on-orbit operation and space situational awareness. Solar wings and main body are the major components of most spacecrafts, and can be described by geometric primitives like planes, cuboid or cylinder. Based on this prior, pipeline to automatically detect the basic components of spacecraft in 3D point clouds is presented, in which planes, cuboid and cylinder are successively detected. The planar patches are first detected as possible solar wings in point clouds of the recorded object. As for detection of the main body, inferring a cuboid main body from the detected patches is first attempted, and a further attempt to extract a cylinder main body is made if no cuboid exists. Dimensions are estimated for each component. Experiments on satellite point cloud data that are recovered by image-based reconstruction demonstrated effectiveness and accuracy of this pipeline.

Keywords: Component detection · Structure analysis · Spacecraft
Point clouds

1   Introduction

Three dimensional (3D) models, compared to two dimensional (2D) images, are free of perspective projection and can represent the spatial characters of objects, e.g. position, orientation, dimensions and shape. 3D models of space objects have enormous potential for aids in advanced space missions such as autonomous rendezvous, docking and on-orbit self-serving [1,9,10,13]. And detection of specific components, such as solar wings and main body, is a critical task. However, the raw and unstructured point cloud data, which could be acquired by laser scanning [1] or recovered from multi-view images [19], is still primary and can not directly represent the structural information of the recorded object. Addressing on this problem, this paper proposes an automatic pipeline to detect the basic components of spacecrafts, i.e. solar wings and main body.

Recent advances made in 3D acquisition technologies result in a broad availability of 3D models and point clouds, and it further facilitates development of

© Springer Nature Singapore Pte Ltd. 2018
Y. Wang et al. (Eds.): IGTA 2017, CCIS 757, pp. 210–218, 2018.
https://doi.org/10.1007/978-981-10-7389-2_21

approaches to process and analyze these data [2, 6]. For most of these approaches, detection of geometric primitives in the scene is a crucial procedure [8, 15]. To construct 3D building models, plane detection is generally employed for rooftop segmentation [3, 14], and to model installations in industrial sites, cylinders, which are frequently encountered in industrial scenes, are detected as description of pipes or part of other complex installations [11, 12]. As for spacecrafts, most of their solar wings and main bodies can be described as specific geometric shape like plane, cuboid and cylinder. Therefore, higher-level structural representations could be generated by detection of such geometric primitives.

In our proposed pipeline, planar primitives are first detected by Hough transform (HT) paradigm [4, 7], and subsequently updated to planar patches which are treated as possible solar wings. Next, through checking pair-wise geometry relations among these detected patches, existence of cuboid main body is identified. Then the cuboid main body is further estimated with the patches (faces) belong to it if there exists one, otherwise, the detection of cylinder main body is performed in the residual points. Simultaneously, dimension information is estimated for each detected component. Experiments are conducted on point cloud data of satellites that are recovered by image-based method [5, 16, 17, 19]. The results of detection and dimension estimation demonstrate the effectiveness and accuracy of the proposed pipeline.

The rest of this paper is organized as follow. Section 2 gives a detailed description of the proposed pipeline of successive detections for planes, cuboid and cylinder, along with the dimension estimation. Experiment results of the proposed pipeline is presented and analyzed in Sect. 3. A final conclusion of this paper is presented in Sect. 4.

2 Detection Pipeline

The block diagram of the proposed pipeline is shown in Fig. 1. It consists of four stages of processing, namely preprocessing, successive detections of possible solar wings, cuboid main body and cylinder main body. All the four stages are respectively explained as follow.

2.1 Preprocessing

The point cloud data used in our cases are generated by reconstruction from images. These data, compared to laser scanning data, contain severe noise and outliers. Statistical analysis of the k nearest neighbor (knn) can effectively identify outliers that are randomly distributed. However, outliers can be also more structured, as shown in Fig. 3(a), outliers in form of high-density clusters exist separating from the object points. To remove such outliers, clustering method implemented by region growing is used. The input point clouds is clustered into groups by region growing, and only the biggest group is regarded as set of object points.

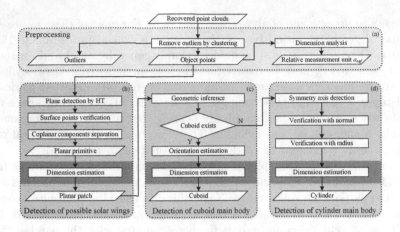

Fig. 1. Block diagram showing the proposed pipeline. (a) Preprocessing; (b) detection of possible solar wings; (c) detection of cuboid main body; and (d) detection of cylinder main body.

Furthermore, to handle the scale variation in different point cloud data, a relative dimensional unit a_{ref} is adaptively defined. In our experiments a_{ref} is set as kD_3, where D_3 is the dimension along the last eigenvector ($\lambda_1 \geq \lambda_2 \geq \lambda_3$) of the covariance tensor of the object points. To keep a balance between the precision and efficiency, k is set to 0.01.

2.2   Detection of Solar Wings

In our plane detection approach, a 3D plane Π is formulated as $s_x X + s_y Y + s_z Z + s_d = 0$, and three separate Hough detections are performed in parallel. For each Hough detection, to uniquely define the plane, one parameter among s_x, s_y and s_z is fixed to 1 and the other two parameters are discretized in range $[-1, 1]$. Π is finally defined as the plane that has the most points among the three separate detection results. In this way, planes with all possible orientations are considered, and trade-off between the accuracy and computation consumption can be easily adjusted too. Besides, only neighborhood of the normal vector need to be voted for each point, when putting the noisy normal information into detection, it accelerates the computation a lot.

Surface points, which belong to the detected plane, are then verified by distance proximity and orientation proximity. However, these points may belong to multiple coplanar solar wings and part of component surfaces that intersect the determined solar wing. To separate these points, a distance proximity based region growing approach is utilized. The group that has the maximum size is kept and finally accepted as possible solar wing if its size is big enough.

Since a solar wing is a bounded planar patch rather than a infinitely extended plane, we update the detected plane primitive to a patch in the dimension estimation step. First the surface points are fitted by the least squares method and all these surface points are projected to the fitted plane. Then two edge directions u, v, as well as the dimensions along these edge directions, are estimated by finding the minimum bounding rectangle (MBR) of the projected points.

Multiple patches are iteratively detected, until no point is residual or the current detected patch is too small. Before inferring the cuboid faces, all these detected patches are treated as possible solar wings.

2.3   Detection of Cuboid Main Body

Faces of the cuboid main body, if exist, may also be detected as patches, as shown in Fig. 3(c-1). An inferring approach is proposed to distinguish these patches. As for a cuboid, there are two kinds of pair-wise geometry relations among its 6 faces, the opposite faces and the adjacent faces. To identify the existence of such cuboid, criteria to verify there relations are exploited.

1. **Criterion for two opposite faces**: (a) their plane normals are parallel and edges of them are respectively parallel too; (b) the line passing their centers is parallel to the plane normal.
2. **Criterion for two adjacent faces**: (a) their plane normals are perpendicular and edges of them are respectively parallel or perpendicular; and (b) they have one common edge.

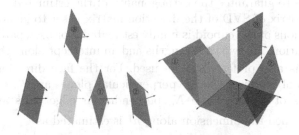

Fig. 2. Criteria for opposite (left) and adjacent (right) faces. The gray patch is a reference patch, the green one passes all the criteria, while the red ones do not satisfy the orientation (case 1 and 2) or position (case 3) requirements. (Color figure online)

For criteria of both opposite and adjacent faces, condition (a) constrains the orientation relations so that case 1 and case 2 in Fig. 2 can be filtered, condition (b) constrains the position relations so that case 3 in Fig. 2 can be filtered. A group of cuboid faces, among which each pair of patches satisfy the opposite or adjacent criterion, can be extracted if there exists a cuboid. Then orientation and dimensions of this cuboid is further estimated as follow.

First, the edge confidence coefficient is estimated. For one edge E of some patch Π_q, all the surface points are projected to E, and the distribution range of the projected points along E is split into N_{Bin} ($N_{Bin} = 10$ in our experiments) bins. The confidence associated with E is then estimated as

$$conf = \frac{-\Sigma_{i=1}^{N_{Bin}}(p_i \ln p_i)}{\ln N_{Bin}} \qquad (1)$$

Where $p_i = n_i/N_{Pts}$, n_i is the number of points that fall in the i-th bin, N_{Pts} is the total number of surface points of Π_q. $En = -\Sigma_{i=1}^{N_{Bin}}(p_i \ln p_i)$ represents the distribution entropy, and $En_{Max} = \ln N_{Bin}$ is the maximum value that En can reach when these points are uniformly distributed.

Then, three orthogonal directions are estimated to define the orientation. Each patch has three orthogonal direction vectors, i.e. one plane normal and two edge vectors. The plane normal is preferred as it is generally more accurate and credible than the edge ones. For a face direction n^f of the cuboid, assume there are N_n ($N_n \le 2$) plane normals n_i^n, $i = 0, 1, ..., N_n$, and N_e ($N_e \le 4$) edge directions n_j^e, $j = 0, 1, ..., N_e$, that are associated with n^f. Then n^f is estimated as

$$\hat{n^f} = \begin{cases} \frac{e_2^2 n_1^n + e_1^2 n_2^n}{e_1^2 + e_2^2} & N_n = 2, \\ n_1^n & N_n = 1, \\ \frac{\Sigma_{j=1}^{N_e} conf_j^2 n_j^e}{\Sigma_{j=1}^{N_e} conf_j^2} & N_n = 0. \end{cases} \qquad (2)$$

Where e is the fitted error of the surface plane, $conf_i$ is the confidence associated with n_i^e. To guarantee the orthogonality of the estimated face directions, the diagonal matrix of SVD of the direction matrix is set to identity.

The dimensions of the cuboid is finally estimated. For each patch, it can offer 2.5 size information, i.e. two edge lengths and an intercept along the face vector. The intercept is also preferred to be used. For the face direction $\hat{n^f}$, assume the projections of center of the N_n perpendicular planes are l_i^n, $i = 1, 2, ..., N_n$, and projections of center of the N_e perpendicular edge pairs are a_j^e and b_j^e, $j = 1, 2, ..., N_e$, then the dimension along $\hat{n^f}$ is estimated as

$$D_{\hat{n^f}} = \begin{cases} abs(l_1^n - l_2^n) & N_n = 2, \\ \max_{q=a,b}\{abs(l_1^n - med(q_j^e))\} & N_n = 1, \\ abs(med(a_j^e) - med(b_j^e)) & N_n = 0. \end{cases} \qquad (3)$$

Note that, due to the noise and detail of the cuboid main body, a face might be detected as multiple patches. To handle these cases, patches that are close to a face of the detected cuboid and can be mostly included by that face will be merged into the cuboid.

2.4   Detection of Cylinder Main Body

If no cuboid main body is detected in Sect. 2.3, a subsequent attempt will be made to detect a cylinder one, on the assumption that there is at least one cuboid or cylinder main body in one spacecraft.

Based on the observation that the surface normals would always intersect with the symmetry axis, an axial-symmetry-based method to detect cylinder is proposed. First, normal of each point is drawn in a discretized 3D space, points (voxels) at which more than 5 normals intersect are then used to estimate the symmetry axis by PCA. The axis is defined as the line that is parallel to the first eigenvector and passes the mean location of these intersections.

To verify the surface points of the determined cylinder, normal vector and radius are successively used. A point is initially accepted as a surface point if the vertical distance of its normal to the symmetry axis is small. Then a mean radius R is evaluated with these verified points. And for each verified points, it is re-verified with the radius information. Only points located around the cylinder faces with radius R are final accepted. R is updated at last, and the length of the cylinder is defined as the dimension of the surface points along the axis.

3   Experiment

Point cloud data used in our experiments are recovered from simulated images sequences [18, 19]. The objects recorded in these data are Helios-2A (1st row in Fig. 3) and Tiangong-1 (2nd row in Fig. 3). Thresholds and parameter values used in our experiments, which have been obtained by trial and error experiments, can be found in Table 1.

Table 1. Parameters for detections in the proposed pipeline

Parameters	Value
Discretization accuracy for s_x, s_y and s_z	0.01
Discretization accuracy for s_d	$1 \times a_{ref}$
Distance threshold in planar surface points verification (T_{dis})	$(2-4) \times a_{ref}$
Angle threshold in planar surface points verification (T_{ang})	$15°$
Angle deviation for parallel and perpendicular patches	$5°$
Distance deviation for adjacent planes	$5 \times a_{ref}$

The component detection results of Helios-2A and Tiangong-1 are illustrated in Fig. 3. Note that the main body detection result of Helios-2A do not include the loads below, which complicate the shape of main body. And the main body of Tiangong-1 is treated as a whole cylinder while it actually contains two capsules. Our pipeline effectively detect the solar wings and main bodies except for solar wing of Helios-2A. Due to the lack of texture, the solar wing of Helios-2A is few recovered except for its frame, and our pipeline failed to detect plane in such sparse points.

To quantitatively evaluate the accuracy of the detection results, the relative dimension ratio ($Ratio_{Est}$) of each detected component is computed, along with

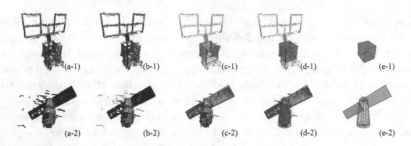

Fig. 3. Results of component detection. (a) Input point clouds that contain severe noise and high-density clustering outliers. (b) Outliers (in green) are effectively identified. (c) Planes are detected and updated to planar patches. (d) Infer a cuboid main body from the patches or detect a cylinder one from the residual points. (e) A clear view of the detected components. (Color figure online)

its ground truth ($Ratio_{GT}$), which is directly measured from the models. The comparison is presented in Table 2, dimension ratios of solar wing and cuboid main body are in form that $l1 : l2 : l3$ ($l1 \leq l2 \leq l3$), and dimension ratio of a cylinder is ratio of its length to its radius. The deviations are all less than 20%.

Table 2. Relative dimension ratio of each component

Object	Component	$Ratio_{GT}$	$Ratio_{Est}$	Deviation (%)
Helios-2A	Cuboid MB	1 : 1 : 1.25	1 : 1.00 : 1.17	0.03, 6.4
	Solar wing	1 : 2.43	Undetected	–
Tiangong-1	Cylinder MB	1 : 5.94	1 : 6.09	2.5
	Solar wing	1 : 2.54	1 : 2.08	18.1
			1 : 2.24	11.8

4   Conclusion

In this paper, a pipeline is proposed to automatically detect the basic components of spacecrafts, which results in a higher structural level representations. The basic components are treated as geometric primitives such as planes, cuboid or cylinder. Therefore, detections for such primitives are successively conducted. To detect the cuboid, an approach to infer a cuboid from group of patches is proposed. Specifically, criteria to determine cuboid faces are proposed, as well as methods to estimate the orientation and dimensions of the cuboid. And a novel axial-symmetry-based cylinder detection approach is also presented, in which the cylinder is robustly detected through detection of its axis and verification of its surface points. The experiment performance on the recovered point cloud data, which are relative sparse and inhomogeneous on the one hand, and surfer from severe noise and outliers on the other hand, verified the effectiveness and accuracy.

To further improve this pipeline, more structure details, such as antennas, imaging sensors and supporting structure, should be considered in, as well as shape refinement of the detected components. Global structure properties of the object and relations of different components could be further exploited to improve the accuracy.

Acknowledgements. This work was supported in part by the National Natural Science Foundation of China (Grant Nos. 61501009, 61371134 and 61071137), the National Key Research and Development Program of China (2016YFB0501300, 2016YFB0501302), the Aerospace Science and Technology Innovation Fund of CASC, and the Fundamental Research Funds for the Central Universities.

References

1. Benninghoff, H., Boge, T., Rems, F.: Autonomous navigation for on-orbit servicing. KI-Knstliche Intell. **28**(2), 77–83 (2014)
2. Berger, M., Tagliasacchi, A., Seversky, L.M., Alliez, P., Guennebaud, G., Levine, J.A., Sharf, A., Silva, C.T.: A survey of surface reconstruction from point clouds. Comput. Graph. Forum **36**, 301–329 (2016). Wiley Online Library
3. Cao, R., Zhang, Y., Liu, X., Zhao, Z.: Roof plane extraction from airborne lidar point clouds. Int. J. Remote Sens. **38**(12), 3684–3703 (2017)
4. Duda, R.O., Hart, P.E.: Use of the Hough transformation to detect lines and curves in pictures. Commun. ACM **15**(1), 11–15 (1972)
5. Furukawa, Y., Ponce, J.: Accurate, dense, and robust multi-view stereopsis. In: 2007 IEEE Conference on Computer Vision and Pattern Recognition, pp. 1–8 (2007)
6. Grilli, E., Menna, F., Remondino, F.: A review of point clouds segmentation and classification algorithms. Int. Arch. Photogramm. Remote Sens. Spatial Inf. Sci. **XLII–2/W3**, 339–344 (2017)
7. Hough, P.: Method and means for recognizing complex patterns (1962)
8. Limberger, F.A., Oliveira, M.M.: Real-time detection of planar regions in unorganized point clouds. Pattern Recogn. **48**(6), 2043–2053 (2015)
9. Opromolla, R., Fasano, G., Rufino, G., Grassi, M.: Pose estimation for spacecraft relative navigation using model-based algorithms. IEEE Trans. Aerosp. Electron. Syst. **53**(1), 431–447 (2017)
10. Ouyang, B., Yu, Q., Xiao, J., Yu, S.: Dynamic pose estimation based on 3D point clouds. In: 2015 IEEE International Conference on Information and Automation, pp. 2116–2120. IEEE (2015)
11. Pang, G., Qiu, R., Huang, J., You, S., Neumann, U.: Automatic 3D industrial point cloud modeling and recognition. In: 2015 14th IAPR International Conference on Machine Vision Applications (MVA), pp. 22–25. IEEE (2015)
12. Rabbani, T., Van Den Heuvel, F.: Efficient Hough transform for automatic detection of cylinders in point clouds. In: ISPRS WG III/3, III/4, vol. 3, pp. 60–65 (2005)
13. Ruel, S., Luu, T., Berube, A.: Space shuttle testing of the tridar 3D rendezvous and docking sensor. J. Field Rob. **29**(4), 535–553 (2012)
14. Tarsha-Kurdi, F., Landes, T., Grussenmeyer, P.: Hough-transform and extended ransac algorithms for automatic detection of 3D building roof planes from lidar data. In: Proceedings of the ISPRS Workshop on Laser Scanning, vol. 36, pp. 407–412 (2007)

15. Vosselman, G., Gorte, B.G., Sithole, G., Rabbani, T.: Recognising structure in laser scanner point clouds. Int. Arch. Photogramm. Remote Sens. Spat. Inf. Sci. **46**(8), 33–38 (2004)
16. Wu, C.: Towards linear-time incremental structure from motion. In: 2013 International Conference on 3D Vision - 3DV 2013, pp. 127–134 (2013)
17. Wu, C., Agarwal, S., Curless, B., Seitz, S.M.: Multicore bundle adjustment. In: CVPR 2011, pp. 3057–3064 (2011)
18. Zhang, H., Liu, Z., Jiang, Z., An, M., Zhao, D.: BUAA-SID1. 0 space object image dataset. Spacecr. Recovery Remote Sens. **31**(4), 65–71 (2010)
19. Zhang, H., Wei, Q., Jiang, Z.: Sequential-image-based space object 3D reconstruction. J. Beijing Univ. Aeronaut. Astronaut. **42**(2), 273–279 (2016)

Research on 3D Modeling of Geological Interface Surface

Qianlin Dong[1], Qing-yuan Li[1,2(✉)], Zhu-bin Wei[1], Jie Liu[1], and Minghui Zhang[1]

[1] College of Geoscience and Surveying Engineering,
China University of Mining and Technology, Beijing 100083, China
dql2008@126.com
[2] Key Laboratory of Geo-Informatics, Chinese Academy of Surveying and Mapping,
Beijing 100830, China
liqy@casm.ac.cn

Abstract. With the steady and fast economical development and the protection of resource and environment, the demand for high accuracy of coal resource exploration is strict. Generally, conventional coal exploration results are shown in two-dimensional geological maps. It is very difficult to represent three-dimensional spatial distribution of geological body in direct and visual way. Based on borehole, two-dimensional topographic and geologic map, coal seam floor contour maps and geological cross sections, this paper reconstructs 3-dimensional spatial distribution of ground surface, coal seam, shape of main faults in study area. Based on multi-source geological data, three-dimensional geological modeling results clearly show us coal seam shape features, coal accumulating scope and intensity of each sedimentary cycle, structural outline characteristics. Therefore, it is a very effective means using three-dimensional geological modeling for the analysis of the coal bed deposition, structure.

Keywords: Three-dimensional modeling · Constrained triangulation
Coal seam floor reconstruction · Faults reconstruction

1 Introduction

The concept of three-dimensional geological modeling (3DGM) was firstly proposed by Canadian scholar Houlding in the early 1990s [1]. As a newly developing technology, 3DGM is very useful for the study of Coal geological structure [2]. Coal seam roof, floor, unconformity and fault are very important interfaces of geological body. The reconstruction methods for these interfaces have always been the basis and hot issues of geological 3D modeling [3]. Surface spline interpolation method was firstly introduced by Yu [4] to reconstruct coal seam floor surface and it had acquired very good application effect. Fractal method was used by Yfantis [5] and Rakawak [6] to simulate geological interface and ground surface. NURBS method was used by Fisher [7] and Zhong et al. [8] to simulate geological surface and entity. 3-D Bezier was used to simulate complex geological structures by De Kemp [9]. Complexly folded surfaces was reconstructed by mathematic methods by Moore and Johnson [10]. Wu and Xu [11] mathematically described the spatial geometry of faults using the method of single plane or multiple plane fitting fault plane, Because the sampling data is usually spatially sparse

© Springer Nature Singapore Pte Ltd. 2018
Y. Wang et al. (Eds.): IGTA 2017, CCIS 757, pp. 219–231, 2018.
https://doi.org/10.1007/978-981-10-7389-2_22

and heterogeneously distributed. The data model is also usually not uniform [12], meanwhile, the geological data have characteristics such as multi-source, multi-scale and multi-temporal, etc. These all above make geological study objects have classic typical characteristics of gray information [13] which determines the complexity and uncertainty of 3DGM. At present, the data for 3-dimensional mining modeling is usually single which are mostly confined to borehole data and ground surveying data. A great deal of geological cross-section maps which include abundant expert knowledge have not been fully utilized. This paper has integrated multi-source geological data (including 43 boreholes, 3 coal seam floor maps, 1 ground topographic & geological map, 13 cross sections) by converting data from different sources and types (including converting original MapGIS data, CAD data and text file into corresponding file format of 3-dimensional geological modeling platform "3D geological engineer assistant" (D3A software). The authors have reconstructed three-dimensional geological model of Sanlutian exploration area in Muli area of Qinghai province in China by expanding function module of D3A software through VC++, OpenGL programming.

2   Coal Seam Floor and Ground Surface Reconstruction of Sanlutian

2.1   Basic Modeling Principle

2.1.1   Two Dimensional-Delaunay Triangulation

Triangle is the simplex in plane domain, triangulation network is particularly suitable for fitting complex topography surface, geological interface, etc. In other words, triangulation network mainly represents surface in the 3D solid geometric modeling system. The circumcircle of each triangle in Delaunay Triangulation does not contain any other point inside. 2D Delaunay triangulation has strict mathematical definition and complete theoretical basis. Meanwhile, it has good capability of representing boundaries and constrained adaptability, so it is widely used in three dimensional geological modeling fields. Complex geological bodies often contain a lot of faults. The relationship among these faults is also very complex. These faults can be seen as constrained condition of triangulation for geological interfaces cut by faults. Currently the most popular constrained Delaunay triangulation algorithm was proposed by Chew in 1989. The basic idea is that constrained lines are divided into smaller sub-lines and then triangulation is carried out. 3D scattered point set on the non-overlapping single-value surface is generally transfered through projection transformation into 2D plane points and then Delaunay triangulation is carried out to fulfill the construction of 3D TIN surface. For multi-Z value geological surface such as overturned folds, they are usually divided into two single-value surfaces and are reconstructed separately [14]. In this paper, constrained Delaunay triangulation is carried out based on constrained condition such as fault lines, coal seam boundary lines, contour lines, etc. to reconstruct coal seam floor surface and ground surface.

2.1.2   Fault Line, Boundary Line and Contour Line Intersection Algorithm

In China, Coal seam floor contour map is always drawn by MapGIS/AutoCAD software. When geological engineering technicians draw the map, they only label elevation value beside the contour lines, while seam floor contour map is still 2-dimensional graphic. It does not reflect ups and downs of coal seam floor surface from real 3D angle. So we need to set these 2D floor contour lines with elevation value to transfer into 3D contour lines. Then Delaunay triangulation is carried out based on constrained condition of seam floor contour lines to make it real 3D coal seam floor map.

Similarly, both fault line and boundary line in the floor contour map are 2D lines. Compared with floor contour lines, they even do not have elevation attribute values. Therefore, we need to obtain three-dimensional both fault lines and floor contour lines. To achieve this aim, this paper carries out line intersecting operation between each fault line and its adjacent floor contour line. In the same way, the line intersecting operation is done between each coal seam boundary line and its adjacent floor contour line. As results, a series of new intersection points are generated both in fault line and coal seam boundary line, then we set them with elevation value in association with corresponding contour line. So we obtain a series of intersection points with real 3D coordinate. Finally, 3D fault line and coal seam boundary line are obtained through linear interpolation. Here the key algorithm is 2D line intersection algorithm. It is basic problem of CAD, Computer Graphics, GIS, etc. Line section can be expressed by mathematical formula below:

$$
\begin{cases}
x = x_m + s * (x_n - x_m) \\
y = y_m + t * (y_n - y_m)
\end{cases}
\quad (0 \leq s \leq 1, 0 \leq t \leq 1)
\tag{1}
$$

where (x_m, y_m), (x_n, y_n) are two endpoints of a line section, s, t are the two parameters to be solved. Given two lines MN and KL in which the start point and end point are (x_m, y_m), (x_n, y_n), (x_k, y_k), (x_l, y_l) separately. Two variables can be calculated based on the line formula in Eq. (1).

$$
s = \frac{(x_n - x_m)(y_m - y_k) - (y_n - y_m)(x_m - x_k)}{(x_n - x_m)(y_l - y_k) - (y_n - y_m)(x_l - x_k)}
\tag{2}
$$

$$
t = \frac{(x_l - x_k)(y_m - y_k) - (y_l - y_k)(x_m - x_k)}{(x_n - x_m)(y_l - y_k) - (y_n - y_m)(x_l - x_k)}
\tag{3}
$$

If the value of s, t are between [0,1], then there is a intersection point of Line MN and Line KL. We substitute s into parametric equation of Line MN or substitute t into parametric equation of Line KL, then we can obtain the coordinate of intersection point. If the value of s,t are out of [0,1], there is no intersection point between Line MN and Line KL.

In this paper, we integrate 43 boreholes, 1 ground surface and geological map, 3 coal seam floor contour maps, 13 cross sections to reconstruct 3D geological model.

2.2 Data Preprocessing

In this paper, the original coal seam floor surface contour map and ground surface and geological map are drawn by MapGIS software. We need to do some work about data preprocessing before 3D geological modeling. Firstly, irrelevant lines and characters in the map should be deleted. For coal seam floor surface contour map, only floor contour lines, fault lines and boundary lines should be left. For geological ground surface map, only contour lines should be left. Secondly, there are some cases in which contour lines are discontinuous when cartographers draw the map using MapGIS software: (1) in order to mark elevation value, contour lines are broken off; (2) when topographic-geological map is drawn, cartographers usually need to add lithologic symbol in some area of the map which cover the contour lines; (3) sometimes the same long contour line is made up of several small line segments because of some kinds of reason. In such cases above, we need to re-connect these line segments. In this paper, the authors carry out constrained triangulation based on constrained condition of boundary lines, fault lines, floor contour lines. to reconstruct coal seam bottom surface (Fig. 1).

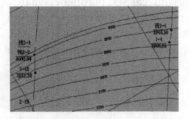   

(a)The contour line is disconnected by   (b) The contour line is disconnected by
elevation value   lithology character

(c) Original Contour line is made up of several sub-lines

Fig. 1. Three cases of Incontinuity of original contour line

2.3 Coal Seam Floor and Ground SurFace 3D Reconstruction

Coal seam floor contour map contains elevation level of coal seam in stratum, geological structure and their mutual relationship, etc. It is foundation of coal mining design, improvement, extension, etc. It is also basis of coal reserve calculation, dynamic change management and mining engineering production design [15]. Meanwhile, it is a good and effective way to reconstruct 3D coal seam using floor contour map with its abundant geological information.

The coal seam floor contour maps collected in study area include floor contour map of top-4 top-5 and bottom-1 coal seam. Topographic-geological map and 43 borehole data are also collected. Based on the geological data above, floor surfaces of the three coal seam and ground surface are reconstructed. Meanwhile, modeling result is validated by borehole data. The overall technique route map of coal seam floor surface reconstruction of Sanlutian exploration area is shown in Fig. 2.

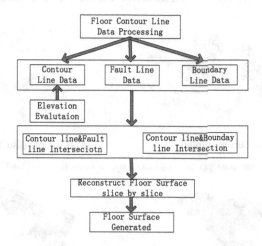

Fig. 2. Coal seam floor surface reconstruction technology route map

Processing of bottom-1 coal seam floor contour map data is taken as example. The original data of bottom-1 coal seam floor contour map is MapGIS file. Firstly, original data should be preprocessed and input the data into D3A software. Secondly, both fault lines and coal boundary lines are intersected with coal seam floor contour lines with elevation value to get real 3D fault lines and coal boundary lines. The original coal seam is cut by faults into several pieces of small coal seams. In order to make 3D modeling convenient, each piece of small coal seam is reconstructed separately. Each small piece of coal seam is carried out constrained delaunay triangulation by relevant coal seam boundary, fault lines and floor contour lines. Figure 3(a) is the constrained delaunay triangulation mesh of bottom-1 coal seam floor in which Y axis points to the North. According to the same principle, 3D topographical-geological map is constructed based on 2D topographical-geological map, as shown in Fig. 3(b). Figure 3(c) is the borehole distribution map in exploration area. In order to show borehole data effectively, transparent display is adopted for ground surface to show how each borehole extend to the depths of underground. Figure 3(d) is the three coal seam floor overlay map in which top-4 coal seam is displayed in red color, top-5 coal seam is displayed in blue and bottom-1 coal seam is displayed in black. The ground surface and coal seam floor overlay map is as shown in Fig. 3(e).

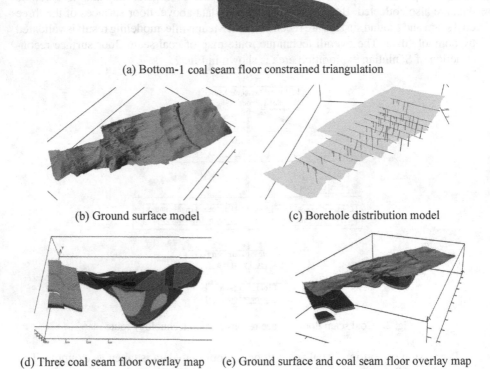

(a) Bottom-1 coal seam floor constrained triangulation

(b) Ground surface model   (c) Borehole distribution model

(d) Three coal seam floor overlay map   (e) Ground surface and coal seam floor overlay map

Fig. 3. Coal seam floor and ground surface 3D reconstruction (Color figure online)

3 Main Fault Surface Reconstruction

There are both normal faults and reserve faults in the exploration area. For normal faults, constrained triangulation is carried out with intersection line of broken coal as constrained line to reconstruct normal fault surface. For reverse faults, constrained triangulation is carried out with fault lines in 13 cross sections as constrained line to reconstruct reverse fault surface. Because reconstruction procedure of normal fault is relatively easy, it is not introduced in detail. Here the process of reserve faults 3D modeling is explained in detail.

3.1 Real 3D Cross Section Generating

It is an important method to reconstruct 3D fault surface using cross sections generated by coal geological exploration. Firstly, conventional 2D cross sections should be converted into real 3D ones. In other words, real 3D cross sections need to be generated.

Here the key point is how 2D points in cross sections are converted into 3D spatial coordinate system. The transformation principle and implementation method of 2D cross section converted to real 3D ones is: (1) Firstly, 2D cross section is divided into several small parts based on the start point, the end point of cross section line and borehole orifice point in the prospect line; (2) Secondly, 3D cross section framework is established based on 2D prospect polyline; (3) Finally, feature points in 2D cross section is transformed into 3D spatial coordinate system step by step. Meanwhile, turning control points are added for the long lines which step across turning points of cross section.

Concretely speaking, as original cross section is two-dimensional, the points on the cross section only have the x and y coordinates. The y coordinate usually corresponds to the z coordinate in real three-dimensional coordinate system, while the x coordinate corresponds to the x or y coordinate. So the y coordinate values can be transformed to the z coordinate in real three-dimensional space based on the reference of elevation line and map scale. For the exploration lines with multi directions, the directions of every sub-line need to be determined through the angle between sub-line and x axis, then the three-dimensional coordinates of all nodes on the prospecting polyline can be calculated. Through programming, the transformation from two-dimensional exploration lines to three-dimensional ones is realized. There are 13 cross sections in the exploration area and the format of the original map is MAPGIS data format. Firstly, the data should be transformed to DXF format and then imported into D3A platform to transform them into D3A format. To make it convenient for establishing three-dimensional model, the cross sections in D3A format should be pre-processed, and the lines of cross sections should be divided into many sub-layers, such as fault line layer, stratum interface line layer, drill line layer, ground surface line layer, elevation line layer and so on. Then, the same code number for fault lines on 13 cross sections of the same fault is assigned. The code

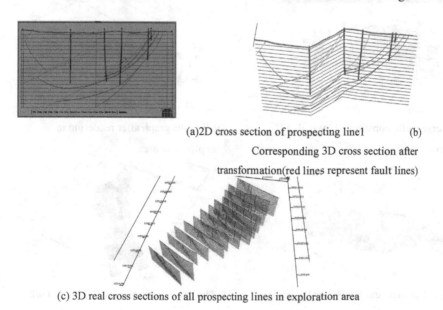

(a)2D cross section of prospecting line1   (b)

Corresponding 3D cross section after

transformation(red lines represent fault lines)

(c) 3D real cross sections of all prospecting lines in exploration area

Fig. 4. Transformation from 2D cross sections to real 3D cross sections (Color figure online)

numbers are like F1, F2, F26, F27, F28, and so on. The original 2D cross section of prospecting line 1 drawn in MapGIS software is shown in Fig. 4(a) Meanwhile, the corresponding 3D real cross section transformed by programming is shown in Fig. 4(b). Figure 4(c) is the overall effect map of real 3D cross sections in exploration areas.

3.2 Fault Surface Reconstruction

Based on fault line coding number above, minimum span length distance algorithm is adopted to carry out constrained triangulation with the same code of fault line as constrained boundary. Minimum span length distance algorithm is also called minimum diagonal line algorithm which is the most common local optimized algorithm. It is archived by three steps: (1) Step1: All outlines or fault lines should be projected, zoomed

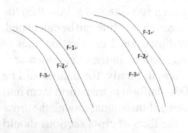

(a)Code number for faults in adjacent cross sections

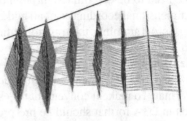

(b)Fault surface triangular mesh reconstruction

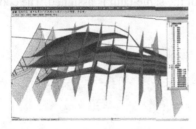

(c)Reverse faults constructed by real 3D cross sections

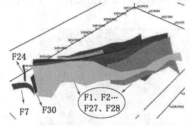

(d)All faults graph after rendering in exploration area

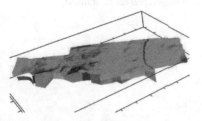

(e)Ground surface and faults overlay map

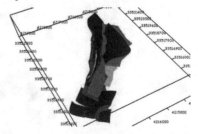

(f) The cut of bottom-1 coal seam by faults

Fig. 5. Faults 3D reconstruction

and moved to similar-size rectangle to make sure that two adjacent line have the same shape and center; (2) Step2: Search the best starting point; (3) Step3: Extend the triangular mesh step by step and choose the shorter one between two diagonal lines as extended line. The minimum diagonal line algorithm is simple and easy to be implemented. Generally speaking, it would generate model with good quality when outlines have similar trend, shape and location. Based on the principle above, 3D reverse fault surface of all coding number is generated. It is a simple example of coding number for fault lines in adjacent cross sections as shown in Fig. 5(a). The triangulation mesh of each reverse fault is constructed based on fault lines with the same coding number is shown in Fig. 5(b). The final 3D graph of reverse fault is shown in Fig. 5(c) which has no illumination rendering effect. The illumination rendering effect graph of all fault surfaces including both normal faults and reverse faults is shown in Fig. 5(d). The ground surface and fault overlay graph is shown in Fig. 5(e). Figure 5(f) shows us that how the faults in exploration area cut bottom-1 coal seam. The reconstructed result of faults clearly shows us that how the faults extend to the depths of underground and how the faults cut the main coal seam and make the coal seam move. Obviously, it provides important reference to mining engineering technician about how they could design and arrange laneway. Due to the inefficiency of original data, the reconstructed fault surface is only part of real fault, how to extend these faults both to ground surface and to the depth of underground deep in the earth should be further considered.

4 Fault Surface Smooth

The fault surfaces generated by the method above always tend to be stiff, so they need to be processed to become more smooth. In short, virtual fault line between original fault lines should be added to reconstruct fault surface triangular mesh in order to make reconstructed fault surface become more smooth. Because points in original fault line are homogeneously distributed, they do not need any processing. In the smoothing process of original fault triangulation mesh, it must meet this constraint condition: the post-processed fault surface must go through original fault lines. In other words, it must go through all the points of original fault lines. In this paper, Cardinal spline curve is used to transform surface smooth processing into polyline smooth processing to reconstruct fine triangular mesh. Cardinal spline is piecewise interpolation cubic curve, and furthermore tangent is appointed at every endpoint location. Meanwhile, it is not necessary to provide tangent value of endpoint. In Cardinal spline, slope value of control point can be calculated by adjacent control point coordinate. A Cardinal spline is fixed by four consecutive control points in which two control point is endpoint of curve segment while the other two points are used to compute slope value of endpoint. It is assumed that there are four consecutive control points P_{k-1}, P_k, P_{k+1}, P_{k+2} and P(u) is parameter cubic function formula of P_k and P_{k+1} (u is parameter), then the constraint condition for building Cardinal spline using four control points from P_{k-1} to P_{k+2} is:

$$P(u) = \begin{bmatrix} u^3 & u^2 & u & 1 \end{bmatrix} * M_c \begin{bmatrix} P_{K-1} \\ P_K \\ P_{K+1} \\ P_{K+2} \end{bmatrix} \tag{4}$$

In which Cardinal matrix is

$$M_C = \begin{bmatrix} -s & 2-s & s-2 & s \\ 2s & s-3 & 3-2s & -s \\ -s & 0 & s & 0 \\ 0 & 1 & 0 & 0 \end{bmatrix} \tag{5}$$

where $s = (1 - t)/2$, t is tension coefficient.

The concrete step using Cardinal spline to achieve fault surface fine expression is as below: (1) Step1: the elevation scope should be determined. Meanwhile, the upper boundary should both rounded up and the lower boundary should be rounded down in order to expand the scope a little (e.g. from 2650 to 4200); (2) Step2: Appropriate elevation interval should be chosen; (3) Step3: For each fault line, maximum and minimum elevation value should be determined (e.g. 3000, 3850); (4) Step4: For each fault line, a series of adopting elevation points with the same interval should be produced using linear interpolation (e.g. 3000, 3050, 3100, …, 3800, 3850); (5) Step5: For the lower boundary point of fault curve surface, the larger adopting elevation value between the lowest adopting elevation points of two adjacent fault lines is used to determine appropriate interpolation point number based on the distance between the two adopting elevation points and then carry out interpolation using Cardinal spline. The same interpolation method is used for upper boundary points of fault curve surface; (6) Step6: For both upper and lower boundary, a virtual elevation point should be generated at the same elevation interval using linear interpolation; (7) Step7: For sampling points and virtual points with the same elevation value, appropriate interpolation point number should be determined by the distance between points, then Cardinal spline is used; (8) Step8: triangulation is carried out for all fault points and interpolation points.

Figure 6(a) is the triangular mesh of F27 fault before smooth in the exploration area and Fig. 6(b) is corresponding illumination rendering effect map. Meanwhile, Fig. 6(c) is the triangular mesh of F27 fault after smooth and Fig. 6(d) is corresponding illumination rendering effect map. The illumination rendering effect map of main reverse faults in the exploration area is shown in Fig. 6(e). It is obvious that both the boundary and inside of fault surface are much more smooth than original graph after Cardinal spline function is used.

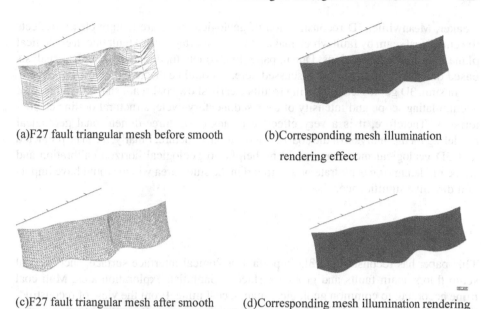

(a)F27 fault triangular mesh before smooth

(b)Corresponding mesh illumination rendering effect

(c)F27 fault triangular mesh after smooth

(d)Corresponding mesh illumination rendering

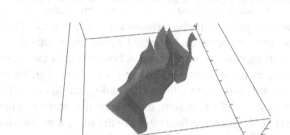

(e) The overall effect map of reverse faults after rendering

Fig. 6. 3D surface smooth results of faults

5   Brief Geological Analysis Based on 3D Modelling

This paper has established fine 3D geological model based on multi-source geological data in the exploration area. The 3D modeling results clearly show the shape feature of coal seam, coal accumulation range and intensity of each sedimentary cycle, structure outline, etc. The faults in the study area are divided into three group of faults including Northwest directional reverse faults, Northeast directional normal faults and Northwest directional normal faults according to 3D modeling results. It is clearly found that, from bottom-1 coal seam to top-5 coal seam to top-4 coal seam, coal seam distribution range is becoming smaller and smaller based on 3D reconstruction of coal seam floor. Meanwhile, the thickness of coal seam is becoming thinner and thinner according to borehole data. Combined with geological survey data, it can be concluded that from Jurassic period coal accumulating intensity of each sedimentary cycle is becoming weaker and weaker. Meanwhile, 3D reconstruction of geological structure feature clearly reflects the cut of coal seam by fault which make up for the shortage of 2D fault line in geological plane map and cross sections. Due to paper limited length, detailed geological analysis based on 3D modeling are not discussed here, it would be discussed in another paper.

In sum, 3D geological modeling results clearly show coal seam shape features, coal accumulating scope and intensity of each sedimentary cycle, structural outline characteristics. Therefore, it is a very effective means using three-dimensional geological modeling for the analysis of the coal bed deposition, structure. Finally, it can be predicted that 3D geological modeling would be helpful to geological horizon calibration and shape modeling of gas hydrate newly found in the study area which would have important directive significance.

6   Conclusion

This paper has reconstructed 3D important geological interface surface, such as coal seam floors, main faults and ground surface in Sanlutian exploration area, Muli coal mine according to common geological map in coal mine. From the view of reconstruction of 3D model, it is obviously economic, quick and accurate method to reconstruct real 3D coal seam floor by adopting constraint Delaunay triangulation technique based on coal seam floor map compared with the methods used in references [8, 9, 12]. Based on cross sections, the reconstructed underground faults are relatively accurate and reasonable because of strong constraint condition of borehole data and reasonable inference from geological expert when cross sections are drawn. However, the reconstructed faults above tend to be stiff, this paper adopts Cardinal spline to smooth fault surface and it is proved to obtain good effect. In sum, it is an effective method proposed by this paper to reconstruct 3D geological interface model in the study area. Obviously, the 3D modeling result is very useful to carry out tectonic analysis, sedimentation analysis and it would strengthen our profound comprehension of geological phenomenon in the study area.

Acknowledgement.   This work is supported by National Nature Science Foundation of China project "Theory and method of anisotropic property field inner geology body based on volume function" (Projec number 41272367) and "Coupled deposit mechanism and basin kinetic control of coal measure gas in Juhugeng mining of Muli coalfield" (Projec number 41572141).

References

1. Houlding, S.W.: 3D Geoscience Modeling, Computer Technique for Geological Characterization. Springer, Heidelberg (1994). https://doi.org/10.1007/978-3-642-79012-6
2. Qingyuan, L., Qianlin, D., Huiling, J.: 3D geological modeling technology and its application in coalfield structure. Coal Geol. China 26(8), 39–44 (2014). (In Chinese)
3. Jing, M.: 3D geological modeling research. J. Geogr. Geogr. Inform. Sci. 27(4), 14–20 (2011). (In Chinese)
4. Yu, Z.: A new method for interpolating geological surface. J. China Univ. Min. Technol. 16(4), 69–76 (1987). (In Chinese)

5. Yfantis, E.A.: Simulation of geological surfaces using fractals. Math. Geol. **20**(6), 667–672 (1988)
6. Rakawak, A., Krotkov, E.: Fractal modeling of natural terrain: analysis and surface reconstruction with range data. Graph. Models Image Process. **58**(5), 413–436 (1996)
7. Fisher, T.R., Wales, R.Q.: 3D solid modeling of sandstone reservoirs using NURBS. Geobyte **5**(1), 39–41 (1990)
8. Zheng, D., Li, M.: Water Conservancy and Power Geological 3D Modeling and Analysis, vol. 168. China Water Conservancy and Power Industry, Beijing (2005). (In Chinese)
9. De Kemp, E.A.: Visualization of complex geological structures using 3-D Bezier construction tools. Comput. Geosci. **25**(5), 581–597 (1999)
10. Moore, R.R., Johnson, S.E.: Three-dimensional reconstruction and modeling of complexly folded surfaces using Mathematiac. Comput. Geosci. **27**(4), 401–418 (2001)
11. Wu, Q., Xu, H.: 3D fault modeling technique in Virtual mining system. J. Liaoning Eng. Tech. Univ. **24**(3), 316–319 (2005). (In Chinese)
12. Wu, Q., Xu, H.: 3D geological modeling method and application in digital mine. China Sci. (earth edn.) **43**(12), 1996–2006 (2013). (In Chinese)
13. Shanjun, M.: Gray geographical information system-the theory and technology of correct geological spatial data dynamically. Acta Scicentiarum Naturalum Universitis Pekinesis **38**(4), 556–562 (2002). (In Chinese)
14. Zhangang, W., Mao, P.: Delaunay triangulation algorithm of 3D folded cross-section. Comput. Eng. Appl. **44**(1), 94–96 (2008). (In Chinese)
15. Song, X., Xu, F.: Coal seam floor surface best fitting under Stratum attitude and elevation. Journal of Coal Science **35**(5), 782–786 (2010). (In Chinese)

Image Segmentation via the Continuous Max-Flow Method Based on Chan-Vese Model

Guojia Hou[1,3], Huizhu Pan[2], Ruixue Zhao[1(✉)], Zhonghua Hao[3],
and Wanquan Liu[4]

[1] College of Computer Science and Technology, Qingdao University, Qingdao,
People's Republic of China
hgjouc@126.com, 1803236530@qq.com
[2] KingKen Technology Company Ltd., Qingdao, People's Republic of China
1013420734@qq.com
[3] College of Automation and Electrical Engineering, Qingdao University,
Qingdao, People's Republic of China
haozhonghua@qdu.edu.cn
[4] Department of Computing, Curtin University, Perth, Australia
W.Liu@curtin.edu.au

Abstract. The Chan-Vese model using variational level set method (VSLM) has been widely used in image segmentation, but its efficiency is a challenge problem due to high computation costs of curvature as well as the Eiknal equation constraint. In this paper, we propose a continuous Max-Flow (CMF) method based on discrete graph cut approach to solve the VSLM for image segmentation. Firstly, we recast the original Chan-Vese model to a continuous max-flow problem via the primal-dual method and solve it using the alternating direction method of multipliers (ADMM). Then, we use the projection method to recover the continuous level set function for image segmentation expressed as a signed distance function. Finally, some numerical examples are presented to demonstrate the efficiency and accuracy of the proposed method.

Keywords: Image segmentation · Variational level set method
The Chan-Vese model · Continuous Max-Flow method

1 Introduction

Image segmentation is of great importance in image analysis, which has found a lot of applications in the fields of computer vision, medical imaging processing, remote sensing imaging analysis, etc. Its task is to divide an image into different parts according to image features without vacuum and overlapping. It can be accomplished by variational methods through minimizing a specific energy functional. Among of the existing approaches, the Mumford-Shah model [1] is a fundamental approach, but it is difficult to solve due to different space definitions of variables. The Chan-Vese model [2] can overcome this problem based on a reduced Mumford-Shah model and variational level set method (VSLM) [3, 4] with the concept of total variation (TV) [5].

© Springer Nature Singapore Pte Ltd. 2018
Y. Wang et al. (Eds.): IGTA 2017, CCIS 757, pp. 232–242, 2018.
https://doi.org/10.1007/978-981-10-7389-2_23

The Chan-Vese model not only can solve a lot of problems of two-phase image segmentation, but also has become fundamental approach to various variational multi-phase image segmentation models [6]. Moreover, its idea can be extended to solve the related variational multi-phase image segmentation models, thus have received a lot of attentions recently. For the problem of two-phase segmentation $\Omega = \Omega_1 \cup \Omega_2$, $\Omega_1 \cap \Omega_2 = \emptyset$, the Chan-Vese model based on the reduced Mumford-Shah model can be described as

$$\underset{c_1,c_2,\phi}{Min}\left\{ \int_\Omega Q_1 H(\phi)dx + \int_\Omega Q_2(1 - H(\phi))dx + \gamma \int_\Omega \delta(\phi)|\nabla\phi|dx\right\} \tag{1}$$

where, $Q_1 = \alpha_1(c_1 - f)^2$, $Q_2 = \alpha_2(c_2 - f)^2$, c_1 and c_2 represent piecewise constant approximations of the original image f in regions Ω_1 and Ω_2 respectively. The function $\phi(x)$ denotes a level set function. $H(\phi)$, $\delta(\phi)$ are Heaviside function and Dirac function of $\phi(x)$. $H(\phi)$, $1 - H(\phi)$ are characteristic functions of Ω_1 and Ω_2 respectively. If $\phi(x)$ is defined as a signed distance function, it must fulfill the following Eiknal equation

$$|\nabla\phi| = 1 \tag{2}$$

Equations (1) and (2) constitute a constrained optimization problem. After c_1 and c_2 are estimated, $\phi(x)$ can be obtained by solving the following gradient descent equation [2]

$$\begin{cases} \frac{\partial\phi}{\partial t} = \left(\nabla\cdot\left(\frac{\nabla\phi}{|\nabla\phi|}\right) + (Q_2 - Q_1)\right)\delta(\phi) & x \in \Omega \\ \nabla\phi\cdot\vec{n} = 0 & x \in \partial\Omega \end{cases}, \tag{3}$$

$$\begin{cases} \frac{\partial\psi}{\partial t} + sign(\phi)(|\nabla\psi| - 1) = 0 \\ \psi(0,x) = \phi(t,x) \end{cases}. \tag{4}$$

In order to avoid the re-initialization process of (4), [7] has augmented the constraint (2) into (1) via the penalty function method as below:

$$\underset{\phi}{Min}\left\{ \int_\Omega Q_1 H(\phi)dx + \int_\Omega Q_2(1 - H(\phi))dx + \gamma \int_\Omega \delta(\phi)|\nabla\phi|dx + \frac{\theta}{2}\int_\Omega (|\nabla\phi| - 1)^2 dx\right\}, \tag{5}$$

Thus, (3), (4) can be replaced with

$$\begin{cases} \frac{\partial\phi}{\partial t} = \left(\nabla\cdot\left(\frac{\nabla\phi}{|\nabla\phi|}\right) + (Q_2 - Q_1)\right)\delta(\phi) + \theta\left(\Delta\phi - \nabla\cdot\left(\frac{\nabla\phi}{|\nabla\phi|}\right)\right) & x \in \Omega \\ \nabla\phi\cdot\vec{n} = 0 & x \in \partial\Omega \end{cases}. \tag{6}$$

But the computation of the curvature in (6) using finite difference scheme is highly complex. The Split Bregman projection (SBP) method designed by [8] can circumvent this difficulty by making use of a generalized thresholding formula and projection method in the alternating optimization process. The alternating iterative formulation can be presented as below.

$$
\left(\phi^{k+1}, \vec{w}^{k+1}\right)
$$

$$
= Arg \min_{\phi, \vec{w}:|\vec{w}|=1} \left\{ \begin{array}{l} \int_{\Omega} Q_1 H(\phi)dx + \int_{\Omega} Q_2(1 - H(\phi))dx \\ + \gamma \int_{\Omega} \delta(\phi)|\vec{w}|dx + \frac{\theta}{2} \int_{\Omega} \left|\vec{w} - \nabla\phi - \vec{b}^{k+1}\right|^2 dx \end{array} \right\}, \tag{7a}
$$

$$
\vec{b}^{k+1} = \vec{b}^k + \nabla\phi^k - \vec{w}^k, \ \vec{b}^0 = \vec{w}^0 = \vec{0}. \tag{7b}
$$

A similar alternating direction method of multipliers projection (ADMMP) method is proposed in [8], which is given by

$$
\left(\phi^{k+1}, \vec{w}^{k+1}\right)
$$

$$
= Arg \min_{\phi, \vec{w}:|\vec{w}|=1} \left\{ \begin{array}{l} \int_{\Omega} Q_1 H(\phi)dx + \int_{\Omega} Q_2(1 - H(\phi))dx \\ + \gamma \int_{\Omega} \delta(\phi)|\vec{w}|dx + \int_{\Omega} \vec{\tau}^k \cdot (\vec{w} - \nabla\phi)dx + \frac{\theta}{2} \int_{\Omega} |\vec{w} - \nabla\phi|^2 dx \end{array} \right\}. \tag{8a}
$$

$$
\vec{\tau}^{k+1} = \vec{\tau}^k + \theta\left(\vec{w}^{k+1} - \nabla\phi^{k+1}\right). \tag{8b}
$$

The SBP method and ADMMP method are motivated by the SB method and ADMM method for the equivalent model of Chan-Vese model [9]

$$
\min_{c, \lambda(x)\in\{0,1\}} \left\{ \int_{\Omega} Q_1 \lambda dx + \int_{\Omega} Q_2(1 - \lambda)dx + \gamma \int_{\Omega} |\nabla\lambda|dx \right\}. \tag{9}
$$

After c is estimated, λ can be obtained via the fast SB method [10], and ADMM method [11] which were originally proposed to solve TV models for image restoration.

Another fast method to solve (9) is the graph cut approach [12] which recasts it to a Max-Flow/Min-Cut problem on a graph [13]. Also its continuous Max-Flow counterpart was proposed by [14–16] to avoid graph construction and complex data structures. In this paper, we will design the Continuous Max-Flow (CMF) method for (1) to provide a new fast implementation of it and lay the foundation for multi-phase image segmentation, 3D image segmentation, etc.

The paper is organized as follows. Section 2 briefly introduces the Continuous Max-Flow method for Chan-Vese model of convex optimization. The CMF method for classic Chan-Vese model under VSLM framework is designed in Sect. 3. In Sect. 4, the numerical experiments are conducted to compare the proposed method with some current fast approaches. Finally, concluding remarks and outlook are given in Sect. 5.

2 The Continuous Max-Flow Method for Equivalent Chan-Vese Model

As one can see that (9) is a minimization problem with two variables, it can be tackled using the alternating optimization strategy. After c is estimated, another sub-problem of minimization on λ is as follows.

$$\underset{\lambda(x)\in\{0,1\}}{Min}\left\{\int_\Omega Q_1\lambda dx + \int_\Omega Q_2(1-\lambda)dx + \gamma\int_\Omega |\nabla\lambda|dx\right\}. \tag{10}$$

The procedure of convex optimization to solve it is based on the relaxation of $\lambda\in\{0,1\}$ to $\lambda\in[0,1]$, and the thresholding formula for the final results. The relaxified version of (10) can be transformed into the Max-Min problem [14–17] as below.

$$\underset{p_t:0\le p_t\le Q_1}{Max}\ \underset{p_s:0\le p_s\le Q_2}{Max}\ \underset{\vec{p}:|\vec{p}|\le\gamma}{Max}\ \underset{\lambda(x)\in[0,1]}{Min}\left\{\begin{array}{l}\int_\Omega p_t\lambda dx + \int_\Omega p_s(1-\lambda)dx + \int_\Omega \nabla\cdot\vec{p}\lambda dx \\ = \int_\Omega p_s dx + \int_\Omega (p_t - p_s + \nabla\cdot\vec{p})\lambda dx\end{array}\right\}. \tag{11}$$

Due to the following dual formulas

$$\int_\Omega Q_1\lambda dx = \underset{p_t:0\le p_t\le Q_1}{Max}\int_\Omega p_t\lambda dx, \tag{12a}$$

$$\int_\Omega Q_2(1-\lambda)dx = \underset{p_s:0\le p_s\le Q_2}{Max}\int_\Omega p_s(1-\lambda)dx, \tag{12b}$$

$$\gamma\int_\Omega |\nabla\lambda|dx = \underset{\vec{P}:|\vec{p}|\le\gamma}{Max}\int_\Omega \nabla\cdot\vec{p}\lambda dx. \tag{12c}$$

Then, (11) can become the following Continuous Max-Flow optimization problem

$$\underset{p_s}{Max}\int_\Omega p_s dx, \tag{13a}$$

$$s.t.\, p_t - p_s + \nabla\cdot\vec{p} = 0, 0\le p_t\le Q_1, 0\le p_s\le Q_2, |\vec{p}|\le\gamma. \tag{13b}$$

which can be solved via the ADMM method as given by

$$\left(p_t^{k+1}, p_s^{k+1}, \vec{p}^{k+1}\right),$$

$$= Arg\ \underset{\substack{p_t:0\le p_t\le Q_1 \\ p_s:0\le p_s\le Q_2 \\ \vec{p}:|\vec{p}|\le\gamma}}{Max}\int_\Omega \left(p_s + \lambda^k(p_t - p_s + \nabla\cdot\vec{p}) - \frac{\mu}{2}|p_t - p_s + \nabla\cdot\vec{p}|^2\right)dx, \tag{14a}$$

$$\lambda^{k+1} = \lambda^k - \mu\left(p_t^{k+1} - p_s^{k+1} + \nabla\cdot\vec{p}^{k+1}\right). \tag{14b}$$

where μ is a penalty parameter, λ is a Lagrangian multiplier.

3 The Continuous Max-Flow Method for the Chan-Vese Model

For the classic Chan-Vese model (1), (2) under the VLSM, after c has been estimated, it can be transformed into the following constrained optimization problem

$$\begin{cases} \underset{\phi}{Min}\{\int_\Omega Q_1 H(\phi)dx + \int_\Omega Q_2(1 - H(\phi))dx + \gamma \int_\Omega |\nabla H(\phi)|dx\} \\ s.t. \quad |\nabla\phi| = 1 \end{cases} \tag{15}$$

In order to solve it, [2] has introduced the regularized Heaviside function $H_\varepsilon(\phi)$ and the regularized Dirac function $\delta_\varepsilon(\phi)$ as

$$H_\varepsilon(\phi) = \frac{1}{2} + \frac{1}{\pi}\arctan\left(\frac{\phi}{\varepsilon}\right), \tag{16a}$$

$$\delta_\varepsilon(\phi) = \frac{1}{\pi}\frac{\varepsilon}{\phi^2 + \varepsilon^2}. \tag{16b}$$

Here ε is a small positive parameter and $H_\varepsilon(\phi) \in [0, 1]$. Let $\lambda = H_\varepsilon(\phi)$, then (15) becomes

$$\begin{cases} \underset{\lambda \in [0,1]}{Min}\{\int_\Omega Q_1 \lambda dx + \int_\Omega Q_2(1 - \lambda)dx + \gamma \int_\Omega |\nabla\lambda|dx\} \\ s.t. \quad \begin{cases} \lambda = H_\varepsilon(\phi) \\ |\nabla\phi| = 1 \end{cases} \end{cases} \tag{17}$$

The first formulation is just the relaxified version of (10), so its solution can be obtained via the CMF method as (14a), (14b) i.e.

$$(p_t^{k+1}, p_s^{k+1}, \vec{p}^{k+1}) = Arg \underset{\substack{p_t : 0 \le p_t \le Q_1 \\ p_s : 0 \le p_s \le Q_2 \\ \vec{p} : |\vec{p}| \le \gamma}}{Max} \int_\Omega \left(\vec{p}_s + \lambda^k(p_t - p_s + \nabla \cdot \vec{p}) - \frac{\mu}{2}|p_t - p_s + \nabla \cdot \vec{p}|^2\right)dx$$

$$\tag{18a}$$

$$\lambda^{k+1} = \lambda^k - \mu(p_t^{k+1} - p_s^{k+1} + \nabla \cdot \vec{p}^{k+1}), \lambda^{k+1} \in [0, 1]. \tag{18b}$$

In fact, (18a) can be divided into the following sub-problems of minimization in terms of alternating optimization respectively,

$$(p_t^{k+1}) = Arg \underset{p_t : 0 \le p_t \le Q_1}{Max} \int_\Omega \left(\lambda^k(p_t - p_s^k + \nabla \cdot \vec{p}^k) - \frac{\mu}{2}|p_t - p_s^k + \nabla \cdot \vec{p}^k|^2\right)dx, \tag{19a}$$

$$\left(p_s^{k+1}\right) = \underset{p_s:0 \le p_s \le Q_2}{Arg\ Max} \int_\Omega \left(p_s + \lambda^k\left(p_t^{k+1} - p_s + \nabla \cdot \vec{p}^k\right) - \frac{\mu}{2}\left|p_t^{k+1} - p_s + \nabla \cdot \vec{p}^k\right|^2\right)dx,$$

(19b)

$$\left(\vec{p}^{k+1}\right) = \underset{\vec{p}:|\vec{p}| \le \gamma}{Arg\ Max} \int_\Omega \left(\lambda^k\left(p_t^{k+1} - p_s^{k+1} + \nabla \cdot \vec{p}\right) - \frac{\mu}{2}\left|p_t^{k+1} - p_s^{k+1} + \nabla \cdot \vec{p}\right|^2\right)dx.$$

(19c)

And their solutions are given by

$$\begin{cases} \tilde{p}_t^{k+1} = p_s^k - \nabla \cdot \vec{p}^k + \frac{\lambda^k}{\mu} \\ p_t^{k+1} = Max\left(0, Min\left(\tilde{p}_t^{k+1}, Q_1\right)\right) \end{cases},$$

(20a)

$$\begin{cases} \tilde{p}_s^{k+1} = \left(p_t^{k+1} + \nabla \cdot \vec{p}^k\right) + \frac{1-\lambda^k}{\mu} \\ p_s^{k+1} = Max\left(0, Min\left(\tilde{p}_s^{k+1}, Q_2\right)\right) \end{cases},$$

(20b)

$$\begin{cases} \begin{cases} -\nabla \lambda^k + \mu\nabla\left(p_t^{k+1} - p_s^{k+1} + \nabla \cdot \vec{p}^{k+1}\right) = 0 & x \in \Omega \\ \lambda^k - \mu\left(p_t^{k+1} - p_s^{k+1} + \nabla \cdot \vec{p}^{k+1}\right) = 0 & x \in \partial\Omega \end{cases} \\ \vec{p}^{k+1} = \frac{\vec{\tilde{p}}^{k+1}}{Max\left(1, |\vec{\tilde{p}}^{k+1}|\right)} \end{cases}.$$

(20c)

Also, the solution of (18b) is given by

$$\begin{cases} \tilde{\lambda}^{k+1} = \lambda^k - \mu(p_t^{k+1} - p_s^{k+1} + \nabla \cdot \vec{p}^{k+1}) \\ \lambda^{k+1} = Max\left(0, Min\left(\tilde{\lambda}^{k+1}, 1\right)\right) \end{cases}.$$

(21)

One can see that the constraints in (17) can recast the continuous level set function as a signed distance function. It can be implemented by the ADMMP method as

$$\begin{cases} \left(\phi^{k+1}, \vec{w}^{k+1}\right) \\ = \underset{\phi, \vec{w}}{Arg\ Min}\left\{\frac{1}{2}\int_\Omega (\lambda - H_\varepsilon(\phi))^2 dx + \int_\Omega \vec{\sigma}^k \cdot (\vec{w} - \nabla\phi)dx + \frac{\mu_0}{2}\int_\Omega |\vec{w} - \nabla\phi|^2 dx\right\}, \\ s.t.\ |\vec{w}^{k+1}| = 1 \end{cases}$$

(22a)

$$\vec{\sigma}^{k+1} = \vec{\sigma}^k + \mu_0\left(\vec{w}^{k+1} - \nabla\phi^{k+1}\right).$$

(22b)

Now, by applying the alternating optimization strategy to (22a), we can obtain ϕ^{k+1} using the standard variational method while fixing $\vec{w}^k$ as

$$\begin{cases} (H_\varepsilon(\phi) - \lambda)\delta_\varepsilon(\phi) + \nabla \cdot \vec{\sigma}^k - \mu_0\nabla \cdot (\nabla\phi - \vec{w}^k) = 0 \\ (-\vec{\sigma}^k + \nabla\phi - \vec{w}^k) \cdot \vec{n} = 0 \end{cases}.$$

(23)

Finally, (23) can be solved through Gauss-Seidel scheme approximately. Then, we can get $\vec{w}^{k+1}$ while fixing ϕ^k as

$$\begin{cases} \vec{\sigma}^k + \mu_0 \cdot \left(\tilde{\vec{w}}^{k+1} - \nabla\phi^{k+1} \right) = 0 \\ \vec{w}^{k+1} = \frac{\tilde{\vec{w}}^{k+1}}{Max(|\tilde{\vec{w}}^{k+1}|,1)} \end{cases} . \tag{24}$$

Now we summarize the algorithm introduced in this section as follows.

Algorithm A.   Fast algorithm based on the CMF for the Chan-Vese model

Set the starting values p_s^1, p_t^1, p^1 and λ^1, let $k = 1$ and start $k-th$ iteration, which includes the following steps, till converge:

1)   Compute p_t^{k+1} according to (20a);

2)   Compute p_s^{k+1} according to (20b);

3)   Compute p^{k+1} according to (20c);

4)   Compute λ^{k+1} according to (21);

The constraints in (16) can be realized by the ADMMP method as:

5)   Compute ϕ^{k+1} according to (23);

6)   Compute w^{k+1} according to (24);

Let $k = k+1$ return to the $k+1$ iteration till converge.

---

4   Numerical Experiments

In this section, we present some numerical experiments to compare the effectiveness and efficiency of our proposed continuous max-flow method with the current fast algorithms (SBP, ADMMP) through the segmentation of three classic images. The experiments are implemented on PC (Intel (R) Core (TM) i5 Duo CPU @3.30 GHz 3.30 GHz; memory: 4 GB; code running environment: Matlab R2010b). Figure 1 shows the three images for segmentation. The segmentation results using SBP, ADMMP and the CMF method are shown in Figs. 2, 3, and 4. Here, we draw a red outline to represent the segmented contour.

(a)   (b)   (c)

Fig. 1. Tested images for image segmentation: (a) liver image, (b) cameraman image, (c) irregular graphic picture.

One can observe from Fig. 2 that the blood vessels of liver are more accurately separated by the proposed CMF method than SBP, ADMMP (see the middle blood vessels of liver). Figure 3 demonstrates that the cameraman and the background are separated more clearly by the proposed CMF than the SBP, ADMMP (see the right of the cameraman image). The results in Fig. 4 shows that the CMF method provides better segmentation of irregular picture components than the SBP and ADMMP methods (see the edge of the irregular graphic picture).

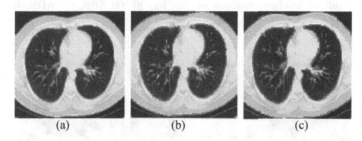

(a)   (b)   (c)

Fig. 2. Segmentation results of Fig. 1(a) by (a) SBP, (b) ADMMP, (c) CMF, respectively. (Color figure online)

(a)   (b)   (c)

Fig. 3. Segmentation results of Fig. 1(b) by (a) SBP, (b) ADMMP, (c) CMF, respectively. (Color figure online)

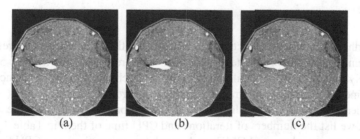

(a)   (b)   (c)

Fig. 4. Segmentation results of Fig. 1(c) by (a) SBP, (b) ADMMP, (c) CMF, respectively. (Color figure online)

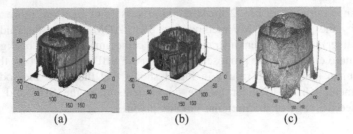

Fig. 5. The result of level set function of Fig. 1(a) by (a) SBP, (b) ADMMP, (c) CMF, respectively.

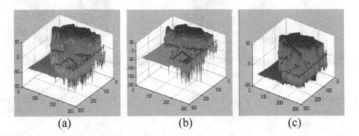

Fig. 6. The result of level set function of Fig. 1(b) by (a) SBP, (b) ADMMP, (c) CMF, respectively.

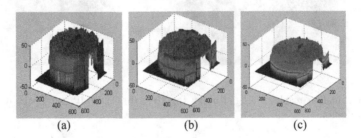

Fig. 7. The result of level set function of Fig. 1(c) by (a) SBP, (b) ADMMP, (c) CMF, respectively.

To further illustrate the effectiveness of CMF method, the processing result using level set function of the three tested images are compared, as shown in Figs. 5, 6 and 7, respectively. It can be seen that all the three method achieve good performance on liver image, cameraman image and irregular graphic picture.

In order to compare the efficiency of the proposed CMF with the SBP and ADMMP, we list the numbers of iterations and CPU time of them in Table 1. It can be seen that our proposed method CMF needs much fewer iterations and CPU time, which proves that the computational efficiency of CMF method is faster than the current fast SBP method and ADMMP method.

Table 1. Comparison on the number of iterations and CPU times of SBP, ADMMP and CMF methods.

Image (size)	SBP		ADMMP		CMF	
	Iterations	CPU time (s)	Iterations	CPU time (s)	Iterations	CPU time (s)
Picture 1 (105 × 128)	24	0.077	24	0.061	20	0.048
Picture 2 (256 × 256)	50	0.613	48	0.426	41	0.329
Picture 3 (512 × 512)	80	5.661	60	4.060	50	1.526

5 Conclusions and Future Topics

Graph cut is a fast algorithm for the min-cut on graphs in computer vision, it is dual to the max-flow method on networks. The continuous max flow method inspired by its discrete counterpart has been proposed to solve some variational model in image processing. In this paper, we design the continuous max flow method for classic Chan-Vese model for image segmentation under the framework of variational level set with constraints of Eiknal equations. Firstly, the Chan-Vese model is transformed into a max-min problem by using dual formulations, based on it, the continuous max flow method is proposed using the alternating direction method of multipliers. Then, the Eiknal equation is solved by introducing an auxiliary variable and ADMM method. Numerical experiments demonstrate that this method is better than the current fast methods in efficiency and accuracy. The investigations in this paper can be extended to the problems of multiphase image segmentation and 3D image segmentation naturally.

Acknowledgments. The work has been partially supported by China Postdoctoral Science Foundation (2017M612204, 2015M571993), and the National Natural Science Foundation of China (61602269). Authors thank Prof. Xue-Cheng Tai, Department of Mathematics at University of Bergen, Prof. Xianfeng David Gu, Department of Computer Science, State University of New York at Stony Brook for their instructions and discussions.

References

1. Mumford, D., Shah, J.: Optimal approximations by piecewise smooth functions and associated variational problems. Commun. Pure Appl. Math. **42**, 577–685 (1989). http://onlinelibrary.wiley.com/journal/10.1002/(ISSN)1097-0312
2. Chan, T.F., Vese, L.A.: Active contours without edges. IEEE Trans. Image Process. **10**, 266–277 (2001)
3. Zhao, H.K., Chan, T.F., Merriman, B., Osher, S.: A variational level set approach to multiphase motion. J. Comput. Phys. **127**, 179–195 (1996)
4. Osher, S., Sethian, J.A.: Fronts propagating with curvature-dependent speed: algorithms based on Hamilton-Jacobi formulations. J. Comput. Phys. **79**, 12–49 (1988)
5. Rudin, L.I., Osher, S., Fatemi, E.: Nonlinear total variation based noise removal algorithms. Physica D **60**, 259–268 (1992)

6. Vese, L.A., Chan, T.F.: A multiphase level set framework for image segmentation using the Mumford and Shah model. Int. J. Comput. Vision **50**, 271–293 (2002)

7. Li, C., Xu, C., Gui, C., Fox, M.D.: Distance regularized level set evolution and its application to image segmentation. IEEE Trans. Image Process. **19**, 3243–3254 (2010). http://www.imagecomputing.org/∼cmli/paper/DRLSE.pdf

8. Duan, J., Pan, Z., Yin, X., Wei, W., Wang, G.: Some fast projection methods based on Chan-Vese model for image segmentation. Eurasip J. Image Video Process. **2014**, 1–16 (2014)

9. Chan, T.F., Esedoglu, S., Nikolova, M.: Algorithms for finding global minimizers of image segmentation and denoising models. SIAM J. Appl. Math. **66**, 1632–1648 (2006)

10. Goldstein, T., Osher, S.: The Split Bregman method for L1 regularized problems. SIAM J. Imaging Sci. **2**, 323–343 (2009)

11. Goldstein, T., O'Donoghue, B., Setzer, S., Baraniuk, R.: Fast alternating direction optimization methods. SIAM J. Imaging Sci. **7**, 1588–1623 (2014)

12. Boykov, Y., Veksler, O., Zabih, R.: Fast approximate energy minimization via graph cuts. IEEE Trans. Pattern Anal. Mach. Intell. **23**, 1222–1239 (2001)

13. Strang, G.: Maximum flows and minimum cuts in the plane. Adv. Mech. Math. **3**, 1–11 (2008)

14. Yuan, J., Bae, E., Tai, X.-C.: A study on continuous max-flow and min-cut approaches. In: IEEE Conference on Computer Vision and Pattern Recognition (CVPR), San Francisco, USA, pp. 2217–2224 (2010)

15. Bae, E., Tai, X.-C., Yuan, J.: Maximizing flows with message-passing: computing spatially continuous min-cuts. In: Tai, X.-C., Bae, E., Chan, T.F., Lysaker, M. (eds.) EMMCVPR 2015. LNCS, vol. 8932, pp. 15–28. Springer, Cham (2015). https://doi.org/10.1007/978-3-319-14612-6_2

16. Yuan, J., Bae, E., Tai, X.-C., Boykov, Y.: A spatially continuous max-flow and min-cut framework for binary labeling problems. Numer. Math. **126**, 559–587 (2014)

17. Wei, K., Tai, X.-C., Chan, T.F., Leung, S.: Primal-dual method for continuous max-flow approaches. In: Computational Vision and Medical Image Processing V - Proceedings of 5th ECCOMAS Thematic Conference on Computational Vision and Medical Image Processing, VipIMAGE 2015, pp. 17–24 (2016)

18. Merkurjev, E., Bae, E., Bertozzi, A.L., Tai, X.-C.: Global binary optimization on graphs for classification of high-dimensional data. J. Math. Imaging Vis. **52**, 414–435 (2015). https://link.springer.com/journal/10851

19. Bae, E., Merkurjev, E.: Convex variational methods on graphs for multiclass segmentation of high-dimensional data and point clouds. J. Math. Imaging Vis. **58**, 468–493 (2017)

Deep-Stacked Auto Encoder for Liver Segmentation

Mubashir Ahmad[1], Jian Yang[1(✉)], Danni Ai[1], Syed Furqan Qadri[2], and Yongtian Wang[1,2]

[1] Beijing Engineering Research Center of Mixed Reality and Advanced Display, School of Optics and Electronics, Beijing Institute of Technology, Beijing, China
jyang@bit.edu.cn
[2] School of Computer Science and Technology, Beijing Institute of Technology, Beijing, China

Abstract. Deep learning methods have been successfully applied to feature learning in medical applications. In this paper, we proposed a Deep Stacked Auto-Encoder (DSAE) for liver segmentation from CT images. The proposed method composes of three major steps. First, we learned the features with unlabeled data using the auto encoder. Second, these features are fine-tuned to classify the liver among other abdominal organs. Using this technique we got promising classification results on 2D CT data. This classification of the data helps to segment the liver from the abdomen. Finally, segmentation of a liver is refined by post processing method. We focused on the high accuracy of the classification task because of its effect on the accuracy of a better segmentation. We trained the deep stacked auto encoder (DSAE) on 2D CT images and experimentally shows that this method has high classification accuracy and can speed up the clinical task to segment the liver. The mean DICE coefficient is noted to be 90.1% which is better than the state of art methods.

Keywords: Deep learning · Liver · Segmentation · Classification

1 Introduction

Liver detection is the most difficult task where the intensity level of each pixel is almost similar to nearby organs. In many clinical treatments, an accurate detection and segmentation of a liver are the most challenging job in CT images. The most progressive treatments are radiotherapy [1], liver resection, and transplantation. Some senior radiologists reported the accurate results using manual segmentation but it is a time-consuming job. Therefore, automatic and semi-automatic methods are most promising in this manner. However, there are still several problems and challenges in computer aided liver segmentation reported previously (see Fig. 1). The first challenge is the low contrast among the different organs which is difficult to detect the liver boundaries. Another challenge is the high intensity of a tumor in the liver. In addition, under segmentation and leakage problem is also occur in the abnormal liver where the intensity based method is used for segmentation. In some cases, shape prior methods are used to distinguish the neighboring organs where the high variation of the liver shapes makes it a challenging task.

© Springer Nature Singapore Pte Ltd. 2018
Y. Wang et al. (Eds.): IGTA 2017, CCIS 757, pp. 243–251, 2018.
https://doi.org/10.1007/978-981-10-7389-2_24

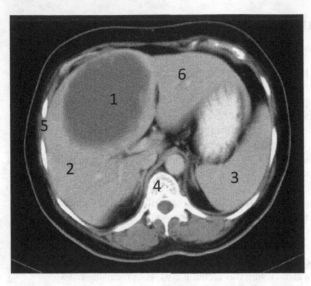

1= Liver Tumor
2 = Liver
3 = Spleen
4 = Spine
5 = Fuzzy Boundaries
6 = Liver

Fig. 1. Represent the challenges in liver segmentation. The presence of pathologies in the liver and weak boundaries.

The image based methods having low-level image information can be addressed as gradient, intensity, and low-level features. These methods are thresh-holding [2], region-growing [3] and graph-cut [4] which might be automatic or semi-automatic. The organs with similar intensities are the challenging job in the gray level method to cause the leakage and under segmentation. In semi-automatic liver segmentation methods need the limited interaction of the user to complete the task which required thresh-holding or morphological operations, achieved better results [5]. To deals with fuzzy boundaries, vibrational energy method [6] is used for surface smoothness and regional appearance while a convex vibrational model is used which based on seed constraint in the fore-ground and background [7]. These methods need user interaction and are very sensitive to initial contours but achieved a better result and good performance.

In recent years, deep learning (Convolutional Neural Network - CNNs) [8, 9] achieved better results in image segmentation. CNNs are the multilayer neural networks in which raw images captures the hierarchy of features from a low level to high-level features and a special information is also encoded in extracted features. Several works on CNNs have been reported as infant brain segmentation [10] and Knee cartilage segmentation [11]. Many researchers have been addressed as a fully CNN and graph cut approaches to achieve automatic CT scan segmentation. Some learned information and probability map of the liver generated by CNN combined into the graph cut as a penalty term [12].

Comparing with the shape based methods, these methods are fully automatic and no deformation and initialization of complex shape positions. However, there are some limitations of heterogeneous due to the presence of pathologies and intrahepatic veins. Stacked de-noising auto encoder [13] is used for segmentation of brainstem in MRI images. This method is successfully applied to get the promising results against other deep learning and SVM techniques. In recent years, stacked auto-encoders have been used for different classification task in deep learning literature [14].

In this work, we focus on Deep Stacked Auto-Encoders (DSAE) to learn the unsupervised features and then fine-tuned with a Soft-max layer using the given labels of the images. Moreover, instead of using a pixel by pixel mapping, we are using a patch based learning which reduced the complexity of our training algorithm and giving very efficient classification results for liver segmentation. Our contribution in this work is, to reduce the classification error among the liver and other organs. We found that, to increase the number of datasets in DSAE, that effect on the classification accuracy. It improves the performance of segmentation as well. Our whole model is represented below (see Fig. 2). The paper is structured as follows, Sect. 2 and 3 describe the proposed method and results, respectively and finally, Sect. 4 concludes the report.

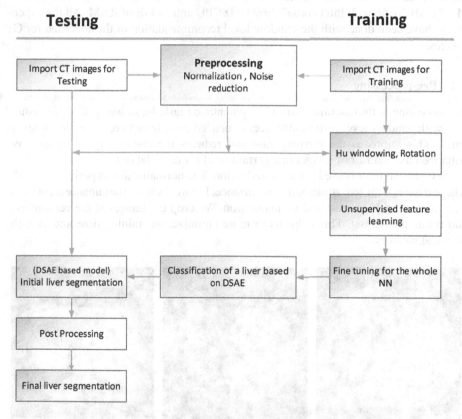

Fig. 2. Model of our system. Training (Right) and Testing (Left).

2   Proposed Method

2.1   Clinical Datasets

In our experiment, we used SLiver07 dataset that consists of 20 training and 10 testing datasets. This dataset available online by the organizers of SLiver07 website (http://sliver07.org). It is the combination of different types of pathologies which include cysts, metastases, and different size of tumors. Using different scanners all the images are contrast enhanced in the central venous phase. Each dataset varies the slice number from 64 to 502, the axial dimension of 512 × 512 pixels. The other dataset is 3dircadb which is also publically available having 20 datasets with their ground truths, having a large number of variations and pathologies. The number of slices varies from 64 to 502. The 3dircadb dataset has been segmented by a single radiologist. This work is done in MATLAB 2016b with Intel core i7 3.60 GHz CPU and 24 GB of RAM. All the experiments have been done with the window level recommendation of the abdomen for CT images.

2.2   Pre-processing

Preprocessing is the essential part of a segmentation task. First, we applied Hounsfield unit with window level [−100, 400] recommended for a liver to remove the irrelevant parts. This improves the learning rate and reduces the complexity of dataset. We enhanced the contrast of images at a certain level for each dataset.

A Gaussian filter is used for noise reduction. The normalization is performed on the whole dataset with zero mean and unit variance. Figure 3 shows the enhancement of the liver images with contrast and normalization. We crop the images at the certain level and rotate the dataset. This helps us to more optimize our training time and save the physical memory.

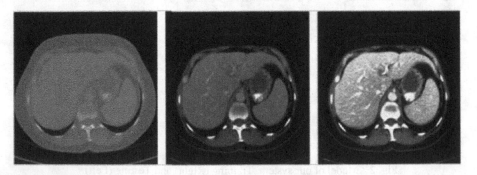

Fig. 3. Raw liver image (left), Applied Hounsfield unit on an image with windowed level [−100 400] (middle), the final contrast-enhanced and normalized image (right)

2.3 Feature Learning and Fine Tuning

Our method is based on classification to segment the liver from CT images. For this purpose, we have learned the features from Stacked Auto-Encoder which is an unsupervised learning method. In this method, we distributed each image into the number of patches which are given as an input to the Stacked Auto-Encoder. We designed the overlapping patches from CT images with a stride of 1 and selected those patches which are over the boundaries of a liver and within the liver. It helps us to separate the liver from the abdominal parts.

Figure 4 shows the orange and blue patches. However, orange patches exist within a liver and boundary of the liver which is given as an input to DSAE without labeling. The architecture of our deep stacked auto-encoder is shown below (see Fig. 5). We trained different patch sizes on our model but 19×19 patch size exhibit promising classification results. For this purpose, two auto-encoder layers are designed to learn the representation of the patches. In first auto-encoder (AE1) layer, we trained the features from 50 hidden neurons with the feature vector of 361 for each patch. The output of AE1 is given as an input to second auto-encoder (AE2) layer with 25 hidden neurons.

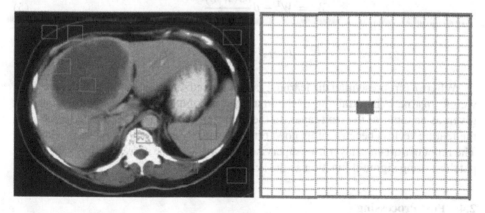

Fig. 4. Orange patches are selected for feature learning from the boundary of a liver and within the liver. The blue patches are not selected for training (left). Central pixel is selected for patch labeling (right), each patch size is 19×19 pixels. (Color figure online)

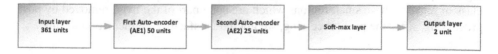

Fig. 5. An architecture of DSAE for the proposed method.

In the feed forward propagation method of auto-encoder, the sigmoid function is used to calculate the weighted sum from input layer [15].

$$f(x) = \frac{1}{(1 + \exp(-x))} \tag{1}$$

$$a^2 = f(z1) = f \sum\nolimits_{i=1}^{m} w^1 x^1 + b^1 \tag{2}$$

Where x is the input to the network, a^2 is the activation values of layer 1, z1 is the weighted sum from the input layer, w^1 is the weight matrix for the input layer, and b^1 is the bias for the first layer. The following formula is used for calculating an error between decoding representation and input using the cost function.

$$J(W,b) = \frac{1}{m} \sum\nolimits_{i=1}^{m} \left[\frac{1}{2} \|h_{W,b}(x) - x\|^2 \right] + \frac{a}{2} \sum\nolimits_{i=1}^{2} \sum\nolimits_{i=1}^{sl} \sum\nolimits_{j=1}^{sl+1} \left(W_{ji}^l \right)^2 \tag{3}$$

$$h_{w,b}(x) = a^3 = f\left(z^3 \right) \tag{4}$$

Where W represents the weighting matrix of the whole network, b is the bias matrix of the entire network, the number of training cases represented by m, and a is the weight decay parameter. The minimum value of J(W, B) is the goal of the encoder. The input representation of the x is $h_{w,b}(x)$.

$$W^1 = W^1 - \beta \frac{\partial J(W,b)}{\partial W^1} \tag{5}$$

$$b^1 = b^1 - \beta \frac{\partial J(W,b)}{\partial b^1} \tag{6}$$

Where β is representing the learning rate of the auto encoder and W is the connecting weight matrix. When training of the first layer is completed then learned features are given as an input to the next layer. In the next step, Soft-max layer is used to classify the feature vectors because of its good fitting capability and computational proficiency. The input of Soft-max layer is unsupervised features with the corresponding label of the patches, using sigmoid function as the activation function.

2.4   Post Processing

The initial segmentation is performed through DSAE based classification. There are some holes in the liver surface. These holes are filled by post processing using morphological operations. Due to misclassification, the other muscles are also included in the class of a liver. These small regions which are not a part of the liver, removed by post processing. After the post processing, we got the satisfactory segmentation results.

3   Results and Discussion

In this section, we have discussed the results of classification and segmentation. We trained the system on 2D CT data for liver segmentation. Table 1 shows the comparative training results of DSAE and SVM. Using deep learning, it is observed that increasing the number of datasets in training constantly improve testing performance. The segmentation results are also improved with a good training. Therefore, we have randomly selected Sliver07 and 3dircadb datasets for feature learning and training. The details of classification parameters are given in [16].

Table 1. Classification accuracy of training using deep stacked auto-encoder with soft-max layer and SVM

Classification methods	Specificity (%)	Sensitivity (%)	Accuracy (%)
DSAE (our)	99.1%	95.7%	98.6%
SVM	99.1%	91.3%	96.2%

We trained DSAE and SVM on the same datasets for classification. The performance of DSAE is obvious in Table 1. To compare with other methods DSAE is simple and faster. Patch selection process is more simple and robust which reduce the complexity of algorithm during a training process. For labeling, we got the central pixel of the patch from a labeled image.

It is also observed that Deep Stacked Auto Encoder based feature learning needs larger data for training. On smaller datasets, there are more misclassifications. Patch based technique for feature learning helps the system to reduce training time. Selection of patches from the image around the liver and within the liver is the best for optimizing

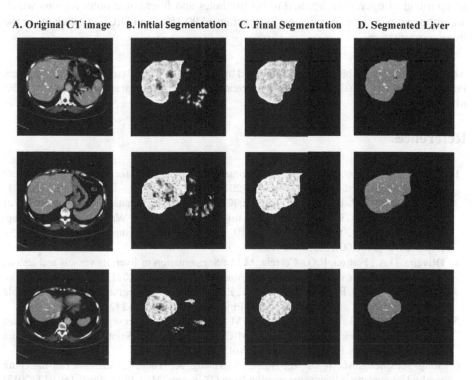

Fig. 6. Column A shows original CT Abdominal images after preprocessing, column B represents the initial results of liver segmentation, column C is the final refined liver using post processing and column D is the segmented liver.

the training time and save the system physical memory. The results of the liver segmentation are given above (see Fig. 6), where the liver is segmented from the CT scan images.

We tested the performance of our model on 650 CT abdominal images where 420 of them are normal and 230 having the abnormality. It has been concluded that Mean DICE coefficient score is 90.1%, which is better than state of the art techniques. The results of segmentation are given in Table 2 below.

Table 2. Segmentation results of the liver using Deep Stacked Auto-Encoders.

Patients	Number of images	Mean dice coefficient
Normal liver	420	92.5%
Abnormal liver	230	87.7%
Total	650	90.1%

4   Conclusion

Deep Stacked Auto-Encoder (DSAE) is proposed for liver segmentation. DSAE learned the features in an unsupervised manner. Soft-max layer fine-tuned the network and also classify the liver region among other parts in the abdomen. After the initial segmentation morphological operations applied to fill the holes and filter some outer regions which are not a part of a liver. We successfully achieved 90.1% mean DICE coefficient for the liver segmentation.

Acknowledgement. This work was supported by National Hi-Tech Research and Development Program (2015AA043203), and the National Science Foundation Program of China (81430039, 81627803, 61572076).

References

1. Li, D., Liu, L., Kapp, D.S., Xing, L.: Automatic liver contouring for radiotherapy treatment planning. Phys. Med. Biol. **60**(19), 7461 (2015)
2. Seo, K.-S., Kim, H.-B., Park, T., Kim, P.-K., Park, J.-A.: Automatic liver segmentation of contrast enhanced CT images based on histogram processing. In: Wang, L., Chen, K., Ong, Y.S. (eds.) ICNC 2005. LNCS, vol. 3610, pp. 1027–1030. Springer, Heidelberg (2005). https://doi.org/10.1007/11539087_135
3. Oliveira, D.A., Feitosa, R.Q., Correia, M.M.: Segmentation of liver, its vessels and lesions from CT images for surgical planning. Biomed. Eng. **10**(1), 30 (2011)
4. Peng, J., Hu, P., Lu, F., Peng, Z., Kong, D., Zhang, H.: 3D liver segmentation using multiple region appearances and graph cuts. Med. Phys. **42**(12), 6840–6852 (2015)
5. Rusko, L., Bekes, G., Nemeth, G., Fidrich, M.: Fully automatic liver segmentation for contrast enhanced CT images. In: Proceedings of MICCAI Workshop 3D Segmentation in the Clinic: A Grand Challenge, Brisbane, Australia, vol. 2 (2007)
6. Song, X., Cheng, M., Wang, B., Huang, S., Huang, X., Yang, J.: Adaptive fast marching method for automatic liver segmentation from CT images. Med. Phys. **40**(9), 091917 (2013)
7. Peng, J., Dong, F., Chen, Y., Kong, D.: A region-appearance-based adaptive variational model for 3D liver segmentation. Med. Phys. **41**(4), 43502 (2014)

8. Krizhevsky, A., Sutskever, I., Hinton, G.E.: Image-net classification with deep convolutional neural networks. In: Advances in Neural Information Processing Systems, pp. 1097–1105. MIT Press, Cambridge (2012)

9. Long, J., Shelhamer, E., Darrell, T.: Fully convolutional networks for semantic segmentation. In: IEEE Conference on Computer Vision Pattern Recognition, pp. 3431–3440 (2015)

10. Zhang, W., Deng, R., Li, H., Wang, L., Lin, W., Ji, S., Shen, D.: Deep convolutional neural networks for multi-modality iso-intense infant brain image segmentation. Neuro-Image **108**, 214–224 (2015)

11. Prasoon, A., Petersen, K., Igel, C., Lauze, F., Dam, E., Nielsen, M.: Deep feature learning for knee cartilage segmentation using a triplanar convolutional neural network. In: Mori, K., Sakuma, I., Sato, Y., Barillot, C., Navab, N. (eds.) MICCAI 2013. LNCS, vol. 8150, pp. 246–253. Springer, Heidelberg (2013). https://doi.org/10.1007/978-3-642-40763-5_31

12. Roth, H.R., Lu, L., Farag, A., Shin, H.-C., Liu, J., Turkbey, E.B., Summers, R.M.: DeepOrgan: multi-level deep convolutional networks for automated pancreas segmentation. In: Navab, N., Hornegger, J., Wells, W.M., Frangi, A.F. (eds.) MICCAI 2015. LNCS, vol. 9349, pp. 556–564. Springer, Cham (2015). https://doi.org/10.1007/978-3-319-24553-9_68

13. Dolz, J., et al.: Stacking de-noising auto-encoders in a deep network to segment the brainstem on MRI in brain cancer patients: a clinical study. Comput. Med. Imaging Graph. **52**, 8–18 (2016)

14. Vincent, P., Larochelle, H., Lajoie, I., Bengio, Y., Manzagol, P.A.: Stacked de-noising auto encoders. learning useful representations in a deep network with a local de-noising criterion. J. Mach. Learn. Res. **11**, 3371–3408 (2010)

15. Lei, Y., Yuan, W., Wang, H., Wenhu, Y., Bo, W.: A skin segmentation algorithm based on stacked autoencoders. IEEE Trans. Multimedia **19**(4), 740–749 (2017)

16. Zhu, W., Zeng, N., Wang, N.: Sensitivity, specificity, accuracy, associated confidence interval and ROC analysis with practical SAS® implementations. In: NESUG Proceedings: Health Care and Life Sciences, Baltimore, Maryland, vol. 19 (2010)

A Flattened Maximally Stable Extremal Region Method for Scene Text Detection

Quan Qiu[1,2], Yuan Feng[1], Fei Yin[1], and Cheng-Lin Liu[1,2(✉)]

[1] National Laboratory of Pattern Recognition (NLPR), Institute of Automation of Chinese Academy of Sciences, 95 Zhongguancun East Road, Beijing 100190, China
{qqiu,liucl,fyin}@nlpr.ia.ac.cn, yuan.feng@ia.ac.cn
[2] University of Chinese Academy of Sciences, Beijing, China

Abstract. The detection of texts from natural scene images is a challenge due to the clutter background and variation of illumination and perspective. Among the methods proposed so far, the maximally stable extremal region (MSER) method, as a connected component based one, has been pursued and applied widely. In this paper, we propose an efficient method, called flattening method, to quickly prune the large number of overlapping MSERs, so as to improve the speed and accuracy of MSER-based scene text detection. The method evaluates the character-likeliness of MSERs and retains only one MSER in each path of the MSER tree. Our experimental results on the ICDAR 2013 Robust Reading Dataset demonstrates the effectiveness of the proposed method.

Keywords: Scene text detection · Maximally stable extremal region (MSER) Flattening

1 Introduction

The detection and recognition of scene texts plays an important role in image data mining and semantic understanding. With the popular use of digital cameras, smartphones and tablets, the number of digital images is increasing rapidly. This poses the need and challenge of information extraction from images. Since many images contain texts, which carry direct and easily understandable information, the detection and recognition of texts from scene images draw high attention from both researchers and users. Scene text detection and localization, as a pre-requisite of text recognition, is a non-trivial problem and has attracted numerous research efforts.

Texts in natural scenes include those on buildings, signboards, goods and so on. Due to the clutter background of texts, the variation of illumination and perspective of imaging (Fig. 1), text detection from scene images remains a challenge. In the past two decades, many efforts have been devoted to scene text detection, as evidenced by the many propose methods and some competitions of Robust Reading at ICDAR 2003 [1], ICDAR 2005 [2], ICDAR 2011 [3] and ICDAR 2013 [4]. The public datasets released at the competitions have triggered the research significantly.

© Springer Nature Singapore Pte Ltd. 2018
Y. Wang et al. (Eds.): IGTA 2017, CCIS 757, pp. 252–262, 2018.
https://doi.org/10.1007/978-981-10-7389-2_25

Fig. 1. Examples of text in natural scene images.

The methods of scene text detection proposed so far can be grouped into two categories: sliding window based methods [5] (also known as texture-based method) and region-based methods [6–8] (also known as connected component based). Sliding window methods extract text candidate regions by shifting a text/non-text classifier on windows. The text/non-text classifiers usually extract texture features such as histogram of oriented gradient (HOG), local binary pattern (LBP) [13], or original pixel features.

Depending on the connected components segmentation method, region-based methods can be divided into ones of binarization, stroke width transform (SWT) [7], maximally stable extremal region (MSER) method [9], and so on. The binarization method obtains text candidate regions by binarizing image. Classic image binarization methods include the OTSU algorithm [10] and the Niblack's local binarization algorithm [11]. Epshtein et al. proposed a stroke width transform [7] which calculates the local stroke width and transforms the origin image to stroke width map. This method segments the image according to the width of the strokes. MSER method is based on the stability of region to segment image. This method can achieve high recall rates. However, MSER method produces a lot of redundant regions that affect efficiency.

In recent years, deep neural networks, especially the convolutional neural network (CNN) has been applied to scene detection and recognition with superior performance [17–19]. CNNs are powerful in learning discriminative features and can separate better texts from non-texts. Despite the superior performance of them, however, CNNs consume much higher computation resource in both training and testing. It's hard to run them on PC and mobile phone. In order to save computations, the method based on connected component and simple classification still has large potential of application.

In this paper, we propose a method to improve the speed and accuracy of maximally stable extremal region (MSER) based scene text detection. The proposed method, called flattened maximally stable extremal region (FMSER), is aimed to prune the large number of MSERs in the MSER tree, so as to save computation and reduce noise disturbance in filtering MSERs. The flattening algorithm is simple without the need of training, but can eliminate about 70% of MSERs without losing the accuracy of text detection.

The rest of paper is organized as follows. Section 2 presents our approach in details. Section 3 presents the experimental results, and Sect. 4 provides concluding remarks.

2   Proposed Method

The overall process of our text detection approach is shown in Fig. 2. First, we use MSER method [9] to extract character candidates. Then, flattened MSER (FMSER) method is used to prune the MSER tree so that a large number of redundant MSERs could be removed. And then, we use the AdaBoost trained character classifier to verify the extracted character candidates. Finally, we group the refined character candidates into text regions to get the result.

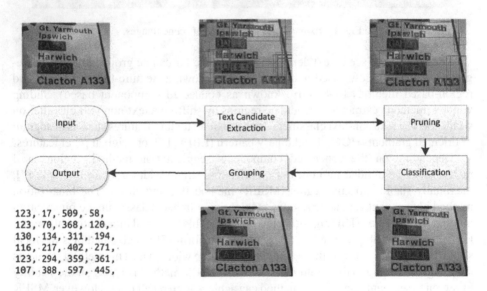

Fig. 2. Overall process of our approach

2.1   Maximally Stable Extremal Region (MSER)

Let **I** denote an *image*

$$\mathbf{I}{:}\mathbf{S} \rightarrow \mathbf{G}, \tag{1}$$

which is a mapping from two dimensional pixel space $\mathbf{S} \subset \mathbf{N}^2$ to grey value space $\mathbf{G}$. $\mathbf{N}$ is natural number set and $\mathbf{G}$ is $\{0, 1, ..., 255\}$. $\mathbf{A} \subset \mathbf{S} \times \mathbf{S}$ is an *adjacency* relation set when all $\left((p_x, p_y), (q_z, q_y) \right) \in \mathbf{A}$ satisfy that $|p_x - q_x| \leq 1$, $|p_y - q_y| \leq 1$, (p_x, p_y) and (q_x, q_y) are not the same point.

Region $\mathbf{R}$ of an image $\mathbf{I}$ is a subset of $\mathbf{S}$ that is $\forall$ p, q $\in$ $\mathbf{R}$, $\exists$ $a_1, a_2, ..., a_n \in \mathbf{R}$ that (p, a_1), (a_1, a_2), ..., $(a_n, p) \in \mathbf{A}$. *Outer region boundary* $\underline{\mathbf{R}} = \{p \in \mathbf{S} \backslash \mathbf{R} \mid \exists q \in \mathbf{R}, (p, q) \in \mathbf{A}\}$.

Extremal Region (ER) is a region whose outer boundary pixels have strictly higher (or lower) values than the region itself that is $\forall p \in \mathbf{ER}$, $\forall q \in \underline{\mathbf{ER}}$ satisfying $\mathbf{I}(q) > \mathbf{I}(p)$ (or $\mathbf{I}(q) < \mathbf{I}(p)$). We can easily obtain ERs of an image by thresholding the image and building an ER tree using an inclusion relationship between the extracted ERs. As shown in Fig. 3, an exemplary input image and some of the threshold images are analyzed during the creation of the ER tree. Each node of the ER tree is assigned the corresponding gray value t at which it was determined.

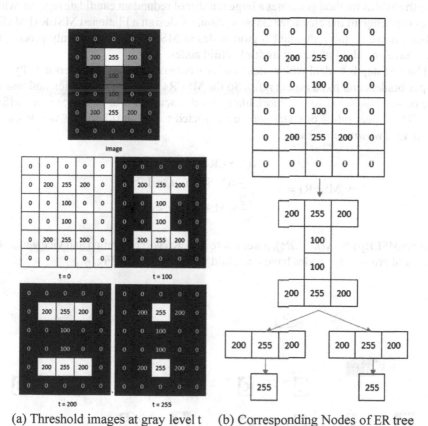

(a) Threshold images at gray level t   (b) Corresponding Nodes of ER tree

Fig. 3. ERs of an image and ER tree.

Maximally Stable Extremal Region (MSER) is an ER whose variation is locally minimal. The *variation* is defined as

$$v(ER_t) = \frac{|ER_{t-t'}| - |ER_t|}{|ER_t|} \tag{2}$$

where $ER_{t-t'}$ represents the parent node of ER_t and $|ER_t|$ represents the pixel number of ER_t. ER_t is a MSER if and only if

$$v(ER_t) < v(ER_{t+t'}), \ v(ER_t) < v(ER_{t-t'}). \tag{3}$$

According to this condition, we can get all MSERs in **ER** and construct MSER tree by traversing the ER tree.

2.2 Flattened MSER

Since the MSER method generates a large number of redundant candidate regions, which brings challenge to the character classification, we design a Flattened MSER (FMSER) method to reduce the redundant region nodes in MSER tree. We mainly process the nodes have one child node and multiple child nodes.

The first step is to deal with nodes that have only one child. Characters usually have sharper borders and fixed aspect ratio. So the MSERs with larger variation and unusual large or small aspect ratios are more likely not characters. Let ar be the ratio of a MSER node. The aspect ratios of characters are expected to fall in 0.2 to 1.2. We define the *regularized variation (rv)* as

$$rv(MSER) = \begin{cases} v(MSER), 0.2 \leq ar \leq 1.2 \\ \dfrac{ar}{1.2} v(MSER), ar > 1.2 \\ \dfrac{0.2}{ar} v(MSER), ar < 0.2 \end{cases} \tag{4}$$

If $rv(MSERp) > rv(MSERc)$, parent note MSERp will be pruned and vice versa. The process of pruning for nodes have one child node is shown in Fig. 4.

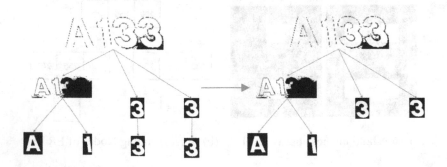

Fig. 4. The process of pruning for nodes have one child.

The next step is to deal with nodes that have multiple child nodes. The stroke width is a very important feature for a character. In general, characters tend to maintain fixed stroke width, therefore we prune nodes that have unstable stroke width. Stroke width can be calculated from a stroke boundary to another along gradient direction. For a pixel (x, y) in a connected component, we define h(x, y), v(x, y), b1(x, y), b2(x, y) as the connected pixels number of horizontal, vertical, 45° inclined, 135° inclined direction respectively. Let

$$sw(x, y) = min(h(x, y), v(x, y), b1(x, y), b2(x, y)) \qquad (5)$$

and sw(x, y) can roughly measure the stroke width of this point(x, y). If a MSER node is a character, stroke width of the node tends to be uniform. The standard deviation of sw in text node should be less than the non-text one. For each path from the root node to the leaf node, the node with the minimum standard deviation is selected as the result of flattened MSER. The result is shown in Fig. 5.

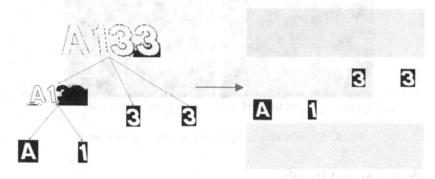

Fig. 5. The process of pruning for nodes have multiple child nodes.

2.3 Text Regions Classification and Grouping

After character candidates are extracted by FMSER method, we use double threshold classification and text tracking by hysteresis method mentioned in literature [16] to obtain credible characters. These character candidates are represented using the MLBP feature and verified using an AdaBoost trained classifier [12]. The overall structure consists two blocks of cascaded classifiers, each with a threshold value that satisfies precision of 99.0% and 90.0% in the training set, respectively. For training the classifiers, we gathered about 62,000 positive samples, together with about 71,000 negative samples. These samples are normalized to a size of 18*18. In double threshold classi-fication, all candidates goes through the first cascade block, and are classified as strong text or non-strong text. Non-strong text candidates goes through the second cascade block, and are classified as weak text or non-text. Whenever weak text satisfies the similar text properties against strong text, the status is converted from weak text to strong text. We include all these strong texts in the final result.

In the text grouping stage, letter candidates are grouped into word. We also apply the same rules for grouping mentioned in literature [16], two candidates are compared on spatial location, size, color and aspect ratio using the same threshold values in text tracking by hysteresis. If two letters satisfy the properties, they will be grouped into the same word. Finally, we can get the word bounding box. The final grouping results are shown in Fig. 6.

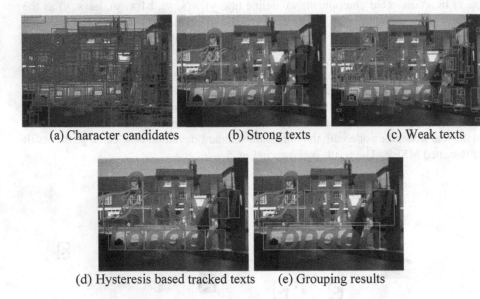

(a) Character candidates   (b) Strong texts   (c) Weak texts

(d) Hysteresis based tracked texts   (e) Grouping results

Fig. 6. Classification and grouping results on a scene image.

3   Experimental Results

We evaluated the performance of the proposed approach on ICDAR 2013 robust reading competition dataset [4]. The dataset is comprised of 229 images for training and 233 images for validation. For the evaluation of text detection results we make use of the framework proposed by Wolf and Jolion [14].

Our method was coded with C ++ in Windows 7 on a PC with Intel(R) Core(TM) i5-2400 CPU-3.1 GHz. 756,755 MSERs are extracted and 233,761 are reserved as FMSERs. We reduce the redundant regions by about 70%. The average processing time per image is reduced from 1.43 s to 0.89 s.

The test performance is shown in Table 1. We can see that the recall of FMSER is almost the same as the recall of MSER and FMSER obtains higher precision. The result demonstrates FMSER could effectively reduce noise and get better performance.

Table 1. A comparison of text detection using MSER and FMSER on ICDAR 2013 competition test set

Method	Recall (%)	Precision (%)	F (%)
MSER	71.2	83.0	76.7
FMSER	71.2	92.8	80.6

We also make a comparison between text detection with ER and with flattened ER. Table 2 shows that Flattened ER also obtains higher performance than ER and slightly higher than flattened MSER. But the speed of the program will drop significantly, Flattened ER method spends 1.7 times as much as FMSER method.

Table 2. A comparison of text detection using ER and flattened ER on ICDAR 2013 competition test set

Method	Recall (%)	Precision (%)	F (%)
ER	67.4	71.9	69.5
Flattened ER	71.7	93.7	81.2

We compare the performance of our method with the results of other systems in ICDAR 2013 (Table 3).

Table 3. Text detection results on ICDAR 2013 competition Test Set

Method	Recall (%)	Precision (%)	F (%)
Our method	71.2	92.8	80.6
USTB TexStar [4]	66.5	88.5	75.9
Text spotter [8]	64.8	87.5	74.5
I2R_NUS_FAR [4]	69.0	75.1	71.9
I2R_NUS [4]	66.2	72.5	69.2
TH-TextLoc [4]	65.2	69.9	67.5
Text detection [15]	53.4	74.1	62.1

Some text detection examples of the proposed algorithm are presented in Fig. 7. Some characters with large stroke width are mistakenly removed in FMSER method leads to these unsuccessful result (see Fig. 7(b)).

(a)Successful samples

(b)Unsuccessful samples

Fig. 7. Examples of text detection result by the proposed method.

4   Conclusions

In this paper, we propose an efficient algorithm to prune and flatten the MSER tree for improving the speed and accuracy of MSER-based scene text detection. Our experimental results on the ICDAR 2013 Competition dataset show that our method can prune about 70% of MSERs while the text detection accuracy (F measure) is improved slightly. Our results show that the recall rate of text components extraction by MSER is not high though the precision is very high. In the future, we will consider other candidate component extraction. We will also consider adjusting the parameters of MSER extraction so as to improving the recall rate though the number of MSERs may increase.

Acknowledgements. This work has been supported by the National Natural Science Foundation of China (NSFC) Grant No.61411136002.

References

1. Lucas, S.M., Panaretos, A., Sosa, L., Tang, A., Wong, S., Young, R.: ICDAR 2003 robust reading competitions. In: Proceedings of the Seventh International Conference on Document Analysis and Recognition (ICDAR), pp. 682–687 (2003)
2. Lucas, S.M.: ICDAR 2005 text locating competition results. In: Proceedings of the Eighth International Conference on Document Analysis and Recognition (ICDAR), pp. 80–84 (2005)
3. Shahab, A., Shafait, F., Dengel, A.: ICDAR 2011 robust reading competition challenge 2: Reading text in scene images. In: Proceedings of the 11th International Conference on Document Analysis and Recognition (ICDAR), pp. 1491–1496 (2011)
4. Karatzas, D., Shafait, F., Uchida, S., Iwamura, M., i Bigorda, L.G., Mestre, S.R., Mas, J., Mota, D.F., Almazan, J.A., de las Heras, L.P.: ICDAR 2013 robust reading competition. In: Proceedings of the 12th International Conference on Document Analysis and Recognition (ICDAR), pp. 1484–1493 (2013)
5. Kim, K.I., Jung, K., Kim, J.H.: Texture-based approach for text detection in images using support vector machines and continuously adaptive mean shift algorithm. IEEE Trans. Pattern Anal. Mach. Intell. 25(12), 1631–1639 (2003)
6. Pan, Y.-F., Hou, X., Liu, C.-L.: A hybrid approach to detect and localize texts in natural scene images. IEEE Trans. Image Process. 20(3), 800–813 (2011)
7. Epshtein, B., Ofek, E., Wexler, Y.: Detecting text in natural scenes with stroke width transform. In: Proceedings of the International Conference on Computer Vision and Pattern Recognition (CVPR), pp. 2963–2970 (2010)
8. Neumann, L., Matas, J.: Real-time scene text localization and recognition. In: Proceedings of the International Conference on Computer Vision and Pattern Recognition (CVPR), pp. 3538–3545 (2012)
9. Matas, J., Chuma, O., Urbana, M., Pajdlaa, T.: Robust wide-baseline stereo from maximally stable extremal regions. Image Vis. Comput. 22(10), 761–767 (2004)
10. Otsu, N.: A threshold selection method from gray-level histograms. IEEE Trans. Syst. Man Cybern. 9(1), 62–66 (1979)
11. Niblack, W.: An Introduction to Digital Image Processing. Strandberg Publishing Company, Birkeroed (1985)
12. Freund, Y., Schapire, R.E.: A decision-theoretic generalization of on-line learning and an application to boosting. In: Vitányi, P. (ed.) EuroCOLT 1995. LNCS, vol. 904, pp. 23–37. Springer, Heidelberg (1995). https://doi.org/10.1007/3-540-59119-2_166
13. Ojala, T., Pietikainen, M., Maenpaa, T.: Multiresolution gray-scale and rotation invariant texture classification with local binary patterns. IEEE Trans. Pattern Anal. Mach. Intell. 24(7), 971–987 (2002)
14. Wolf, C., Jolion, J.-M.: Object count/area graphs for the evaluation of object detection and segmentation algorithms. Int. J. Document Anal. Recogn. (IJDAR) 8(4), 280–296 (2006)
15. Fabrizio, J., Marcotegui, B., Cord, M.: Text segmentation in natural scenes using toggle-mapping. In: Proceedings of the 16th International Conference on Image Processing (ICIP), pp. 2373–2376 (2009)
16. Cho, H., Sung, M., Jun, B.: Canny text detector: fast and robust scene text localization algorithm. In: Proceedings of International Conference on Computer Vision and Pattern Recognition, pp. 3566–3573 (2016)
17. Zhang, Z., Zhang, C., Shen, W., Yao, C., Liu, W., Bai, X.: Multi-oriented text detection with fully convolutional networks. In: CVPR 2016, Las Vegas (2016)

18. Zhu, S., Zanibbi, R.: A text detection system for natural scenes with convolutional feature learning and cascaded classification. In: CVPR 2016, Las Vegas (2016)
19. Jaderberg, M., Simonyan, K., Vedaldi, A., Zisserman, A.: Reading text in the wild with convolutional neural networks. Int. J. Comput. Vis. **116**(1), 1–20 (2016)

A Combinational De-Noising Algorithm
for Low-Dose Computed Tomography

Wei Zhang[1,2] and Yan Kang[1(✉)]

[1] Sino-Dutch Biomedical and Information Engineering School,
Northeastern University, Shenyang, China
wzhang@sina.cn, kangyan@bmie.neu.edu.cn
[2] Computer School, Jilin Normal University, Siping, China

Abstract. To improve the image quality of low-dose CT, this paper proposes a modified algorithm which combined with the projection domain de-noising and reference-based non-local means (RNLM) filtering in the image domain. A generalized Anscombe transformation (GAT) is used to improve the effectiveness of the stabilization and filtering. The exact unbiased inverse of the GAT is also applied to ensure accurate de-noising results. The experimental results demonstrate that the proposed method could significantly improve the quality and preserve the edges of low-dose CT images.

Keywords: Computed tomography · Low-dose · Non-local means

1 Introduction

As an X-ray imaging technique, computed tomography (CT) is widely used in disease diagnosis and screening [1]. Due to the risk of inducing secondary harm through radiation exposure, low-dose CT has become a popular research topic in recent years [2–4]. It is desirable to apply lower-intensity X-rays or to use fewer projection views or less angular coverage [5]. Low-dose collection schemes increase noise contamination, yielding poor image quality. Noise reduction approaches are applied to improve the raw data (sinogram) followed by standard FBP based reconstruction in projection domain [6, 7]. In addition, iterative reconstruction algorithms and image field noise reduction approaches can be utilized to reduce noise [8]. In previous work [9], a pipeline with effective de-noising was demonstrated in the low-dose CT. On account of photon starvation, the feature of projection data noise approximately follows a non-stationary Gaussian distribution [10], an improved low-dose CT image reconstruction based on joint the projection domain de-noising and the adaptive RNLM filtering in the image domain is presented in this paper.

In the following section, the noise model is introduced firstly. Then, the schemes involved in the proposed method are described in Sect. 3. The results and discusses are presented in Sect. 4, and the conclusions are summarized in Sect. 5.

© Springer Nature Singapore Pte Ltd. 2018
Y. Wang et al. (Eds.): IGTA 2017, CCIS 757, pp. 263–270, 2018.
https://doi.org/10.1007/978-981-10-7389-2_26

2   Noise Model

X-ray photons are produced with high-speed electrons from cathode to the anode impact on the target materials in CT imaging system. The radiation composed of X-ray photons possesses exclusive statistical properties [11]. Although the compound Poisson model is more accurate for the description of the noise [10], it is numerically challenging to implement this model for data noise simulation. To describe the nature of measured data, the compound Poisson-Gaussian statistical model is used, that is assumed in [6] and is also verified in [12]. The model is defined as

$$\tilde{P}(\beta_k, u, v) = Possion(P(\beta_k, u, v)) + Gaussian(m_E, \sigma_E^2) \tag{1}$$

Consider $\tilde{P}(\beta_k, u, v)$ as pixels from the noisy datum under the β_k-th projection view, where (u, v) are spatial coordinates. $P(\beta_k, u, v)$ is the mean number of photons or the noise-free transmission datum, m_E and σ_E^2 are the mean and variance of the electronic noise respectively.

3   Methodologies

The projection domain de-noising with the RNLM filtering in the image domain is combined in the proposed method. It consists of three major steps in the scheme: (a) Direct Feldkamp–Davis–Kress (FDK) image reconstruct from the original low-dose projection data $\tilde{P}(\beta_k, u, v)$ [13], and then get the denoised image $\tilde{I}_{TV-denoised}^{FDK}$ by total variation (TV) method; (b) Projection domain restore using data adjustment with block-matching and 3D filtering (BM3D) de-noising, and get FDK reconstruction image $\tilde{I}_{sinodenoised}^{FDK}$ from the final projection data P_{IVST}; (c) RNLM filtering with an average weights related to both step (a) and (b). An overview of the proposed pipeline is given in Fig. 1. In the following subsections, the steps (b) and (c) are presented in detail.

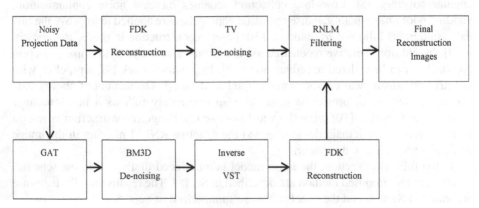

Fig. 1. Overall schematic of the proposed pipeline.

3.1 Projection Domain Restoration

3.1.1 Data Adjustment for De-Noising Processing

It is difficult to accomplish directly on account of having signal-dependent noise in CT imaging [14]. According to the noise model (1), it is commonly executed by using variance stabilizing transformations (VST) to adjust the signal-dependent projection data [15, 16]. The generalized Anscombe transformation (GAT) is one of the well-known VST for Poisson-Gaussian variables [17]. For all projection angles β_k of the original low-dose projection data $\tilde{P}(\beta_k, u, v)$, where u, v are pixel locations at the β_k-th projection angle, the GAT is defined as

$$f\left(\tilde{P}(\beta_k, u, v)\right) = \begin{cases} 2\sqrt{\tilde{P}(\beta_k, u, v) + \dfrac{3}{8} + \sigma_E^2}, & \tilde{P}(\beta_k, u, v) > -\dfrac{3}{8} - \sigma_E^2 \\ 0, & \tilde{P}(\beta_k, u, v) \le -\dfrac{3}{8} - \sigma_E^2 \end{cases}. \tag{2}$$

Where $f\left(\tilde{P}(\beta_k, u, v)\right)$ is the stabilized projection data, which can be modeled as corrupted exclusively by standard Gaussian noise. The noise parameter σ_E^2 could be estimated by fitting a global parametric model into locally estimated expectation/standard deviation pairs [18].

3.1.2 Remove the Projection Data Noise

The noise could be treated as additive independent Gaussian white noise with unitary variance after stabilizing the variance by GAT. The denoised projection data $P_{denoised}$ could be gotten by using BM3D approach from the projection data $f\left(\tilde{P}(\beta_k, u, v)\right)$. There are two main steps in the BM3D de-noising method. First, the denoised image is estimated using hard-thresholding of the transformed coefficients during filtering, and then the original noisy image and the basic estimate image obtained from the first step are combined to yield the final estimate.

3.1.3 Inverse VST

The final projection data is obtained by inverting the denoised data $P_{denoised}$ with the exact unbiased inverse of the generalized Anscombe transform f_{EUI}^{-1}, as proposed in [19]:

$$P_{IVST} = f_{EUI}^{-1}\left(P_{denoised}\right) = \frac{1}{4}P_{denoised}^2 + \frac{1}{4}\sqrt{\frac{3}{2}}P_{denoised}^{-1} - \frac{11}{8}P_{denoised}^{-2}$$
$$+ \frac{5}{8}\sqrt{\frac{3}{2}}P_{denoised}^{-3} - \frac{1}{8} - \sigma_E^2. \tag{3}$$

3.2 RNLM Filtering

Using the NLM method to reduce noise in k^{th} slice of images I_{direct}^{FDK} reconstructed by FDK from the original projection $\tilde{P}$, and let related k^{th} slice of images $\tilde{I}_{direct}^{FDK}$ serve as the reference image, this yields the final images $\hat{I}$. This method uses the following expression:

$$\hat{I} = \sum_{j \in N_i} \omega(i,j) I_{direct,k}^{FDK}. \tag{4}$$

Where the weight ω is defined as follows:

$$\omega(i,j) = \frac{exp\left(-\left\|I_{direct,k}^{FDK}(N_i) - \tilde{I}_{sinoDenoised,k}^{FDK}(N_j)\right\|_{2,a}^2 / h^2\right)}{\sum_j exp\left(-\left\|I_{direct,k}^{FDK}(N_i) - \tilde{I}_{sinoDenoised,k}^{FDK}(N_j)\right\|_{2,a}^2 / h^2\right)}. \tag{5}$$

Where the neighborhood windows N_i and N_j in size 7×7 are located at i and j, respectively; $\|\cdot\|_{2,a}^2$ denotes the Gaussian distance between two similarity windows with a standard deviation a; h is usually a function of the standard deviation σ of the image noise, which controls the decay of the exponential function in Eq. (5), it can be determined with

$$h^2 = k\bar{\sigma}^2 \tag{6}$$

Where $\bar{\sigma}$ is the standard deviation of the images $I_{direct,k}^{FDK}$ which can be estimated by using the reference image $\tilde{I}_{sinoDenoised,k}^{FDK}$.

4   Results and Discussion

By using the Matlab environment, the algorithm was implemented and tested on sets obtained from the RANDO head phantom images. The images and parts of codes are provided by courtesy of the tomographic iterative GPU-based reconstruction (TIGRE) toolbox project [20]. The images were reconstructed by using the FDK algorithm. The CT image reconstruction parameters are given in Table 1. Figure 2 presents the 64th slice image reconstructed by the different schemes. The image profiles along the central lines of the images are illustrated in Fig. 3. It could be observed that the profile of our result is much closer to the original image. The quantitative comparisons are carried out to

Table 1. The parameters of CT image reconstruction.

Parameter	Value
Detector unit number	512×512
Distance source detector/mm	1536
Distance source origin/mm	1000
Image resolution	256×256
Pixel size/mm	2.0
Number of views	200

further prove the validity of our method. The signal to noise ratio (SNR) of the reconstructed images in Fig. 2 is defined by

$$\text{SNR} = -20 \log_{10}\left(\|x - y\|_2 / \|x\|_2\right). \tag{7}$$

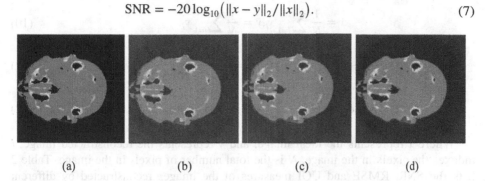

(a)   (b)   (c)   (d)

Fig. 2. The 64th reconstructed image of different processing procedures (a) Reconstructed from noise-free projection data; (b) Reconstructed from noisy projection data directly; (c) Reconstructed image with TV de-noising; (d) Reconstructed image using the proposed algorithm.

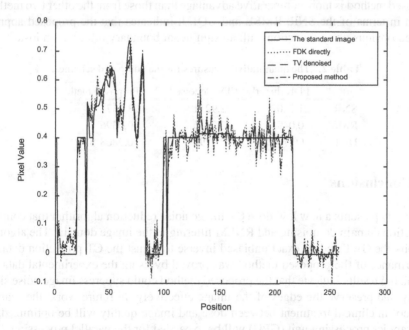

Fig. 3. Image profiles along the central line of the images

In addition, the root mean square error (RMSE) is calculated and the degree of similarity between the reconstructed and phantom images is evaluated by universal quality index (UQI) [21], which are formulated as follows:

$$\text{RMSE} = \sqrt{\|x - y\|_2 / N}. \tag{8}$$

$$UQI = \frac{4\sigma_{xy}\bar{x}\bar{y}}{\left(\sigma_x^2 + \sigma_x^2\right)\left[(\bar{x})^2 + (\bar{y})^2\right]}. \tag{9}$$

$$\bar{x} = \frac{1}{N}\sum_{i=1}^{N} x_i, \bar{y} = \frac{1}{N}\sum_{i=1}^{N} y_i. \tag{10}$$

$$\sigma_x^2 = \frac{1}{N-1}\sum_{i=1}^{N}(x_i - \bar{x})^2, \sigma_y^2 = \frac{1}{N-1}\sum_{i=1}^{N}(y_i - \bar{y})^2 \tag{11}$$

$$\sigma_{xy} = \frac{1}{N-1}\sum_{i=1}^{N}(x_i - \bar{x})(y_i - \bar{y}). \tag{12}$$

Where x represents the ideal image, and y represents the reconstructed image, i indexes the pixels in the image. N is the total number of pixels in the image. Table 2 lists the SNR, RMSE and UQI measures of the images reconstructed by different schemes. A higher SNR indicates that the image is of higher quality. An RMSE value close to zero suggests high similarity to the ideal phantom image. A UQI value closer to one suggests better similarity to the true image. It can be seen that the gains from the proposed method is more comparative advantage than those from the other two methods, which in terms of the SNR, RMSE and UQI. It indicates that the proposed approach yielded obvious noise reduction with no significant boundary information lost.

Table 2. The quantitative measures for the compared schemes.

	FDK directly	TV-denoised	Proposed method
SNR	21.3802	22.9211	23.3371
RMSE	0.0496	0.0416	0.0396
UQI	0.9709	0.9791	0.9808

5 Conclusions

This study presents a new low-dose CT image noise reduction algorithm that combines projection domain de-noising and RNLM filtering in the image domain. The algorithm exploits the GAT and its exact unbiased inverse to adjust the CT projection data. The performance of the proposed method was proved by using the experimental data. The de-noising results indicate that the proposed method could suppress image noise significantly and preserve the edges of the image effectively. In future work, the scanning protocol in clinical treatment between dose and image quality will be optimized, and the graphics processing unit (GPU) will be expanded for the parallel processing.

Acknowledgements. This work was supported by the National Natural Science Foundation of China (No. 61372014) and the Scientific and Technological Development Plan Program of Siping (No. 2016062).

References

1. Brenner, D.J., Hall, E.J.: Computed tomography—an increasing source of radiation exposure. N. Engl. J. Med. **357**(22), 2277–2284 (2007)
2. Chen, G.H., Tang, J., Leng, S.: Prior image constrained compressed sensing (PICCS): a method to accurately reconstruct dynamic CT images from highly undersampled projection data sets. Med. Phys. **35**(2), 660–663 (2008)
3. Sidky, E.Y., Pan, X.: Image reconstruction in circular cone-beam computed tomography by constrained, total-variation minimization. Phys. Med. Biol. **53**(17), 4777 (2008)
4. Zheng, Z., Papenhausen, E., Mueller, K.: DQS advisor: a visual interface and knowledge-based system to balance dose, quality, and reconstruction speed in iterative CT reconstruction with application to NLM-regularization. Phys. Med. Biol. **58**(21), 7857 (2013)
5. Kalender, W.A.: Dose in X-ray computed tomography. Phys. Med. Biol. **59**(1), 129–150 (2014)
6. La Riviere, P.J., Bian, J., Vargas, P.: Penalized-likelihood sinogram restoration for computed tomography. IEEE Trans. Med. Imaging **25**(8), 1022–1036 (2006)
7. Zhang, Y., Zhang, J., Lu, H.: Statistical sinogram smoothing for low-dose CT with segmentation-based adaptive filtering. IEEE Trans. Nucl. Sci. **57**(5), 2587–2598 (2010)
8. Beister, M., Kolditz, D., Kalender, W.A.: Iterative reconstruction methods in X-ray CT. Physica Med. **28**(2), 94–108 (2012)
9. Zhang, W., Mao, B., Chen, X.: Low-dose computed tomography image de-noising with variance-stabilizing transformation and noise variance estimation. J. Med. Imaging Health Inform. **6**(5), 1345–1359 (2016)
10. Whiting, B.R.: Signal statistics in x-ray computed tomography. In: Proceedings of SPIE, Medical Imaging 2002, vol. 4682(1), pp. 53–60. International Society for Optics and Photonics (2002)
11. Buzug, T.M.: Computed Tomography: From Photon Statistics to Modern Cone-Beam CT. Springer, Heidelberg (2008). https://doi.org/10.1007/978-3-540-39408-2
12. Hsieh, J.: Adaptive streak artifact reduction in computed tomography resulting from excessive x-ray photon noise. Med. Phys. **25**(11), 2139–2147 (1998)
13. Feldkamp, L.A., Davis, L.C., Kress, J.W.: Practical cone-beam algorithm. JOSA A **1**(6), 612–619 (1984)
14. Lu, H., Hsiao, T., Li, X.: Noise properties of low-dose CT projections and noise treatment by scale transformations. In: 2001 IEEE Nuclear Science Symposium Conference Record, vol. 3, pp. 1662–1666. IEEE (2001)
15. Yu, G.: Variance stabilizing transformations of poisson, binomial and negative binomial distributions. Stat. Probab. Lett. **79**(14), 1621–1629 (2009)
16. Anscombe, F.J.: The transformation of Poisson, binomial and negative-binomial data. Biometrika **35**(3/4), 246–254 (1948)
17. Zhang, B., Fadili, M.J., Starck, J.L.: Multiscale variance-stabilizing transform for mixed-Poisson-Gaussian processes and its applications in bioimaging. In: 2007 IEEE International Conference on Image Processing, ICIP 2007, vol. 6, pp. VI-233–VI-236. IEEE (2007)
18. Foi, A., Trimeche, M., Katkovnik, V.: Practical poissonian-gaussian noise modeling and fitting for single-image raw-data. IEEE Trans. Image Process. **17**(10), 1737–1754 (2008)
19. Makitalo, M., Foi, A.: A closed-form approximation of the exact unbiased inverse of the Anscombe variance-stabilizing transformation. IEEE Trans. Image Process. **20**(9), 2697–2698 (2011)

20. Biguri, A., Dosanjh, M., Hancock, S.: TIGRE: a MATLAB-GPU toolbox for CBCT image reconstruction. Biomed. Phys. Eng. Expr. **2**(5), 055010 (2016)
21. Wang, Z., Bovik, A.C.: Universal image quality index. IEEE Signal Process. Lett. **9**(3), 81–84 (2002)

Author Index

Printed in the United States
By Bookmasters